Faith, Text and History

THE BIBLE IN ENGLISH

Faith, Text and History

THE BIBLE IN ENGLISH

David Lawton

University Press of Virginia
Charlottesville

First published 1990 by Harvester Wheatsheaf

First published 1990 in the United States of America by
The University Press of Virginia
Box 3608 University Station
Charlottesville, Virginia 22903

Printed and bound in Great Britain

Library of Congress Cataloging-in-Publication Data
Lawton, David A., 1948–
    Faith, text, and history: the Bible in English/David Lawton.
      p. cm.
    Includes bibliographical references and indexes.
    ISBN 0–8139–1325–X   0–8139–1326–8 (pbk.)
    1. Bible Criticism, interpretation, etc.—History. 2. Bible
Criticism, interpretation, etc.—History—20th century. 3. Bible.
English—Versions—Authorized. 4. Bible. English—Versions.
5. Bible as literature. 6. Bible and literature. 7. Bible–
Hermeneutics. 8. Bible—Reading. I. Title.
BS500.L38 1990
220.6′09—dc20   90–47688
                                                    CIP

For Edith Lawton, Elizabeth Bradley
and Amanda Beresford.

Contents

Contents

Acknowledgements

I began my work on the Bible in 1983, teaching a course at the University of Sydney on 'The Bible in English'. I owe a great debt to my students over the years, and to colleagues, who have encouraged me to publish a book-length study; also to the University of Sydney, for a University Research Grant in 1986 and 1987. Sonya Jensen has been an invaluable assistant; Annette Krausmann, Cathey Eke, Pat Ricketts and others have helped with the production of my typescript.

Several people have read and commented on some or all of this book, notably Northrop Frye – in whose honour I first delivered as a lecture a draft of 'Difficulty and transference in the Song of Songs', later published in *AUMLA*, 66 (1986).

I am grateful to Faber and Faber Ltd, and Grove Press, New York for permission to quote from Samuel Beckett, *Waiting for Godot*; to Doubleday (Bantam, Doubleday, Dell Publishing Group Inc.) for permission to quote from *Genesis* (Anchor Bible), translated and edited by E. A. Speiser, © 1964 Doubleday, and from *The Song of Songs* (Anchor Bible), translated and edited by Marvin H. Pope, © 1977 Doubleday; The Catholic University of America Press, for permission to quote material from The Fathers of the Church series in Chapter 2; Basil Blackwell, for permission to quote from G. R. Owst, *Literature and Pulpit in Medieval England*, second edition (1961); to Cambridge University Press, for permission to quote from Francis Landy, 'The Case of Kugel: Do we find ourselves when we lose ourselves in the text?', *Comparative Criticism 5*, ed. E. S. Shaffer (Cambridge University Press, 1983), from Edmund Leach and D. Alan Aycock, *Structuralist*

Acknowledgements

Interpretations of Biblical Myth (Cambridge University Press, 1983), and from *The Cambridge History of the Bible*, three volumes (see Chapter 1, note 6); to Editions du Seuil for permission to quote from *Signes et Paraboles: Sémiotique et Texte Evangelique*, Groupe d'Entrevernes, © Editions du Seuil, 1977; Collins Publishers and Richard Scott Simon Ltd, for permission to quote from *The Literary Guide to the Bible*, edited by Robert Alter and Frank Kermode; Martin Secker and Warburg Ltd., for permission to quote from Norman Cohn, *The Pursuit of the Millennium*; Routledge and Kegan Paul, for permission to quote from Northrop Frye, *The Great Code: the Bible and Literature*; The Washington Post, for permission to quote from Ronnie Dugger, 'Reagan's Apocalypse Now'; John Johnson Ltd, for permission to quote from Peter Levi, *The Bible In English* (1974); The University of Chicago Press, for permission to quote from Harold Bloom, *The Breaking of the Vessels* (1982), © The University of Chicago; Yale University Press, for permission to quote from James L. Kugel, *The Idea of Biblical Poetry* (Yale University Press), © Yale University 1981; SCM Press, for permission to quote from James D. G. Dunn, *Unity and Diversity in the New Testament*, © 1977 and from Lucas Grollenberg, *Rediscovering the Bible*, © 1978; Indiana University Press, for permission to quote from *The Poems of St. John of the Cross*, edited and translated by Willis Barnstone; Princeton University Press, for permission to quote from Søren Kierkegaard, *Fear and Trembling*, edited and translated by Howard V. Hong and Edna H. Hong, © Princeton, 1983, and Erich Auerbach, *Mimesis: The representation of reality in Western literature*, translated by Willard R. Trask, © Princeton 1968; André Deutsch Ltd, for permission to quote from A. C. Partridge, *English Biblical Translation*; Methuen, London and William Collins, for permission to quote from Michel Tournier, *The Erl-King*, translated by Barbara Bray, © 1972; and Hill and Wang, New York, for permission to quote from Roland Barthes, *A Lover's Discourse: Fragments*, translated by Richard Howard, © 1978 Farrar, Straus and Giroux, Inc.

CHAPTER 1

Introduction

Words and books

The focus of this study is the Bible's power to signify: not what it means, but what it can be and has been taken to mean. This study deals in poetics, not theology; but it also deals in history, for the history of a book's reception becomes part of our reading of that book.

Modern literary theory of many kinds is often called upon by professional students of the Bible. Some interest in biblical criticism (exegesis) is shown by modern literary theorists, and major incursions into the Bible have been made by scholars in the social sciences. However, until recently, and since the early nineteenth century, there has been surprisingly little systematic study of modes of biblical reading in the light of modern theory.[1] Such relative neglect has not benefited exegesis or literary theory. Modern literary theorists have often shown relatively little awareness of working within a Western intellectual tradition that stemmed above all from biblical commentary: Jacques Derrida, for instance, is a lineal descendant from early allegorists, a new Origen. Modern biblical exegetes for their part do not all show theoretical sophistication or a developed concept of reading and interpretation, such as unfailingly characterised the work of Church Fathers such as Augustine. Neither party quite admits that reading the Bible is an act of reading like any other; and, conversely, that no model of reading can be adequate if it fails to include the kind of commitment with which people have read and read their Bibles. This study, from a critical and historical perspective, aims to help join together what post-medieval readers have put asunder: reading and the Bible.

The study is written by one with little Greek and less Hebrew. I am in the position of Stephen Prickett or Edmund Leach, who confess to their scholarly shortcomings before beginning their writing on the Bible,[2] rather than that of Robert Alter[3] or Northrop Frye,[4] who bring to their reading of the Bible and their interest in interpretation generally a formidable scholarly equipment of biblical languages and studies. I have armed myself with a copy of *The Literary Guide to the Bible*,[5] *The Cambridge History of the Bible*,[6] standard commentaries on various books of the Bible such as the Anchor commentary, general introductions like Lucas Grollenberg's *Rediscovering the Bible*,[7] challenging works on Bible interpretation such as Alter's or Steinberg's or Bal's or Josipovici's or Frye's, and selective reading in journals such as *The Journal of Biblical Literature* or *Semeia*. I am less expert in hermeneutics than Prickett and less qualified to write on the Bible than any of the contributors to *The Literary Guide*. If my work has any claim on the attention it is because of my interest in the interrelatedness of text and reading, in the questions that might be asked by a student of reading. The focus of this study is my attempt to read the text as the history of its possible readings.

To some readers this programme may appear unreasonably limited or, indeed, evasive. The question of the Bible's truth is a crucial one, but it requires a book to deal with it, not a paragraph. If I had an easily labelled position on the question – as militant atheist, say, or fundamentalist Christian – I should now declare it; but I have not, and this whole book must serve as my declaration. Though the book contains a fairly complex and extended argument, it is in some sense introductory: that is, it does not presume that its readers already have a background in hermeneutics and other biblical studies. Much new work is being done to expand such studies in the field of theory; but most published accounts take up the argument, as it were, in the middle. There seems a real need for a book that presents the issues as for the first time, and brings together a discussion of related issues – such as interpretation and translation – within one volume.

Equally, there is a difference between my book and studies that address a specialist literary readership, such as Gabriel Josipovici's *The Book of God*. Josipovici's brilliantly original reading of the Bible as open text is shared with others comfortable in the worlds of Dante,

Proust and Joyce, who are invited to accompany Josipovici in his biblical exploration. If the present book is less assuming, it also wishes to respond more fully to the prevalent readings of modern Christian fundamentalism. Josipovici can trust his readers to have little time for unsophisticated acts of interpretation. I am not sure, however, that professional scepticism is always taken as an adequate reaction to the certainties of fundamentalists: certainties that reach out of the textual, after all, into the institutional and political. I see a need to take them seriously and respond to them seriously: not, probably, to the satisfaction of fundamentalist readers, but to my own satisfaction as one whose qualifications are in the field of reading and who therefore desires to refute what they represent.

It would be cheering to open with a claim like that of Alter and Kermode: 'We are writing to serve the interests of the educated general reader rather than those of some critical party'.[8] A reader could hardly disagree, always provided that one felt sufficiently educated and general – and except that an educated general reader may also happen to subscribe to 'some critical party', if only that of educated generality. The history of reading is the history of parties. Not the least invigorating among them is the enlightened empiricism represented by Alter and Kermode. Ways of reading such as semiotics, structuralism, deconstruction, reader-response theory and other forms of hermeneutics belong to our age and will contribute to subsequent histories of interpretation. If we pretend that they do not exist we deny our own part in history; we set up not only what we read but ourselves as readers as belonging somehow outside time. So my study takes particular note of those forms of reading that we think of as distinctively modern, and sees them in the context of an ongoing history. I do not try to view this history from an objective external vantage point, for I have no access to one – even though my reading has a history, and may have a future, independent of me and largely unknown to me. None of this need mean that I become a narrow subscriber to 'some critical party', or even a broader subscriber to several. Indeed, I have made a conscious effort to avoid more technical terms than I absolutely need; but I would scarcely be writing this book if I were unsympathetic to modern modes of reading. That said, a reader of this book need not be at all expert in modern theory, and I have aimed throughout to supply, rather than to assume, whatever knowledge is needed.

It is sad, in fact, that even in so valuable, up-to-date and intellectually generous an enterprise as *The Literary Guide to the Bible*, the editors feel a need for their disclaimer. As it tries to bridge one gap, between educated general readers and the Bible, it testifies to another, between specialist readers (or literary theorists) and other readers, including specialist readers of the Bible. The present book addresses the second of these gaps. Its intended audience would be that sought by Frye when he set out to shed light on Blake's great claim: 'The Old and the New Testaments are the Great Code of Art'. Such an audience may range all the way from fundamentalist Christians through Jewish readers to relaxed atheists. While I am citing others' formulation of their preferred readers, I would do well to add Frye's:

> At one end of the spectrum of possible readers for this book are those so deeply committed to the existential and the religious issues of the Bible that they would regard such a book as this as a mere exercise in sterile dilettantism. At the other end are those who assume that the Bible must be some kind of 'establishment' symbol, bound up with sexual inhibitions and a primitive view of biology, and that any interest in it must be a sign of some authoritarian or infantile malaise. This book is addressed to readers of good will who are somewhere in between. Some even of these may well feel that to attempt a fresh and firsthand look at the Bible is mere foolhardiness, and of course they may be right, but the years have brought me an elastic conscience and a tenure appointment.[9]

And I should add my own disclaimer. My interests lie in language and the act of reading language: not truth but interpretation (or the range of possible interpretation) is at stake here. My study will not engage polemically with the question of truth or otherwise of the Bible, though it will do so incidentally in referring to others' consideration of it. It will engage, however, historically and theoretically, with the central question of the Bible's textuality.

'The Great Code of Art' is approached historically by asking what the Bible has meant to different people in different cultures in different times: and here, one would begin with the word 'Bible' itself, and its radically different construction in Jewish and Christian traditions. One would also look at the different forms in which different people received it: this relates both to recensions (such as the Septuagint or the Vulgate) and to translations (the Bible of Spenser, Shakespeare and Milton, for example, is not the King James but the Geneva Bible). It is a simple fact that different people read, and have read, different Bibles: in what sense can these be said to be *the* Bible? And this question, like the Bible itself, can be approached as a modern problem. Whatever historically a text meant 'originally', whatever it has meant to countless generations of its dead readers, however alien or remote it might seem, a text is also our contemporary: it becomes our contemporary as soon as we try to read it. On the one hand, then, we should ask: how have long legions of our historic precursors read the Bible? On the other, there is a no less pressing and potentially more embarrassing question: how are we to read the Bible today? If it is the 'Great Code', have we lost the key? Was there ever a key to lose? The issue becomes theoretical as soon as we take this step: for we must then ask how we align the readings of the past with our own, and enquire how these are to be distinguished from, or how they constitute, 'the text'. No resolution of such questions is remotely possible without asking how we read any text – how we understand, try to understand or triumphantly misunderstand anything we read.

This book follows a roughly tripartite structure in its pursuit of such issues. The third and longest part (Chapters 4 to 6) consists of readings of selected books and passages of the Bible: from the Jewish Bible (Old Testament) in Chapter 4, from the Christian supplement (New Testament) in Chapter 5 and the most overtly figurative books of the Old and New Testaments – the Song of Songs, and the Book of Revelation – in Chapter 6. These readings will apply, sparingly, modern theoretical and stylistic instruments of analysis. The second part justifies the need for their application (Chapter 2), and examines the Bible as English text (Chapter 3). The focus of my discussion of the English Bible, and the text from which I normally quote, is the King James Bible of 1611, authorised for use in the Anglican churches and thus known as the Authorised Version. This translation is both a major English literary influence and the closest approximation in its dominant place in English tradition to the Latin Vulgate, which held sway in the international Church from the fourth century to the Reformation and beyond. I am reassured in my choice of the King James Bible by the value placed upon it by Alter, who sees it as the closest English expression of biblical styles in both Hebrew and Greek, and by Gerald Hammond:

> At its best, which means often, the Authorised Version has the kind of transparency which makes it possible for the reader to see the original clearly. It lacks the narrow interpretative bias of modern versions, and is the stronger for it. Through its transparency the reader of the Authorised Version not only sees the original but also learns how to read it.[10]

The interpretative 'transparency' or openness of this version makes it especially suitable for the purpose of my study – though we should not forget that the high value placed on these qualities, and Hammond's insistence that a translation can teach us 'how to read' 'the original', both have their ideological dimension. I discuss this further in Chapter 3.

Hammond's claim is a curious modern echo of Miles Smith's preface on behalf of the translators of the Authorised Version – a preface unfortunately omitted from most modern published editions. Smith's is a far-reaching claim: 'We do not deny, nay we affirm and avow, that the very meanest translation of the Bible in English . . . containeth the word of God, nay *is* the word of God.'[11] It is also a vital claim. The Bible is true, and therefore it is equally true in English as it is in Hebrew, Greek or Aramaic. Yet close historical works on the language of English Biblical translation in different periods and in different styles makes it abundantly clear how much the reader's understanding is conditioned by the particular translation: it is on these very grounds that Hammond recommends 'the Renaissance versions' rather than modern ones with their 'narrow interpretative bias'.

Translation from one language to another involves a constant loss. In Genesis, for instance, we meet much narrative that is aetiological: the narrative exists as the result of a name. When Rebekah is pregnant with Isaac's twins, 'the children struggled together within her' (Genesis 25:22). God explains this as the struggle of two nations, of whom 'the elder shall serve the younger'. At the birth, Esau is the first born, but 'after that came his brother out, and his hand took hold on Esau's heel; and his name was called Jacob' (25:26). Most readers no doubt see that the text highlights the names, Esau and Jacob; and some probably appreciate that there is a disparity between the two names – for whereas Esau bears the name of his nation, Edom, Jacob must acquire the name of his nation, Israel, in his maturity. Relatively few readers, I imagine, would know that the name Jacob is cognate with the Hebrew word 'heel': the detail of verse 26 is a narrative pun on Jacob's name. Such a link between narrative and name in the original Hebrew was perhaps lost on some later Jewish readers (because the name becomes so familiar that etymology is overlooked – as in, say, the royal English name Victoria). Certainly, the link cannot survive translation? This is a relatively simple instance of the way in which a translation, any translation, produces a different book from the original and from other translations. Moreover, each different translation makes for itself a different reception. Generations of God-fearing English-speaking people, terrorised or intimidated by the adage 'Sufficient unto the day is the evil thereof' (Matthew 6:34), might have had a very different response to the more prosaic translation of the Jerusalem Bible: 'Each day has trouble enough of its own'.

The languages of God

To return to Miles Smith, how can 'the very meanest translation of the Bible in English' not just contain but *be* 'the word of God'? What kind of word/Word is this that does not suffer any loss in translation? It is this very question that is taken up by both the beginnings of the Christian Bible.

The first of these beginnings, Genesis 1 and verses 1–3 of Genesis 2, is now the beginning of the Old Testament but, like all good beginnings, was probably a late addition and did not form part of the original design. The second, the first Chapter of St John's Gospel, was designed as a beginning for the New Testament but never achieved the position in canonical order. Both these would-be beginnings locate God in language, word/Word. I shall first cite John 1:1–9 in the familiar King James version:

> In the beginning was the Word, and the Word was with God, and the Word was God.
> The same was in the beginning with God.
> All things were made by him; and without him was not any thing made that was made.
> In him was life; and the life was the light of men.
> And the light shineth in darkness; and the darkness comprehended it not.

> There was a man sent from God, whose name was John.
> The same came for a witness, to bear witness of the Light, that all men through him might believe.
> He was not that Light, but was sent to bear witness of that Light.
> That was the true Light, which lighteth every man that cometh into the world.

There is no better demonstration of the point I have just made – that each new translation produces a new and different book – than by comparing the same passage as translated in the eighteenth century by Dr Edward Harwood:

> Before the origin of the world existed the Logos – who was then with the Supreme God – and was himself a divine person.
> He existed with the Supreme Being, before the foundation of the earth was laid:
> For this most prominent personage did the Deity solely employ in the formation of this world, and of every thing it contains.
> This exalted spirit assumed human life – and from his incarnation the most pure and sacred emanations of light were derived to illuminate mankind:
> This light shot its beams into a benighted world – and conquered and dispelled that gloomy darkness, in which it was inveloped.
> To usher this divine personage into the world, and to prepare men for his reception, God previously commissioned and sent John the Baptist.
> This prophet came to give public notice that a glorious light would shortly appear – to excite all the Jews to credit and receive this great messenger of God.
> John himself openly disavowed all pretensions to this exalted character – declaring, that he was only appointed of God to give public information of this illustrious personage.[12]

It is a remarkable difference – almost as great as that between the account in John 1 and that in Genesis 1:

> In the beginning God created the heaven and the earth.
> And the earth was without form, and void: and darkness was upon the face of the deep. And the Spirit of God moved upon the face of the waters.
> And God said, Let there be light: and there was light.
> And God saw the light, that it was good: and God divided the light from the darkness.
> And God called the light Day, and the darkness he called Night. And the evening and the morning were the first day.

(If we seek a contrast to match that between King James and Dr Harwood, we might do worse than recall the Yorkshire dialect version: 'First up ther wor nobbut God. An 'e said, "Ee, lad, turn th'bloody light on".')

It is stretching credulity to talk of 'The Bible' as if it were historically invariable. Different people have different Bibles; each culture has at least one Bible that is distinctively its own. Comparing Harwood with the King James Bible John, or the Yorkshire dialect version with the King James Bible Genesis, we recognise enough similarity to accept in each case that both translate a common source. We also experience a powerful feeling of difference. And it is just such a sense of simultaneous likeness and difference that the author of John's Gospel exploits in fashioning his Christian equivalent, or free imitation of Genesis 1, echoing in his Greek version the style of the Septuagint translation of the Hebrew Bible into Greek. It is, so to speak, an inspired Christian hijack of the beginning of what then becomes the Old Testament. It depends on two unspoken premises of the Genesis account. First, God creates by speech: 'God *said*, Let there be light'. God is therefore a language. But to whom is this language spoken? Who is God talking to? The Christian answer is that he is talking to Christ, and John insists that Christ had no beginning and is co-existent with God: he is instrumental Word. John substitutes this account for the birth stories of the synoptic gospels, which stress humanity rather than divinity. Secondly, God understands his creation, his speech, not by saying but by seeing: 'God *saw* that it was good'. Most of us cannot see in the dark; even if God can, the reader cannot. That is why God must first say 'Let there be light', in order to dispel the darkness on the face of the deep. Word is therefore light; the Word of God is Christ; Christ is the Light of the World.

This is evidently what the writer of John's Gospel believed that the beginning of Genesis meant. More evidently still, it is not what the writer of the beginning of Genesis would have thought that it meant. What happens when we go beyond the Christian revision, further towards the so-called 'original' meaning?

First, we find that the word for God in this account is not YHWH, the exclusive and unspeakable name of the fire-god of the Jewish people, but the originally plural name, 'Elohim', which originally referred to all gods of the world in which the Jewish people moved. That world was not monotheistic. 'Elohim' however, is probably used here with singular meaning, for the writer of Genesis 1 is aware of the tradition that YHWH did not reveal his name until well after Creation. When the writer of Genesis 1 calls the god of the Jewish people Elohim he answers one question – God speaks not to his son but to other gods; and at the same time audaciously annihilates those other gods and powers. As Harold Bloom puts it:

> The Priestly Author has swept away by his own breath the enormous wars against the abyss and its creatures that God fights and wins, victories celebrated throughout the Psalms, the Prophets, Job, and other Biblical texts. By a magnificent ellipsis of tradition, the Priestly Author has strengthened the creative force of the divine by making that force transcend its traditional opponents to the point where they have vanished wholly.[13]

The one Word wipes the world's ears clean of all interference. Language is God's creative and aggressive main attribute.

Why does Bloom refer to the writer as 'the Priestly Author'? To raise this question is to raise a more formidable one: why are there two inconsistent accounts of creation in Genesis? Modern textual criticism tells us that Genesis 2:4 was once the opening verse of the book. It introduces what is now the second account of creation in the book of Genesis, which appears to conflict with the first in several respects: the earth and heavens were made not in sequence but together, not in six parts but in one (Genesis 2:4); man is formed not in the image of God (1:27) but 'of the dust of the ground' (2:7). Whereas in the first account (1:27) man and woman are created at the same time, we have in Genesis 2 the notorious account of the formation of woman from Adam's rib. Documentary criticism also explains how this came about. Genesis 2, the original – or, at least, antecedent – account is the work of the marvellous Yahwist author (J), writing relatively early (though not as early as Moses): Genesis 1 and 2:1–3 are an addition in the fifth century Before the Christian Era (BCE) by the so-called Priestly writer, or committee (P). P is called Priestly because his revision dates from the time of Ezekiel, not that of Moses; and much of the law of the Pentateuch (the first five books), the Torah, is an addition by P. Moses is expected to behave according to laws formulated nearly a millennium after his death. P is associated with the Temple of Jerusalem and the considerable tightening of Judaic law in Ezekiel's time. Among the laws tightened was that of Sabbatarian observance. Hence the fable retrospectively validates Priestly law (2:3–4). And, as we shall see from the narrative of the sacrifice of Isaac, whereas J is a born fabulist and a consummate maker of myth, P is overtly theological: hence the tone of Genesis 1, which, as it were, puts God in his proper place, at headquarters – a very different God in a very different place from the stroller in the garden of Genesis 2.

The earlier account, that of J, is man-oriented: man, not God, is the focus of Genesis 2. God does not create by speech, but by breath and mist in a kind of impregnation (compare 1:2). It is man to whom the Lord God (YHWH Elohim) brings all the creatures of creation: it is Adam, not God, who gives names and invents language (Genesis 2:19–20), whereas in the Priestly account God is Word, and He gives the names: 'God called the light Day and the darkness he called Night . . . God called the firmament Heaven . . . God called the dry land Earth; and the gathering together of the Waters called he Seas'. J's account of creation is a relatively bare one; it does not have the order or detail of P. Man is both its focus (what it is centred upon) and its focalisation (the direction from which the focus is coming).[14] Adam, not God, is an adequate source for the account. It is as if God told Adam a little of what He had done – not too much; Adam inferred or guessed a little more – again, not too much; Adam told Eve that she was the result of a surgical operation; Adam and Eve passed on the tradition to their children, and they to theirs; and so it went on until someone finally had the presence of mind to write it all down. It reads as an account focused on humans by humans. And it makes Genesis an important book, but, all the same, only a book.

But the Bible is held to be divinely inspired. By the time that the Priestly writer wrote his much later account, it was accepted that Moses was the writer of the Pentateuch, and that he wrote at God's dictation. By this time, then, God is held to be the author of the Book of Genesis. According to this version of events, respect for tradition would have ensured that there would have been no thought of tearing up J's account in Genesis 2; but it was not an ideal beginning, with its all too human focus and focalisation, and it required P's account as a preface and a supplement.

P's solution is bold and brilliant: as John 1 feeds on Genesis 1, so Genesis 1 feeds on Genesis 2. The focus is on God, not human kind; humankind is created late in the account, and P seizes the chance to have male and female created simultaneously: even in the fifth century BCE, Adam's rib does not seem to have been a popular point of origin. The focus is God, and God existed in the beginning, before anything else: this is a new claim, not found in the J account. If God existed before anything else, it follows that only God Himself could have described in detail His own actions in creating: God therefore becomes both the focalisation and the narrator of Genesis. And if this is so, there is therefore no difference between Genesis, the book, and genesis, the act of creating. The book is no longer an ordinary book. It is the book of creation, and God is simultaneously the author of the book and the world. The one entails the other. It follows that the language of that book is no longer our normal human language, an arbitrary language of such sublime unconcern to God in the earlier account that He let Adam invent all the nouns. The book's nouns are now divinely appointed, those which God made when He called light day; the book's words are now Word. The Bible is not literature but language.

The problems I have raised here about language – the language of the Bible in relation to the truth of the Bible – are therefore not questions raised by a modern critic. They are to be located squarely in the opening of the Bible itself, in the juxtaposition of Genesis 1 and Genesis 2, God's nouns and Adam's.

About that second language, ordinary human language, well over two thousand years of linguistic study might well be condensed in one truism: given as an example, as coincidence would have it, by both the father of the Church, St Augustine, and the father of modern linguistics, Ferdinand de Saussure. When I say '*ox*' in English I refer to the same thing as someone who says '*bos*' in Latin or '*boeuf*' in French. I use an arbitrary or conventional sign – a random collection of sounds that the speakers of a language agree to let signify the thing '*ox*' – for that ox, a real, natural thing. The sign I use, the word '*ox*', is not the thing to which I refer. There is no alternative; or rather, there is one alternative only, that when I form my vocal apparatus to say the word '*ox*', the thing, a real ox, pops tumbling out of my mouth. Absurd: yet this is what God does in Genesis 1, for that is precisely the nature of creating Word.

Therefore this book has two poles: *words*, here the English language, bound to specific times and places, to history, to semantic change, to context, to imprecision; and *Word*, the Bible's consciousness of itself as a superlanguage, as natural (the thing itself), as the secret of life and the path of perfect understanding, whose claims are transcendent, absolute, cosmic, thoroughly opaque – and somehow conceptually terrifying, like the voice of God from which Adam hides in the garden.

God and the Bible belong to the second type of language, Word: that is the claim of Genesis 1, that God is language and language is God. But what sort of God is this, who speaks to create? Here I think the Priestly writer took his cue from the scene I have just mentioned: after eating the forbidden fruit, Adam and Eve hide when they hear, in the marvellous phrase of the King James Bible, 'the voice of the Lord God walking in the garden in the cool of the day' (Genesis 3:8). There is a superb ambivalence in the English translation: it is not of course God's voice that is walking in the garden, but God Himself. Are we safe in distinguishing the two? We find, in fact, that we are not: the English phrase comes from the wording in the Hebrew, combining the identity of God with the notion of voice. Adam and Eve hide before God addresses them, not after; when they first hear his voice, then, he is not talking to them. We are told that language cannot exist without dialogue: yet this one does. A fair reading might be that God is talking to Himself. God cannot help talking to Himself, for God is Word. This becomes the God of Genesis 1: a self-enclosed language in search of a conversation. Such a language is not absence but presence. Such a God is not to be found in silence or the peace that passes understanding. The God of Genesis is the primal activity of language. He is all set to begin the primal book.

Notes

1. For documentation and examples of recent developments, see *The Book and the Text: The Bible and literary theory*, ed. Regina M. Schwartz (Oxford: Blackwell, 1990), especially Schwartz's 'Introduction: on Biblical criticism', pp. 1–15. Major recent monographs includes those by Mieke

Bal, 'Sexuality, sin and sorrow: The emergence of female character (A reading of Genesis 1–3)', in *The Female Body in Western Culture: Contemporary perspectives*, ed. Susan Rubin Suleiman (Cambridge, Mass, and London: Harvard UP, 1986), pp. 317–38; *Femmes Imaginaires* (Utrecht and Paris: Hes/Nizet, 1986); *Lethal Love* (Bloomington and London: Indiana UP, 1987) and *Death and Dissymetry* (Chicago and London: University of Chicago Press, 1988); Julia Kristeva, *Tales of Love* (New York and London: Columbia UP, 1987); Meir Sternberg, *The Poetics of Biblical Narrative* (Bloomington and London: Indiana UP, 1985); Letty M. Russell (ed.), *Feminist Interpretation of the Bible* (Oxford: Blackwell, 1985); David Jobling, *The Sense of Biblical Narrative* (Sheffield: Almond Press, 1986); Tzvetan Todorov, *Symbolism and Interpretation*, trans. Catherine Porter (Ithaca: Cornell UP, 1982) and *Theories of the Symbol*, trans. Porter (Ithaca: Cornell UP, 1982). Probably not since S.T. Coleridge, *Confessions of an Inquiring Spirit*, 2nd edn (1849), has any literary theorist grounded his work so strongly in biblical hermeneutics as Paul Ricouer in, for example, *Essays on Biblical Interpretation*, trans. David Pellauer, ed. L.S. Mudge (Philadelphia: Fortress Press, 1980); *Interpretation Theory: Discourse and the surplus of meaning* (Fort Worth, Texas: Christian UP, 1976); *The Rule of Metaphor* (Toronto: Toronto UP, 1977); 'Biblical hermeneutics', *Semeia* 4 (1975), 29–48; 'The task of hermeneutics', *Philosophy Today* 17 (1973), 112–24; 'Temps biblique', *Archivio di Folosofia* 53 (1985), 19–35; and in volume 3 of *Temps et Récit* (Paris: Seuil, 1985), trans. into English as *Time and Narrative*, vol. 3 (Chicago: University of Chicago Press, 1988). A classic modern literary reading is that of Gabriel Josipovici, *The Book of God: A response to the Bible* (New Haven and London: Yale UP, 1988).

2. Stephen Prickett, *Words and 'The Word': Language, poetics and biblical interpretation* (Cambridge: Cambridge UP, 1986); Edmund Leach and D. Alan Aycock, *Structuralist Interpretations of Biblical Myth* (Cambridge: Cambridge UP, 1983): see especially Leach's second essay, 'Anthropological approaches to the study of the Bible during the twentieth century'. My comparison here is unfair: with Prickett and with Leach the profession of relative ignorance is a fine rhetorical strategy, whereas in my case it is safely to be taken at face value.

3. Robert Alter, *The Art of Biblical Narrative* (New York: Basic Books, 1981).

4. Northrop Frye, *The Great Code: The Bible and literature* (London: Routledge and Kegan Paul, 1982).

5. *The Literary Guide to the Bible*, ed. Robert Alter and Frank Kermode

(London: Collins and Cambridge, Mass.: Harvard UP, 1987) – henceforth cited as *Literary Guide*.

6. *The Cambridge History of the Bible*, henceforth cited as *CHB*, 3 volumes (Cambridge: Cambridge UP): I *From the Beginnings to Jerome*, ed. P.R. Ackroyd and C.F. Evans (1970); II *The West from the Fathers to the Reformation*, ed. G.W.H. Lampe (1969); III *The West from the Reformation to the Present Day*, ed. S.L. Greenslade (1963).

7. Lucas Grollenberg, *Rediscovering the Bible* (London: SCM Press, 1978), first published as *A New Look at an Old Book* (New York: Newman Press, 1969).

8. *Literary Guide*, p. 5.

9. *The Great Code*, pp. xx–xxi.

10. *Literary Guide*, p. 64.

11. The preface is reprinted in the facsimile of the 1611 Bible published by Oxford University Press in 1985.

12. This extract from Dr Harwood's New Testament (1768) is published in Peter Levi (ed.) *The English Bible 1534–1859* (London: Constable, 1974), pp. 194–205.

13. Harold Bloom, *The Breaking of the Vessels* (Chicago and London: University of Chicago Press, 1982), pp. 16–17.

14. For these terms, see the valuable introduction by Shlomith Rimmon-Kenan, *Narrative Fiction: Contemporary poetics* (London and New York: Methuen, 1983).

CHAPTER 2

Biblical interpretation

Origen and The Book

Today we are familiar with a situation in which there are two major types of interest in the Bible: the literal (which provides an evangelical blueprint for readers to live by or is rejected by the scientifically minded) and the historical (that which concerns itself with the study of sources, textual history and so on). Each of these is distrustful of the other. We hear, still, debates about whether to teach creation or evolution in certain countries or states. How did such a situation develop? What makes anyone think that there is room for a third type of interest in the Bible, that related to poetics? It may be of more than incidental interest to both parties in the creation/ evolution dispute to know that the early Fathers of the Christian Church would all have considered it irrelevant: for the early Fathers of the Christian Church teach that the creation stories in Genesis are wonderful fable, myths in which God tries to give mortals, with our limited understanding, some small insight into His much more marvellous planning than can be described in human words or conceived by human minds.

The nature of a book is at least in part determined by its readers. In the case of the Bible, we use the word to mean *The Book*; but of course there is an implied plural in the Greek of the title. The Book is also the books, or one large book composed of many smaller ones. At once readers must decide whether to emphasise the unity or the multiplicity. This question lies at the root of theological and exegetical controversy down the ages: and it lies at the root of many responses to reading the Bible, even when readers have never read the whole of it.

'The books' became The Book mainly by majority vote, in the councils of the early Church: here the early Church emulated with the New Testament and the Bible as a whole the committee process that was also taking place in Judaism with what becomes in Christian tradition the Old Testament.[1] For in neither case did all the books that could have been included achieve inclusion. The canon is determined by sifting through all possible books, including some and rejecting others which are then relegated to an apocrypha. New Testament apocrypha is many times longer than the canonical New Testament and contains pseudo-gospels, 'secret' sayings, Manichean doctrine that matter and spirit can never be reconciled, and the story in the Gospel of Nichodemus of Jesus' descent into Hell after his death on the Cross: a story that was expunged from the Biblical canon, but survives in the Creed.[2] How do some books become canonical and others not? The issue should not be oversimplified. Certainly, the criteria are partly scholarly: the spurious is expunged, the fake and the forged are exposed. But they are also critical: readers exclude what they do not wish to read, and they also exclude what appears to conflict with the rest. Such readers begin not with the Book, but with the Faith, and admit into that book only what strengthens the faith. That is what the early Christians did, quite self-consciously.

What we decide to read is very close to how we decide to read it. To set up a canon is to have in mind an interpretation of that canon. And in the early Christian Church that interpretation did not emphasise at all the so-called literal sense. Rather it emphasised the harmony of the parts: everything in the Bible agrees with everything else; and if it does not do so obviously, then it must be made to do so by interpretation. Exegesis, or allegory, of the kind practised by the early Fathers of the Church and in a tradition unbroken till at least the thirteenth century, is more than a historical curiosity. Critically, it is a key to what we do when we read in any systematic way: modern critics, though many would deny it or not be aware of it, are types of allegorical exegetes. Historically, it is a key to European culture and the most coherent model of reading as a social activity ever presented. For many people today, the Bible is one book among many; but it remains true that the Western sense of what a book is depends on the work of many centuries when the Bible was *The Book*.

Much of Western literary tradition feeds off the Bible and the ways in which, historically, it has been read. There is no easy distinction in this between a primary activity, of making new texts, and a secondary one, of interpreting them and the existing text of the Bible. Reading and writing combine so closely that they may sometimes appear to be one creative and interpretative activity. In the sixteenth century, for example, the great Spanish mystic St John of the Cross wrote nine ballads or 'romances', the first six of which are based on the Creation, the last three on the Incarnation. The first takes its cue from Genesis 1:1 and the New Testament equivalent, the first verse of St John's Gospel, and produces an account of Creation in line with the Christian reading outlined in my first chapter. The Father, God, lives in and with the Son, Word, and the love in which they live is the Holy Spirit: the love that they experience for one another makes the three Persons one. Creation arises out of the plenitude of this love; the Father decides to give the Son a present of a bride, the spiritual equivalent of an arranged marriage, and this is the subject of the third ballad. The Bride, who will burn in the arms of the Son with love of the Father, is not quite humanity, for her palace is divided into two rooms above and below. Humankind is placed in the lower room. But 'all are part of one body which is called the bride' (ballad 4). There is no fall in John's poetry. Life on earth is seen as a period of hope and labour, of constant love and yearning for the absent love object. The yearning for the beloved Son is the desire for a cataclysmic intervention of the divine into Time, which will yet 'bring forth that flower that will be the earth's flowering' (ballad 5). It is finally in answer to Simeon's particular pressing request that God agrees the time has come. The celestial birth is announced: the labour pains of the world come to an end. The Son agrees to increase the Bride's delight by allowing her to see him like himself, 'under the law of Moses': that is, in the flesh. The Son's resolve is that of the most loyal Bridegroom (ballad 7): to die in order that his Bride might live, and so, rescuing her, to return her to the Father. The last poem, the birth itself, exploits to the full the potential in the Nativity for the roles of Mother and Bride to combine: the infant Jesus is married to his mother as he assumes mortality, and by a mysterious exchange that foreshadows the Redemption, the child god weeps and humanity rejoices.

St John's poetic version of the Creation and Incarnation is hauntingly beautiful. But it is not truly idiosyncratic; and it is certainly not original. What makes this doctrinal poetry possible is a tradition of commentary, patristic exegesis, that lives very late in St John's poem; and it is evident from such poetry that certain parts of the Bible are particularly privileged and connections are formed that are deeply conventional and yet not at all inevitable. A bridge is built from Genesis to the New Testament, in which humanity assumes the shape of the apocalyptic Bride from Revelation and repeats, speaks anew, the great lament of the Bride for an absent Bridegroom that constitutes the Song of Songs. Such connections bear a good deal of exploration. What should be clear at once from St John's poems, late examples as they are, is that such writing is not a question of trying to find an allegory in which to cast a literal narrative. The imagery and the symbolism with which John unfolds his view of Creation, Incarnation and Redemption are not detachable from the significance of John's work. Nor can a 'literal' understanding of John's work be extrapolated from the imagery and the symbolism. Narrative and discourse are deeply interfused. In the earliest days of the Christian Church, the role of the symbol is structural, not an ornament: it serves, as either straight narrative or a paraphrase of the supposedly literal sense of John's poem would not, to convey doctrine at the level of belief. Thus Christian doctrine from the early Church Fathers onwards depends for its formulation on habits and modes of reading that are more literary than they are literal.

Given that the early Christian Church had taken over the whole Jewish Scripture, called it the Old Testament and by adding the New Testament had given it a radically different meaning, it is no great surprise that the early Christians played down the literal meaning. The new kind of Christian meaning began with St Paul, who preached that the letter – the literal sense – kills; and its first major resource in making a harmonious canon of the Old and New Testaments together, is what we now know as typology. Typology is the central link from the Old Testament to the New Testament. It is built into the Pauline and other Epistles (Christ as New Adam), into Christ's teaching itself (as in the parable reference to Himself as Bridegroom), and it is thoroughly developed in the commentary of the Church which abounds in types of Christ: Abel because he dies, Noah because he saves humanity, Jonah because Christ himself mentions him and the three days Jonah spends in the whale are equivalent to the three days Christ spends harrowing hell, and so on. Typology is one part of the machinery of allegorical exegesis.[3] But it is not an addition by the Church Fathers; it is simply an extension of the principle according to which the narrative of the New Testament was itself constructed. This is particularly true of the Gospel narratives, as will be evident in Chapter 5. Inbuilt into the structure of the gospel are specific references to the Psalms, the Book of Isaiah, the Book of Daniel, and so on; and these references were never treated as if they are incidental: in the view of the early Fathers, aligning Jesus with the Old Testament prophecies, 'He explained the texts and the texts explained Him'.[4] The early Fathers could not have been more aware of the link between the Gospel narratives and the Old Testament.

Far from being an embarrassment of any kind, such links were an invaluable weapon in Christian propaganda against the Jews. Jesus is another form of the name Joshua: like Joshua, Jesus comes after Moses, and leads his people into the Promised Land where the law of Moses had failed. Such cross-references were what allowed for the annexation of the Old Testament. Moreover, typology exists in Judaism and was not a Christian invention. The famous Chapter 53 of the Book of Isaiah offers a prophetic type of the Jewish people itself and the sufferings they will undergo. But in Judaism typology looks forward in time, whereas in Christianity it looks backward: for Christ is the fulfilment of the Scriptures. Hence the need felt in the Christian Church from time to time, a need that often tipped into heresy, for a third level of typology that would again open the reading process into a historical future.

$$\text{Old Testament} \quad \text{New Testament} \begin{array}{l} \longrightarrow \text{the Kingdom (Origen) [Teleology]} \\ \searrow \text{Last Things} \rightarrow \text{[Eschatology]} \end{array}$$

The Last Things are the union of Heaven and Earth, Judgement and the end of the world, as in Revelation; and the end of Time, the mystic marriage of Christ and his bride as is consummated in Revelation and prefigured in the Song of Songs. In this way the Song of Songs achieves its prominent place in Christian exegesis, as in the Jewish canon. It may seem to be a poem about carnal love, 'Solomon and the Shulamite'; but if so, what is it doing in the Bible? It is there because what is hardest to interpret allegorically is the supreme test for the exegete: the harder something seems the more important it is going to be. The Song of Songs is the only Old Testament book which fulfils the need of orthodox Christian typology to look forward as well as back; and in that sense it deserves its place as the mystery of mysteries.[5] Figurative language here and in Revelation mediates belief: or rather, it keeps a text open so that belief may close it.

The types of typology mentioned here determine the Christian reading of 'the little books', τα βιβλια, as The Bible. They make many books parts of a whole that is greater than the sum of its parts. They therefore determine a particular structural approach to the whole as a canon. And they also do something very radical: they displace the literal meaning.[6]

Implicit in this typological approach is the historical understanding that the commentator knows more than the individual human writer of each particular book. This is the role of the Holy Spirit in Christian exegesis: in the iconography of the Church Fathers the Holy Spirit is often represented as a dove perched on the shoulder of the reading commentator, murmuring into the commentator's ear the interpretation of the book that the Spirit had itself constructed, so that commentary is represented as a kind of authorial second edition. It would follow that any kind of literal meaning that can be glossed in terms of the intention of the human author is quite secondary to the true meaning of the part when read in this way as part of the whole. In the later Middle Ages, this distinction is formalised in the school of St Victor by a distinction between sense and 'sentence'.[7] Sense was the grammatical meaning, and the intended meaning. Perhaps Isaiah did not quite know that he meant Jesus when he talked of 'the man of sorrows', but the sentence is unmistakable to the commentator. Sense is the meaning of the part alone; sentence is the meaning of the part in relation to the whole. However, the meaning of the whole is not a literal meaning, but a spiritual one. To find it readers do not read the words; readers read through the words, like looking in a mirror. The letter may not kill, but it constricts; and the literal understanding is not a true or a full understanding. The spiritual understanding is to the soul what the literal sense is to the body. Just as in order to live properly, the soul must govern the body; so in order to read properly, to live in the Word, the sentence must govern the sense. Therefore 'the Bible is one vast allegory, a tremendous sacrament in which every detail is symbolic'.[8] The first readers of the Christian Bible read in a literary manner.

It is this attitude which represents the early historical tradition. A so-called 'fundamentalist' insistence on the Bible's literal meaning is a development so late as to appear decadent. Those who lived closest to the events described in the Gospels were in no doubt that not all was to be taken uniformly as literally true. An extreme example is in the New Testament itself: St Paul's discussion of the resurrection of the body in I Corinthians 15: 42–50. I quote James Dunn:

> The resurrection appearances for St Paul have to be classified as some form of visionary experience. Paul's understanding of the resurrected body ('spiritual', not 'natural') certainly implies that he understood Jesus' mode of risen life as different from physical existence; consequently his seeing 'the risen Jesus' (I Cor. 9: 1), must have been of a different order from 'physical' seeing – that is to say, it must have been some form of visionary seeing.[9]

Christ rises in a spiritual body not a physical one; he is seen with spiritual sight. This is not a literal understanding; it is a spiritual one.

Similarly, the first great exegete, Origen, treats the New Testament text which says that Satan took Jesus up on a high mountain to offer him all the kingdoms of the earth, by stating that this did not literally happen as recounted; the account is figurative, for spiritual understanding. Or to give another example, Origen on Genesis is in no doubt whatever that he is reading an inspired fiction:

> Could any man of sound judgement suppose that the first, second and third days had an evening and a morning, when there was yet no sun or moon or stars? Could anyone be so unintelligent as to think that God made a Paradise somewhere in the east and planted it with trees, like a farmer, or that in that Paradise he put a Tree of Life, a tree you could see and know with your senses, a tree you could derive life from by eating its fruit with the teeth in your head? When the Bible says that God used to walk in Paradise in the evening or that Adam hid behind the tree, no-one, I think, will question that these are only fictions, stories of things that never actually happened, and that figuratively they refer to certain mysteries.[10]

There is another reason for preferring the spiritual sense – a subjective one. Here is St Augustine's comment on Chapter 4:2 of the Song of Songs ('thy teeth are like a flock of sheep'):

> I do not know why I feel greater pleasure in contemplating holy men when I view them as the 'teeth' of the Church, tearing men away from their errors and bringing them into the Church's body with all their harshness softened down, just as if they had been torn off and masticated by the teeth.[11]

Even more bluntly symbolic is Origen's commentary on Genesis 18, where God visits Abraham when he is, according to the King James Bible, 'in the plains of Mamre', but in Origen's Greek Septuagint 'under the tree of Mamre': 'for what does it help me who have come to hear what the Spirit teaches the human race, if I hear that "Abraham was standing under a tree"?'. Origen has a good answer: in this case, the etymology of Mamre as 'vision': 'spiritually sharp sight'.

What has worried many modern commentators on patristic exegesis is that sharpness of sight exists by definition in the eye of the beholder. The charge against medieval exegesis is that it often sounds arbitrary, forced and subjective. The charge can be answered; but in order to appreciate its justice one citation of St Ambrose on the fifth day of Creation serves well as, at first glance, a *reductio ad absurdum* of subjectivity:

> Fish are given to man for his use. They also continue for us a pattern of vices to be observed in our society . . . What is the difference between a rich man driven by his wicked lusts to absorb the patrimony of the weak, and the fish called Silurus whose belly is filled with the flesh and blood of smaller fish? . . . We are justified, therefore, in comparing man to a fish.[12]

It must again be said that in this kind of apparent flight of fancy Ambrose is in fact following a certain kind of Alexandrian commentary which displays quite active distrust of the literal sense in order to concentrate on the spiritual.

The birthplace of Christian biblical exegesis was late second-century Alexandria in an era of persecution of Christians. Its father, and greatest master, was Origen (186–c. 254). He is the only one of the major Church Fathers not to be a saint: some of his views were judged to be heretical in a sixth-century council, although this did not stop Origen from being with Augustine the most influential exegete in the history of the Church. The master of the spiritual sense took two major literal stands in his life. The first was his embracing of martyrdom. In the early Church, teaching took place under the threat of death. Origen's life is lived with integrity and ends in torture: not until the world of *Pilgrim's Progress* do we find so acute a visualisation of martyrdom. The second was an adolescent lapse with permanent consequences. The early Christians believed that the end was imminent, the kingdom was about to come (the doctrine that is called *parousia*) and in anticipation of this end encouraged abstinence from the world and flesh. As a young enthusiast, Origen read in St Paul of the need to be a eunuch for Christ, because in the kingdom of Heaven there is neither male nor female: he took it literally, and castrated himself. Origen's castration arises from a failure to understand allegory, the mode of writing in which truth is concealed figuratively so that the literal level is not, in fact, compelling. In the thirteenth-century French poem, the *Roman de la Rose*, Origen's castration is still recalled in a context dealing with the need for non-literal knowledge and the folly of a literal reading.[13] His action was a major deviation from the spiritual sense, and for Origen it was a uniquely literal misinterpretation of the text.

Origen was also a genius, one of the few great critical minds in Western history. In order to understand his achievement and his exegesis, it is necessary to understand the foundations on which he built: those laid by a fellow Alexandrian, the Jewish exegete, Philo. Philo's important commentary was on Genesis.[14]

I have already discussed the fact that there are two accounts of Creation, in Genesis 1 and Genesis 2 respectively. In the previous chapter I offered a version of the generally accepted modern explanation for this, in the multiple layers that mark the textual history of Genesis. By the time of Alexandrian criticism, however, the pious legend that Moses was the author of the Pentateuch, a legend assiduously cultivated by the Priestly school responsible for the account in Genesis 1, was firmly established. There was no textual scholarship then to pose the problem and then remove it. Yet any criticism remotely sensitive to tone, style or logic must be aware of the duality and presumably provide some explanation. It is the first great problem of biblical exegesis. Philo's explanation makes the modern one seem crass and unsubtle. He looks at the six days of creation in contrast to the one day of creation, and concludes that six days is not a period of time but rather the principle of order and productivity; the reason for specifying six days in the account is that all order involves number. Six, Philo says (with Genesis 1:27 in mind, 'male and female he created them both') is by nature as a number both male and female: 1 and 3 are odd (male) numbers, 2 is even (female); 6 is both the sum and the product of these parts $(1 + 2 + 3; 1 \times 2 \times 3)$.

There are two accounts of Creation because God made the intelligible world before He made the visible world. Before the material world of Genesis 2, there existed in the word and reason of God the incorporeal world, what Philo calls 'the word of God engaged in the act of creating', just as the design of a city exists in the brain of an architect (I, ii). The word of God is equivalent to the image of God and these are equivalent to man (as a part), and the universe (as a whole). The man made in the image of God in Genesis I is the idea of man, who is both male and female because he has both mind (*nous*, male) and soul (*psyche*, female) – man was made 'after the pattern of the single Mind, even the Mind of the Universe as an archetype' – and also because God foreconceived the need for both male and female: he foresaw a species. The 'man' who is made in Genesis 2 is not equivalent to the man made in the image of God in Genesis 1, which is the Platonic idea of man; this is the man made of earth and Divine Breath, man as an object of sense perception, an immortal mind in a mortal body, 'the only world citizen', to whom God brings the animals like a teacher with a pupil – so that Adam might bestow the names that God has foreconceived. There are two accounts because in reality all things took place simultaneously (II, 4), but 'the fact that living organisms were afterwards to come into existence one out of another rendered necessary an adumbration of the principle of order in the narrative'. Philo can therefore speak of the 'exceeding beauty of the chain of sequence which Moses has employed in setting forth the bringing in of life'. 'The Creation story', Philo says, 'is Moses' exordium to the Law, implying that the Law and the world are in harmony by the purpose and will of Nature'.

Philo has set out an important principle: the account of Creation is narrative, but Creation itself was not. We need the idea of 'genesis' and the book Genesis as an ordered narrative because we are subject to the senses and live in time. God is not subject to the senses and does not live in time. Time was born at midnight on Day One, when Day Two began, and with it a sequence both of mathematics and of narrative. God has no beginning. For Philo 'In the beginning God' is a tautology. But these things can only be conceived or represented by means of narrative, which has beginnings. What Genesis does is to translate the otherness of creation into narrative. Narrative, the so-called 'literal', is therefore already metaphor.

Philo is a Jewish commentator, but he represents the true 'genesis' of Christian exegesis. It is Philo who makes Christian use of the Old Testament at all possible. For the implication of what Philo has written here, to a mind as bold as Origen's, is that divine truth transcends narrative. Narrative is a cipher, which we read in the light of truth. It is therefore Philo's technique that Origen adapts to Christian apologetic; and it is Philo's architectural metaphor – surviving right to the seventeenth and eighteenth-century view of God as 'the Divine Architect' – that becomes the standard rule for Christian allegory. I quote what Beryl Smalley calls the definitive formulation for reading, by Gregory the Great:

> First we lay the historical foundations, next by pursuing the typical sense we erect a fabric of the mind to be a stronghold of faith; and moreover as the last step, by the grace of moral instruction, we, as it were, clothe the edifice with an overcast of colouring.[15]

What Gregory calls the 'typical sense' incorporates both allegory and typology; it is what Origen calls the spiritual sense. Thus there are three senses for Gregory, as for Origen and Philo: literal, spiritual and moral. Fourfold exegesis emerges when the Venerable Bede, in later medieval Christianity, subdivides the spiritual sense into the allegorical (typological) on the one hand, and the specialised sense (the anagogical) on the other, related to the Last Things (the forward direction of typology), and the Church as an institution.'

Origen follows Philo closely in the account of the beginning ('Scripture is not speaking here of any temporal beginning'), and in the account of the creation of man. The one small difference is that Origen's account of the literal meaning of 'male and female he made them' is more textual:

> It seems to be worth inquiring in this passage according to the letter how, when the woman was not yet made, the Scripture says, 'Male and female he made them.' Perhaps, as I think, it is because of the blessing with which he blessed them saying, 'Increase and multiply and fill the earth'. Anticipating what was to be, the text says, 'Male and female he made them,' since, indeed, man could not otherwise increase and multiply except with the female. Therefore, that there might be no doubt about his blessing that is to come, the text says, 'Male and female he made them.' For in this manner man, seeing the consequence of increasing and multiplying to be from the fact that the female was joined to him, could cherish a more certain hope in the divine blessing. For if the Scripture had said: 'Increase and multiply and fill the earth and have dominion over it,' not adding this, 'Male and female he made them,' doubtless he would have disbelieved the divine blessing, as also Mary said in response to that blessing which was pronounced by the angel, 'How shall I know this, since I know not a man?'[16]

Here is Origen's characteristic subtlety of argument, his eye moving constantly from Genesis in the direction of the New Testament. And of course Origen, as a Christian commentator must, goes many steps further than Philo. He applies the truth of the spiritual understanding to the cipher of the narrative. The boldest step is the first, Origen's gloss on the very first words of the Bible:

> 'In the beginning God created Heaven': that first heaven indeed which . . . is spiritual, is our mind, which is also itself spirit, that is, our spiritual man which sees and perceives God. But that corporeal heaven, which is called the firmament (Gen. 1:8), is our outer man which looks at things in a corporeal way.[17]

If readers are to break through the corporeal seeing of that 'outer man', and see and perceive God truly – that is, in the spirit – we must take the moral of Genesis 1:7: we too must 'divide the waters'. Readers too must say 'Let there be light' (1:3): these lights are the greater light, Christ ruling the day, and the Church, ruling the night of the body, with stars to guide us such as Moses and all to whom Scripture testifies that they please God. God makes 'fowl that may fly above the earth in the open firmament of heaven' (1:20), and also beasts of the earth and creeping things, 'everything that creepeth upon the earth' (1:25). It is an acute critical intelligence that sets these two together, and suggests that we read 'thoughts of good' for the birds and 'evil thoughts' for the creeping creatures. Likewise, 'the great whales' of 1:21 are identified with 'impious thoughts'. And it is a razor-sharp intelligence that immediately anticipates and triumphantly rebuts the commonsense objection:

> But someone asks how the great whales and creeping creatures are interpreted as evil and the birds as good when Scriptures said about all together, 'And God saw that they were good.'
>
> Those things which are opposed to the saints are good for them because they can overcome them and when they have overcome them they become more glorious with God. Indeed when the devil requested that power be given to him against Job, the adversary, by attacking him, was the cause of double glory for Job after his victory. What is shown from the fact that he received double those things which he lost in the present is that he will, without doubt, also receive in the same manner in the heavenly places. And the Apostle says that 'No one is crowned except the one who has striven lawfully.' And indeed, how will there be a contest if there not be one who resists? How great the beauty and splendour is of light would not be discerned unless the darkness of night intervened. Why are some praised for purity unless because others are condemned for immodesty? Why are strong men magnified unless weak and cowardly men exist? If you use what is bitter then what is sweet is rendered more praiseworthy. If you consider what is dark, the things which are bright will appear more pleasing to you. And, to put it briefly, from the consideration of evil things the glory of good things is indicated more brilliantly. For this reason, therefore, the Scripture says this about everything: 'And God saw that they were good'.[18]

There is another strong and persuasive piece of moral exegesis when Origen identifies the vegetation and the fruit of the earth with bodily affections, which can be used for good or evil: for bodily affections correspond to vegetation, being the part of us that is rooted in the earth.

What underlies this kind of exegesis is Origen's conviction that the Bible is the book of spiritual love, to be read – consumed, eaten – as spiritual food. Spiritual understanding is the reading of Divine Thought which veils itself in biblical narrative. It is the penetration to the spiritual heaven in Genesis 1 which exists before narrative begins. Most of all, the human reader is required to understand the Scripture as God created the world, by an ordering that might literally be called preconception – or foreconceit – like an architect planning a city. The text itself, without form and void, needs the spirit of a reader to move upon it.

It cannot be said, however, that Origen is neglectful of the literal sense. On the contrary, his attention to the exact meaning of Hebrew words and the quality of their Greek translation is exemplary. When he examines Noah's ark, Origen puzzles in great detail over the mathematics of the thing. How could an ark of that size contain so many animals? Here Origen notes that the Egyptian cubit is ten times the usual cubit, and that Moses must have been using that scale, as a man versed in Egyptian science – an example of what the New Critics would call the biographical fallacy. What was the shape of the ark? and so on. But Origen is in no doubt that the greater significance of the story is that we must build our own spiritual ark as the spiritual Noah, who is Christ, requires; and this ark, movingly, is represented as a library of Christian books. Most important of all, Origen's method enables him to do, quite effortlessly, what early Christian exegesis had to do: confront the old law of the Jewish Pentateuch, and de-Judaise it by finding a spiritual sense. Thus he takes on the very unpromising topic of the circumcision of Abraham (a topic of some importance in the early church).[19] Origen is able to quote a figurative meaning to the word 'circumcision' in the Epistles of Paul: circumcision of the lips, circumcision of the ears, and so on. And then he asks: if the Holy Spirit can use circumcision allegorically in reference to lips and ears, why cannot Abraham's foreskin be allegorical too? In short, Origen aligns his commentary with the Gospel to the Gentiles.

The last example may seem bizarre: it is not. It is characteristic of the best critics that they select the most difficult passages, or build a convincing interpretation from what may seem to be small and unpromising details. The incestuous story of Lot and his daughters; the birth of Isaac and the fact that he is weaned; Abimelech, and his wish to take Abraham's wife Sara; the role of wells in Genesis: these are all subjects of Origen's homilies on Genesis. The homilies are invariably satisfying and confident. Of course Origen does not render 'the literal meaning', but he does not purport to. Indeed he seems to doubt the possibility that such a reading exists. The real danger comes with critics who do render an allegorical interpretation and pretend that it is the literal meaning – and this is never a fault of Origen's. He does, masterfully and honestly, just what he says he is doing. That makes him an examplary critic – the first, and perhaps the greatest, critic of the Christian world: the author of the spiritual sense of Scripture.[20] It is true, of course, that Origen read the Bible and found what he wanted to find. When has anyone ever done otherwise, with the Bible of all books?

Medieval exegesis of all kinds follows the path set by Origen, though it often tries to give the literal sense a little more scope. St Ambrose, for example, insists that the 'darkness' and 'abyss' of Genesis 1 should be taken in the literal sense; but he then proceeds to moralise them, and to weave an inspired series of fantastic and eclectic digressions in, around and out of the sequence of the text. But the spiritual sense is primary, as is the double typology by which the Old Testament is treated as the type of the New, and the New Testament is treated as, in Origen's phrase, 'the shadow of the kingdom'.

It is instructive to compare with Origen's homilies on Genesis St Ambrose's fine fourth-century commentary, the *Hexameron* (the Six Days of Creation). Ambrose wrote in Milan, in a more relaxed environment then that in which the besieged Origen wrote. His is a self-consciously literary work, freely quoting from the whole Bible, from the *Physiologus* (the medieval Bestiary), from Horace, Virgil, Lucretius and other Roman poets. Here is the start of Book 6, 'the sixth day':

> This is the sixth day, which brings to a close the account of the origin of created things and at the same time terminates the discourse which we have undertaken on the genesis of matter. This day calls for even greater expenditure of toil, because we have reached a critical point: the culmination of the whole debate. We must realize that during the preliminary stages of contests in music, song, or sport, however numerous and important they may be, there is no award of a wreath of victory. This presentation of a wreath for victory is assigned to the last day. On that occasion the expectant decision is reached, together with the shame or the reward which either defeat or victory brings.[21]

Again, this introduction signifies literariness. The subject and the process of Ambrose's writing is presented as a literary or rhetorical structure. The second chapter of the fourth day opens with Genesis 1:14: 'and God said, Let there be lights in the firmament of the heaven to divide the day from the night; and let them be for signs, and for seasons, and for days and years'.

Who says this? God says it. And to whom is he speaking if not to his son? Therefore, God the Father says: 'Let the sun be made', and the Son made the sun, for it was fitting that the 'Son of Justice' should make the sun of the world. He therefore brought it to light. He illuminated it and granted it the power of light.[22]

Ambrose then follows Origen. The Sun and the Moon represent Christ and the Church; but he is then sidetracked into an accurate scientific description of the moon's waning – even though only the horns shine, the moon is still all there. A theological point is clearly in Ambrose's mind, but it is not articulated as Ambrose warms instead to the natural science. The thought of light leads him to Moses and the burning bush: the word 'fire' leads him to Deuteronomy; he then returns to sunlight in order to speak of shadows, but again in a scientific sense. Ambrose then comes to the notion of time passing, which takes him, by way of an array of biblical texts, to a rejection of astrological determinism. He expounds a passage from the Song of Songs in terms of the seasons, and an array of supporting texts leads him to an allegorical exposition of Psalm 16:8: 'Thou shalt protect me under the shadow of my wings', reading 'shadow' as the shadow of the Cross and the shadow of salvation. But this leads him not to a further exegesis of a biblical text, but to a naturalistic and chatty digression on the properties of shadows. Then he goes on to a similarly scientific treatment of sun and sunrise. All is grist to the mill in Ambrose's description of God's work and its properties: moral theology and natural science are one and the same in the description of Creation. Moralisation, the spiritual sense, scientific detail, humour – all belong in such an account: had not Philo called God the creator of laughter, and called laughter 'the poetry God makes'?

Origen sees in the name 'Isaac' the etymology of the word 'laughter', God's promise to Abraham. Such laughter accounts for the tone of St Ambrose's writing on fish, quoted earlier. He knows that he is stretching the point as far as it will go, and he builds it up into a kind of witty conceit which anticipates John Donne by over one millennium: 'Do not hold in fear, my good fish, the hook of Peter. It does not kill; rather it consecrates.' But Ambrose knows that it is licensed in the New Testament: the kingdom of heaven in Matthew 13: 47–50 is like a catch of fishes. He also knows that the fish is a Christian symbol because the Greek word *ichthous* is taken as an acronymic name of Christ. He is poised throughout for the brilliant sacramental twist, the return to Origen's spiritual sense: human are like fish because they live in water, and water for humans is 'the source for the remission of sins'.[23]

There are not many exegetes quite like St Ambrose; but his happy, and literary, transitions from nature to the spiritual sense are not untypical, and they are seen as a decorous tribute to divine creation. Was not God, for St Ambrose (day two), a master rhetorician, moulding an entire universe to fit the rhetorical doctrine of *discordia concors*? How, St Ambrose asks, could God see that 'it' was good on the second day, when 'it' was incomplete? Because God is an author, and authors know what is coming next:

> He praises each individual part as befitting what is to come. He praises the total work, which is compounded of the elegance of each part. True beauty, in fact, consists of a fitting adjustment in each part and in the whole.

How, one might ask, does St Ambrose know? Because he too is an author, and is thus in a good position to understand his senior colleague. Not just Genesis but creation itself respond to rhetorical theory: both are literary texts.

There is another, unavoidable and more disturbing sense in which the Bible is literary: it is made of human language. Origen asks why the Bible says 'God saw that it was good', rather than 'God *said* that it was good'. It is because true understanding is not spiritual speech but, as I have stressed, spiritual sight. Origen saw clearly that when we read, we take the meaning we want to take. I know no critic of any period more outspoken than Origen in recognising this. If we resist Origen today, it will be because we have other ideological affiliations; but will we be as honest about our preconceptions as Origen was about his?

Origen stressed the consequence, that reading is a matter of ethical choice: we should choose the best possible meaning, which is the spiritual sense. This implies that there are other possible meanings we could take. When Augustine sets out to codify the Christian mode of reading in his *De Doctrina Christiana*, he acknowledges the ambivalence of signs, which can be interpreted *in bono* ('in a good sense') or *in malo* ('in a bad sense').[24] This ambivalence is a powerful resource for meaning: the same sign can mean opposite things in different contexts. The lion, for example, in one context will signify Christ, while in another it will signify the devil. The rule for determining the right reading for the particular context is an ethical one, the doctrine of charity – with which both any Christian's reading of the text and the text itself, insofar as they can be distinguished, must accord. In larger terms too, where the apparent literal meaning of a passage or book would be in conflict with charity, then the passage or book must be interpreted spiritually. For example, the Song or Songs cannot be about sex, because that is carnal love and in conflict with charity: it must therefore be to do with divine love. The criterion for reading here, the doctrine of charity, is what the reader both brings to the passage and finds in it. But there exists at the larger, discursive level of interpretation something resembling the ambivalence of the sign; there exists at both levels a possibility, if both reader and reading should be out of accord with charity, that a bad reader will choose a wrong meaning. Understanding is indeed spiritual sight, but spiritual sight may be in conflict with physical sight: Jesus, after all, said 'If thine eye be evil thy whole body shall be full of darkness' (Matt. 6:23). According to patristic exegesis, the Bible is literary because it necessarily contains, and enshrines, the possibility of its own misunderstanding. For the Bible is a work of language, that inferior language whose nouns God was content to leave Adam to invent; and in earthly language, even the Holy Spirit cannot avoid being misunderstood and misread. What readers read in the Bible are words; only interpretation will make them Word. And inspired interpretation at that: the Holy Spirit must read, as well as write, the Bible.

In this acknowledgement that for a discourse to have meaning, it must also be open to misprision, medieval exegesis is centred on what modern theory – literary, linguistic, semiotic – would regard as a crucial insight. If the desire to write meaningfully in a context of values and ideas reflects a desire to build in some sense a closed system, the fact of writing in language opens that system to multiple interpretation. Many literary theorists, and a modest number of theologians, claim to value such openness; in practice, however, few seem comfortable with it. Some early exegetes, by contrast, seem to have been able to practise their enjoyment. They write as if they were able to foresee, with pleasure rather than alarm, the diversity and multiplicity of subsequent interpretation. We are therefore in no position to dismiss their work as irrelevant.

Modes of interpretation since the Reformation

Various traditions of medieval allegorical exegesis were the staple fare of the European Catholic Church to the Reformation. There are changes, of course, and many modifications; but what is more impressive is the amount that is neither changed nor modified.[25] Two corollaries stem from the doctrine of the spiritual sense. The first is that it is for adepts: one has to be trained to see beyond the letter of the text, the words on the page, and what one sees will depend on what one has been trained to see. It follows that the interpreter's role is a privileged one. Secondly, the interpreter is divinely inspired: the Holy Spirit has not only to write Scripture but also to read it. This does not mean, however, that any reader has access to divine inspiration. On the contrary, according to orthodox Catholic theology, the Church is the sole agent through which divine inspiration works, and it holds a monopoly on that inspiration. Only through the Church have lay people access to God's word. It follows that authority (belonging to the Church) is co-equal in importance with Scripture.

Modern readers may be forgiven for feeling that the tradition of allegorical exegesis practised in the entire medieval period is a very rich one: stimulating in small doses and indigestible in excess. Towards the end of the medieval period, say from the thirteenth century, it came to be seen as rich in another sense too: the equivalent intellectually of the Church's riches materially. Such a critique contrasts the awesome simplicity of the Bible, especially the New Testament – simplicity of style and content, the simply phrased categorical demand to live simply – with the intellectual complexity, the privileged social influence and the corporate earthly wealth of the medieval Church as an institution. In such a comparison, the Church is the loser; it stands judged by the criteria of a Bible that it adulterates by interpretation. The conflict reaches its peak in the thirteenth and fourteenth centuries, with St Francis expounding a lifestyle of real apostolic poverty, and St Thomas Aquinas later replying, in effect, that we do not all have to live like apostles in order to be saved. Rich people can be saved too, by doing what the Church tells them. According to Aquinas, when Christ said to the rich young man 'Give up thy goods and follow me', he was speaking figuratively; in any case this was not necessarily meant to be a general rule. The general rule is given by St Paul, and overrides all others: 'Remain in that station to which you were called'. The notion survives into the nineteenth century as 'the rich man in his castle, the poor man at his gate'.

The reaction against the material wealth of the Church, and the intellectual richness of its authority of interpretation, begins well before the Reformation. So too does an allied but quite separate desire to get away from the labyrinths of the spiritual sense of Scripture to its letter: what do the Scriptures really mean? What do the words on the page really say? This sort of question leads to study of the original languages of the Bible: Hebrew and Greek. It also leads to textual scholarship of an objective and uncommitted kind: what were the original readings of the text? what are the best manuscripts? and so on.

The two sorts of question came together in the Reformation, but they did so quite briefly. The first, the desire to live as Christ ordered and the Apostles obeyed, can be called the literal concern; the second, the desire to discover by textual study just what Jesus actually did order, can be called the historical concern. A great deal of perplexity is caused by the tendency of the Christian tradition at all times to insist that the historical and the literal are the same. They are not. The historical concern is often very literal-minded: hence the development of the communion sacrament from the Last Supper, hence medieval and later inquisitions and burnings based on the biblical order 'Thou shalt not suffer a witch to live'. But the literal is often, in this sense, very unhistorical: the Copernican revolution in biblical scholarship occurred in the seventeenth century when some scholars realised that Moses did not write the Pentateuch and could not have done so, given the date of manuscripts with 'original' readings. It continues today with the insistence of some biblical scholars that the resurrection of Jesus is not necessarily a historical fact: 'The well-known stories about the empty tomb and about Jesus' apparition did not intend to give an account of facts'.[26] In short, historical study of the text often leads to an understanding of the Bible that is quite at odds with the literal urge to live out biblical narrative as if it were true and because it is believed to be true; and in that conflict lies the key to debates about the Bible in the last six hundred years.

The literal and historical concerns came together in the great early sixteenth-century scholar, Erasmus, who edited a good version of the Greek New Testament and regarded disinterested textual study as a way to reform the life of the Church from the inside.[27] But the Reformation was more interested in the reform and less interested in the disinterested study. The reaction against material and intellectual wealth over-shadows scholarship; what matters is a more dramatic challenge to the Church's authority than textual scholarship can ever provide. It is not that the reformers were not interested in textual scholarship; but there came a time when they had to make a choice, at least of priorities, and they chose what could be called historical drama. Luther challenged the authority of the Church in the name of Christ; and the only authority to which he could appeal was therefore the Bible, which he translated into German. He had a very businesslike approach to the question of the biblical canon – which books should be in it, and which not: if a book teaches Christ it is apostolic; if not it should be thrown away. But Luther could not appeal to the authority of traditional interpretation; he could only appeal to the words on the page. 'The Bible is the Holy Spirit's own peculiar book, writing and Word.' 'God is in every syllable.' 'No iota is in vain.' 'One should tremble before a letter of the Bible, more than before the whole world.' 'Everything in the Bible is to be believed because the book constitutes a whole, and he who does not believe one statement cannot believe anything.' Moreover, Luther and the people around him tried not only to read the Bible but to live it. As Roland Bainton puts it, 'The Men of Luther's circle lived in a perpetual Passion Play':

> Luther steeped himself in Scripture, projected himself into the experiences of Biblical personages, thought their thoughts after them, and sometimes with more acuteness of feeling than the record itself relates. How Luther marvelled at Noah, who had the courage to believe in God's word and to build an ark when there was no cloud in the sky! How his neighbours must have mocked him for constructing a seagoing vessel far from the coast! It was all the harder for Noah because he had lived so long. Not only while the ark was under construction, but for hundreds of years beforehand he must have endured the taunts of unbelievers. 'If I had seen such men in the camp of the ungodly opposing me I should have thrown down my ministry in sheer desperation. Nobody knows how hard it is for one man to stand out against the consensus of all the other Churches and against the judgement of his noblest and choicest friends.[28]

This is brilliant and it is also moving; but it is one step back to the old problem. If anybody can have direct access to God in the Scripture, what was to stop someone opposing Luther and the new Protestant Churches on exactly the same grounds as the Protestants opposed the Pope? The discreetly Catholic English poet, John Dryden, put the challenge wickedly but well in the seventeenth century:

> For did not Arius first, Socinus now,
> The son's eternal godhead disavow?
> And did not these by gospel texts alone
> Condemn our doctrine and maintain their own?
> Have not all heretics the same pretence,
> To plead the Scriptures in their own defence?[29]

Once Christianity is divided into interpretative factions, it splits again and again: Luther, and Calvin, face a challenge almost at once from more extreme sectarian sects. Suddenly in the midst of his commendations of Scripture alone, we hear Luther sounding like an allegorical exegete and insisting that there is not a choice between the literal and the spiritual sense of the Scriptures: 'Scripture is its own interpreter, proving, judging and illuminating everything'. Then it is not, after all, the words on the page that are the criteria (since 'Scr001the page. If someone were to argue with you from the Scriptures, you should argue back that they have not understood the spirit of what they cite. So you claim, in fact, to be a privileged interpreter: authority is dethroned, only to be reassimilated. Neither Luther nor Calvin was what today we would call a fundamentalist. In Calvin's Geneva, a textual scholar, Sebastian Castellio, argued against the authority of the Song of Songs. He was refused admission to the ministry and politely asked to leave Geneva. Or, as Calvin wrote: 'Castellio said that it was a lascivious obscene poem in which Solomon described his indecent amours. We told him . . . that he should not be so rash as to despise the perpetual consensus of the Church universal'.[30] Calvin's attitude is a case of old wine in new bottles, authority reinstated by stealth.

Lutheran and Calvinist commentators were as committed as any medieval exegete to a notion of the harmony of the parts. Though there may be certain superficial inconsistencies, which Luther, for instance, brushed aside, everything in the Bible agrees with everything else in the Bible. Francis Turretin, Geneva's city pastor and professor of theology from 1648 to 1687 asks: 'Are there in Scripture true contradictions, or any irreconcilable passages, which cannot be resolved or harmonised in any way?' He answers: 'No'.[31] But although Turretin recognises that the true meaning of the Bible is a spiritual one, and although he recognises very fully that the literal meaning of a passage may actually be figurative, so that he is prepared to recognise allegory in a passage if the language of the passage forces it upon him, he rejects allegorical exegesis; and by so doing he makes the task of harmonising all the parts supremely difficult. The reason for recognising that the true meaning of the Bible is a spiritual one is easy to understand; since it is in the Bible itself it is inescapable: the Bible speaks to believers, and only to believers will its message be 'the truth'. 'Those who have ears to hear, let them hear.' In the language of the Bible the word is the seed which causes rebirth (I Peter 1:23), the lamp by which we are guided (Psalm 119:105), the food by which we are nourished (Hebrews 5:13–14; Isaiah 55:1–2) and the foundation on which we depend (Ephesians 2:20). But how can we be sure that the meaning we find there, if we call ourselves believers, is the 'true' one? Here Turretin takes the fateful step: the true meaning is the one which the author of a particular book intended.

The logic of this interest in authorial intention leads to an increased reliance on textual scholarship. But Turretin's interest in the Bible is of the sort I have called literal. He wishes to follow what the Bible teaches, and therefore accepts the 'words on the page' as a changeless blueprint. He immediately comes into conflict with the textual scholarship whose interest is what I have called historical, which implies that many parts of the Bible cannot be taken literally. This sort of scholarship shows that the books of the Bible are of multiple and diverse authorship: what one author intended might well be different from, and unacceptable to, another biblical author. What happens then to the harmony of the parts?

The problem is acute in Turretin's time because in France in 1678 the great French scholar Richard Simon won his modern title of the 'Father of Biblical Criticism' by publishing his critical history of the Old Testament, 'which using the most accurate available texts and the methods of philology reached the conclusion that Moses was not the author of the Pentateuch, but only of the Mosaic Law, that the chronology of the various parts of the Old Testament was confused, and that within the framework of some of its books, the order of their contents had been transposed'.[32] This is the Copernican revolution in biblical criticism; and Turretin will have absolutely nothing to do with it. He insists: 'that the prophets and apostles were such, and that they wrote the books attributed to them, cannot be called in question without destroying all belief in *historical records*, and giving rise to total scepticism' (my italics). How dare anyone argue that Moses was an impostor? (This is the reverse of what Simon actually argued: he said that an impostor pretended to be Moses.) Turretin proceeds to attack overly detailed textual criticism of the Hebrew manuscripts: 'If the Hebrew of the Old Testament and the Greek of the New Testament are not authentic, there is no authentic version'.[33]

What has happened here is extraordinary. For Turretin, authenticity is seen as equivalent to the letter of the generally received text and this in turn is identified with 'historical records'. Christianity which bases itself on the sole authority of the Bible becomes a belief in the Bible as a true and accurate historical record, and that belief in undermined by biblical criticism itself. Protestant orthodoxy in the seventeenth century falls into the trap neatly sidestepped by Luther, who insisted – inconsistently, perhaps, but wisely – that 'the word of God is not at all that which is written'. Less agile minds now ordain that the Word of God and the words on the page of the Bible are one and the same; to doubt the one is to doubt the other. The uneasy relationship between biblically based faith and biblical criticism subsides into a yawning chasm.

Given Frei's monumental study, and others', there is no need to give an exhaustive study of biblical reading from the seventeenth century to the twentieth century.[34] Biblically based faith, the literal, goes one way; biblical criticism, the historical, another. Those who care work desperately hard to bridge the chasm. Those who do not, scoff – as in Voltaire's comment on Genesis, that God seemed to be weak on geography – or lose interest, as the Bible throughout the period has lost general readers.

There is also no need to document the very literal-minded nature of many appeals to believe in the Bible today, though I confess to a feeling of constant astonishment that those who profess to rely on the Bible so much seem to know so little about it. The way in which the Bible has been consistently pitted against science seems unfortunate, and unfair to both. There is the evolutionary controversy, in modern times as in Victorian England, but at least that raises some serious issues. In many ways a more telling example is the controversy in Victorian England about the introduction of small doses of chloroform given to mothers during childbirth. The issue was finally resolved by Queen Victoria, who bore nine children and hated every moment until she discovered chloroform. The argument was not about natural childbirth; it was about, and was debated by means of, quotations from Genesis. Those who were against chloroform quoted God's words in Chapter 3:16: 'Unto the woman he said, I will greatly multiply thy sorrow and thy conception: in sorrow thou shalt bring forth children'. Those who supported chloroform countered with Genesis 2:21: 'And the Lord God caused a deep sleep to fall upon Adam'. (The first operation in recorded history was therefore by general anaesthetic.) In neither case is this any way to read Genesis, or indeed anything else.

Neither Origen and the Church Fathers nor, I suspect, Luther would have felt the need to defend the Bible against the discoveries of science: they would have admired the accounts of Creation in Genesis 1 and 2 all the more as wonderful spiritual fables. St Ambrose would have added a chapter on chimpanzees to the *Hexameron*. History and science are different fields, not conflicting ones. As Philo puts it: 'Probably there was an actual man called Samuel, but we conceive of the Samuel of the Scripture not as a living compound of soul and body, but as a mind which rejoices in the service and worship of God and that only.'[35] But from the seventeenth century onwards, with the fateful confusion between literal and historical, with the consistent havering between the author's intention and the spiritual benefit gained by the reader, which are two different things, biblical exegetes feel the need to leap onto the scientific bandwagon and all too often land under the wheels. It is a seventeenth-century calculation (1642), not an early Christian one, that the world was created at 9 a.m. on 23 October in the year 4004 BCE: the person who did the sum split his bets between a bid for sainthood and membership of the Royal Society.

Ultimately, of course, it brings discredit on the Bible itself. In 1722 the eminent professor of mathematics, William Whiston, published his *Essay towards restoring the true Text of the Old Testament and for vindicating the Citations made thence in the New Testament*, which addressed what was by now seen as the problem that 'many of the Old Testament prophecies quoted in the New Testament had apparently had a meaning imposed on them which they did not originally have'.[36] Whiston's solution was to conjecture massive textual forgery in the Old Testament by Jewish enemies of Christ, with the intention of discrediting Christianity by making Old Testament prophecies differ from it. This example at least takes us back in the direction of textual scholarship, however bizarre. It reminds us that scholarship provides no defence against prejudice. Along similar lines, but much further down the track, the eminent German scholar Friedrich Delitzsch published in 1921 his book *The Great Deception*, arguing that the Christian Church would be a great deal better off if the Old Testament were abolished. He called it 'an unbroken conglomeration of contradictory reports and whole stories of non-historical, purely fabricated sagas and fables; in short, a book filled with conscious and unconscious deceptions, in part self-deception: a very dangerous book to be used only with the greatest care'.[37] An attack on the Old Testament is an attack on Judaism, and Delitzsch called overtly for the greatest possible attention to be paid to the Jewish Question; in Adolf Hitler he found a critical disciple. This sort of disillusionment occurs when people expect too much from the Bible, more than can be expected from any book: not knowledge, but accurate information; not truth to life but life itself. This sort of demand is hysterical, and it generated extraordinarily shameful scandals. One example will suffice: in 1697, in Edinburgh, one Thomas Aikenhead, aged 18, was hanged for arguing that Ezra, rather than Moses, was the author of the Pentateuch. Modern textual criticism might argue that Aikenhead was somewhat closer to the truth than the piously outraged Calvinists who hanged him.[38]

Meanwhile, textual scholarship grew strong. In 1753 Jean Astruc became the father of what is known as 'the higher criticism of the Bible', the study of whole documents: by taking the instances of the names of God in Genesis, YHWH and Elohim, he demonstrated the hypothesis that two original documents had been conflated, and so laid the cornerstone of modern 'scientific' study of the Scriptures.[39] This sort of study culminated in the magnificent work of Julius Wellhausen in 1878, who demonstrated the further hypothesis that Genesis is the result of a combination of three documents, J, E (the Elohist) and P, at the time of P, the priestly dominance in Jerusalem at the time of Ezekiel in the fifth century BCE.[40] There was also a fourth document in the whole Pentateuch, D for Deuteronomy, third in the documentary series and dating from the time of Jeremiah: the Deuteronomic code, then, contains the law ascribed to Moses, but in fact at least eight centuries later than the probable time of the (now historically problematic) Moses.

In New Testament criticism, a similar situation was postulated: Mark's Gospel comes first in the order; a lost source called Q (for *Quelle*), was combined with Mark to make Matthew; the whole Gospel message was adapted for a non-Palestinian audience by Luke, who added to it a distinctive tradition of his own, which we now celebrate as the Christmas story; all the Gospels are later than the Epistles of St Paul, who shows relatively little knowledge of the stories of the life of Jesus; and the New Testament canon may have taken over a century to form, and reveals everywhere the struggle between the two schools of early Christianity, the Jewish, associated with Peter, and the Gentile, associated with Paul. Among the documents and oral traditions from which the Gospel writers worked would have been collections of the sayings of Jesus, such as the so-called Gospel of Thomas discovered this century and other Qumran material. These sayings show a shift in early Christianity: whereas Jesus, until additions in the latest Gospel of all, John, never speaks on behalf of God, the later writers speak on behalf of God and Jesus; that is, they move from professing the faith *of* Jesus to faith *in* Jesus; and the Bible itself reveals this movement.[41] Most of this was documented by the end of the nineteenth century; it has taken until recently for the views to win widespread acceptance in the churches, and now textual criticism is again in a state of flux. The effects of course are very far-reaching. I will restrict myself here to the Old Testament.

First, it allows modern readers to understand a great deal more about the history and literary types of the books of the Old Testament. These are normally divided into three categories: the Law (the Pentateuch); the Prophets (early: Joshua, Judges, Samuel, Kings; later: Isaiah, Jeremiah, Ezekiel, and 'the Roman XII'); and the third category, the Writings (Psalms, Proverbs, Job, The Song of Songs, Ruth, Lamentations, Ecclesiastes, Esther, Daniel, Ezra/Nehemiah, Chronicles). They span a huge period, and were compiled and put together as a canon later in the history of pre-Christian Judaism. They arise also from diverse historical contexts; they cover a wide range of literary types; and so-called 'historical' works, for example, from the Pentateuch to Chronicles/ Kings, range from myth and oral tradition to written accounts by eyewitnesses. Each must be evaluated on its merits.

Secondly, especially in the Pentateuch, the Old Testament begins to look like a patchwork quilt: all sorts of materials are stitched together. The pattern seen already in Genesis 1 and 2 is in fact the prevalent pattern throughout. In Genesis, an account by one source, say E, will have a verse or two by, say, J inserted, and will have been reshaped and edited by P and possibly D before P. Thirdly, this means that the Old Testament provides reliable historical evidence of the world view of Judaism in the fifth century BCE and very poor historical evidence of Jewish history before, say, David. Wellhausen believed that there was no evidence for an historical Abraham.

Fourthly, the notion of the harmony of the parts is utterly and irredeemably shattered. Interpretation cannot in conscience ignore such textual fragmentation.

How can the situation be retrieved? One answer is provided by Strauss in the nineteenth century and reworked by Bultmann in existentialist terms in the twentieth century:

> We have to realise that the narrators [of the Gospels] testify sometimes, not to outward facts, but to ideas, often the most practical and beautiful ideas, constructions which even eyewitnesses had unconsciously put upon facts, imagination concerning them, reflections upon them, reflections such as were natural to the time and at the author's level of culture. What we have here is not falsehood, but misrepresentation of the truth. It is a plastic, naive, and, at the same time, often most profound apprehension of truth, within the area of religious feeling and poetic insight. It results in narrative, legendary, mythical in nature, illustrative often of spiritual truth in a manner more perfect than any hard, prosaic statement could achieve.[42]

For Bultmann, 'The Bible does not speak to us objectively in general terms which philosophers (or scientists, or historians) can understand; it speaks to us in all the passionate subjectivity of our loneliness as we face the problem of our existence.' We demythologise what might be called the wrapping: that is, we use scholarship to understand how the truths of the Bible came to take the form they have; and inside the parcel we find the truths that speak to us all the more openly. It is somewhere between a paradox and a circular argument. As Bultmann puts it: 'In order to understand the text it is necessary to believe what the text expresses, which itself can only be known through understanding it.'[43]

What has happened here is again extraordinary. It is the grand cyclic motion of the history of biblical interpretation: every objective cycle leads to a subjective one. In order to read the Bible at all, we have to know what we expect, or want, to find.

There are of course more objective approaches than Bultmann's. Archaeology and the study of Mesopotamian documents from other cultures allow us to distinguish, in some cases quite sharply, between myth and history in Genesis. The Flood story, for example, is a myth common to many cultures of the area: as, for example, in the Sumerian *Epic of Gilgamesh*. Why then does it find a place in Genesis? The answer is complicated because there are in fact two accounts of the Flood: that by J, which stresses that God is propitiated by a burnt offering, a sacrifice; and that by E, which is characteristically more theological. But the interest in both cases may be gauged by Genesis 6:1–5:

> And it came to pass, when men began to multiply on the face of the earth, and daughters were born unto them,
>
> That the sons of God saw the daughters of men that they were fair; and they took them wives of all which they chose.
>
> And the Lord said, My spirit shall not always strive with man, for that he also is flesh; yet his days shall be an hundred and twenty years.
>
> There were giants in the earth in those days; and also after that, when the sons of God came in unto the daughters of men, and they bare children to them, the same became mighty men which were of old, men of renown.

The Anchor Bible commentary describes this as an 'isolated fragment' characterised by 'undisguised mythology'. It finds a key to the passage in the reference (KJB to 'giants', '*Nephilim*'), in verse 4, also named as a giant race in Numbers 13:33, and shows parallels in Greek and Phoenician mythology, as well as Hittite texts and Ugaritic culture. But it would follow from such research that the story is told without any real discrimination on the authors' part as to whether it is history or myth: it is told because the tradition exists – and the tradition, after all, whether true or false, is historical fact – and because it can be made to make a moral point. It is there precisely because the authors believed that, historical or not, it is true. It is there for its spiritual sense. On the other hand, we have Genesis 14, a chapter totally unlike anything else in Genesis, on the theme of invasion from the east. Scholars cannot attribute it to any of the four known documentary traditions, and therefore some invoke a fifth, called (appropriately) X. It turns out that it in its turn probably has a source from pre-Hittite Anatolia; if so, Abraham is cited in a quasi-historical narrative written by foreigners. And if this is indeed so, it might also follow that scepticism could be taken too far, and that ancient documentary evidence exists to testify that Abraham was a real historical figure.[44]

One more type of modern biblical criticism deserves to be mentioned, Form-Criticism. It grew up in reaction against the documentary method: there is a real danger, after all, that being trained in finding four sources predisposes one not only to find four sources but also to subdivide them each, say, into four more, and so on *ad infinitum*. The form-critical method has a great deal to teach modern criticism of all kinds, because it combines close attention to language, and the recognition that literary language is different from ordinary spoken utterance, with an equally close attention to historical and social context. The most approachable book on the subject is that by Klaus Koch, *The Growth of the Biblical Tradition*. In form-criticism, form and content are studied at one and the same time: the unit studied may be a whole genre or a formulaic phrase, but in each case it must be an 'established literary type' holding in common with other examples of the type a common 'fund of thoughts and feelings'. These types do not exist in a vacuum: 'they are found in particular forms in particular circumstances'. The purpose of form-criticism is to establish the type and then find its *Sitz im Leben*, its context in life: a literary form of expression found in a particular place at a particular time in particular cultural circumstances. For example, the *Sitz im Leben* of Christ's Beatitudes in the Sermon on the Mount:

> does not refer to the particular occasion upon which Jesus proclaimed the Beatitudes, but to the typical relationship between him and his followers which made a formal utterance of this kind possible. For the Beatitudes are not, as might

be assumed by modern hearers, a spontaneous discourse, but they are carefully formulated *doctrine*, the result of the long history of the literary type.[45]

This is a sophisticated critical method, and it has two golden rules: first that no biblical text can adequately be understood without a consideration of the *Sitz im Leben* of its literary type; and, second, that no way of life in ancient Israel and in the early Christian community can be exhaustively detailed without a thorough study of all literary types relating to it. It also yields some rather fine results. The Beatitudes, for example, are consolation, not a programme of virtues to be followed. The Ten Commandments also are not primarily rules of conduct but rather proclamations of God's power associated with certain sanctuaries and festivals. It is also rather depressing criticism: its logic is that we cannot adequately read the Bible at all except in Hebrew and in Greek, and then only with the enormous learning of form-criticism behind us.

To this sketch or caricature of biblical criticism, I would add a somewhat subversive comment of my own. Scholarship too has its *Sitz im Leben*: its place in time, its cultural fads, its ideological colour, its prejudices. These exist in all discourse, and we cannot pretend that they do not. There is no finality by which criticism can detach itself from its prejudices and win universal consent with a timeless conclusion. There is no compelling one true meaning. Faith may determine otherwise; criticism cannot. All criticism is provisional. All criticism is producer and product of its *Sitz im Leben*, not least the present essay.

For criticism, meaning is always at least double; to use the medieval distinction, sense (the grammatical sense, the words on the page) and 'sentence', or significance, what readers make of those words at different times and in different places. Biblical criticism helps with the sense and indirectly with the sentence (by insisting that it should not be built on top of a 'mistaken sense'). But it cannot dictate significance. It can refine; it can point towards what is wrong (it is wrong, for example, to believe that Moses wrote the Pentateuch); but it cannot identify what is right, because that is a matter ultimately of belief, and of prejudice. In this, the experience of reading the Bible is a perhaps stronger version of the experience of reading literary texts.

Moreover, readers can and do read the Bible without a volume of form-criticism in their hands. We can and do read it in English translation. We can and do make decisions about what it means. Biblical criticism of all kinds is enormously helpful, but it does not, in fact, regulate our reading. And it fails, as all scholarship fails, to establish beyond doubt one true original meaning. The lesson of form-criticism, for example, is to my mind that we have very little hope of practising it: historically we are too far away, we have lost too much information about the nuances of words in the social life of Palestine up to 3,000 years ago. In our reading of the Bible we are like Moses, a community of readers wandering in the wildnerness of significance, always on the point of ultimate discovery, always checked. We are exiles from 'one true meaning' of the Bible; and reading is an exile's way of life. As Francis Landy has written memorably, 'the Bible is outside its own tradition'.[46] In the next chapter, we see how for most readers it is also in exile from its own language.

Notes

1. Frank Kermode, 'The canon', in *Literary Guide* (Chapter 1, note 5, above), pp. 600–10. The debate between James Barr, *Holy Scripture: Canon, authority, criticism* (Oxford: Clarendon, 1983) and Brevard S. Childs, *Introduction to the Old Testament as Scripture* (Philadelphia: Fortress Press, 1979) is refereed by Kermode, 'The argument about canons', in *The Bible and the Narrative Tradition*, ed. Frank McConnell (New York and Oxford: Oxford UP, 1986), pp. 78–96. See also *CHB* I (Chapter 1, note 6, above), pp. 67–158 and 232–307; and Jean Daniélou, *History of Early Christian Doctrine*, trans. J. A. Baker, 2 volumes (London: Darton, Longman and Todd, 1973).

2. M. R. James, trans. *The Apocryphal New Testament* (Oxford: Clarendon, 1924).

3. See Daniélou, *History of Early Christian Doctrine* (n. 1, above); *CHB* I, pp. 377–453; A. C. Charity, *Events and their Afterlife: the dialectics of Christian typology in the Bible and Dante* (Cambridge: Cambridge UP, 1966).

4. Lucas Grollenberg, *Rediscovering the Bible* (London: SCM Press, 1978), p. 331.

5. See below, Chapter 6, for an extended discussion.

6. I am sympathetic to the account of Christian allegory given by David Aers,

Piers Plowman and Christian Allegory (London: Edward Arnold, 1975), though it conflicts with H. de Lubac, *Exégèse Médiévale: Les quatre sens de l'écriture*, 4 volumes (Paris: Aubier, 1959–64). There were protests, especially from Antioch, against Alexandrian allegories: *see CHB* I, pp. 489–509; but, as Frank Kermode writes, such objections 'did not prevail': *The Genesis of Secrecy: On the interpretation of narrative* (Cambridge, Mass and London: Harvard UP, 1979), p. 19, and see p. 148.

7. Beryl Smalley, *The Study of the Bible in the Middle Ages*, 3rd edn (Oxford, Blackwell, 1983), pp. 83–195; *CHB* II, pp. 197–219; and see also Gillian R. Evans, *The Language and Logic of the Bible: The earlier Middle Ages* (Cambridge: Cambridge UP, 1984) on *lectio* and exegesis. See also Martin Irvine, 'Interpretation and the semiotics of allegory in Clement of Alexandria, Origen and Augustine', *Semiotica* 63 (1987), 33–71.

8. Jean Daniélou, *Origen*, trans. Walter Mitchell (New York: Sheed and Ward, 1955), pp. 133–73.

9. James D. G. Dunn, *Unity and Diversity in the New Testament* (London: SCM Press, 1977), p. 177.

10. Daniélou, *Origen*, (n. 8, above), p. 180.

11. *CHB* I, p. 547. The interpretation follows Gregory of Nyssa: Marvin H. Pope, *Song of Songs*, The Anchor Bible (Garden City, New York: Doubleday, 1977), pp. 462–3.

12. St Ambrose, *Hexameron, Paradise*, and *Cain and Abel*, trans. John J. Savage, in *The Fathers of the Church* 42 (New York: Fathers of the Church, 1961), pp. 169–70.

13. Guillaume de Lorris and Jean de Meun, *The Romance of the Rose*, trans. Charles Dahlberg (Princeton: Princeton UP, 1971), p. 286.

14. *Philo*, with an English translation by F. H. Colson and G. H. Whitaker, 10 volumes, Loeb Classical Library (London: Heinemann and Cambridge: Mass.: Harvard UP, 1939): vol I deals with the Creation (*De Opificio Mundi*) and allegorical interpretation (*Legum Allegoriae*).

15. Smalley, *Study of the Bible in the Middle Ages* (n. 7 above), p. 33.

16. Origen, *Homilies on Genesis and Exodus*, trans. Ronald E. Heine, in *The Fathers of the Church* 71 (Washington DC: Catholic University of America Press, 1981), p. 67.

17. *ibid.*, p. 49.

18. *ibid.*, p. 59.

19. The issue relates to the debate between Peter's followers, who regarded Christianity as a Jewish sect, and Paul's mission to the (often uncircumcised) Gentiles.

20. On Origen as the first Christian explorer of 'the pleasure of the text', see

Patricia Cox Miller, ' "Pleasure of the text, text of pleasure": Eros and language in Origen's *Commentary on the Song of Songs', Journal of the American Academy of Religion* 54 (1986), 241–53. For further work on Origen see Peter Brown, *The Body and Society: Men, women and social renunciation in early Christianity* (New York: Columbia University Press, 1988), pp. 162–77; Henri Crouzel, *Origen: The man and his work* (Edinburgh: T.N.T. Clark, 1989); Joseph Wilson Trigg, *Origen: The Bible and philosophy in the third-century Church* (Atlanta: John Knox and Philadelphia: Westminster, 1983); Rowan Williams, 'Ascetic enthusiasm: Origen and the early Church', *History Today* 39 (December 1989), 31–7.

21. Ambrose, *Hexameron*, (n. 12 above) p. 227.
22. *ibid.*, p. 129.
23. *ibid.*, p. 171; p. 190; and the sea, p. 172, is also the Gospel.
24. Augustine, *On Christian Doctrine*, trans. D. W. Robertson Jr (New York: Liberal Arts Press, 1958).
25. See note 6, above, for Aers and his challenge to any strong notion of fidelity to the literal sense; *CHB* II, pp. 155–220; James S. Preus, *From Shadow to Promise: Old Testament interpretation from Augustine to the Young Luther* (Cambridge, Mass.: Harvard UP, 1969). For further references, see John Bossy, *Christianity in the West 1400–1700* (Oxford and New York: Oxford UP, 1985); Jesse M. Gellrich, *The Idea of the Book in the Middle Ages* (Ithaca: Cornell UP, 1985); *The Bible and Medieval Culture*, ed. W. Lourdaux and D. Verhelet (Leuven: Leuven UP, 1979); Robert M. Grant, *A Short History of the Interpretation of the Bible*, rev. edn. with David Tracey (Philadelphia Fortress Press, 1984).
26. Grollenberg, *Rediscovering the Bible*, p. 319: the writer is a Dominican and the first (Dutch) version (Amsterdam: Elsevier, 1968) carried a 'Nil Obstat'.
27. *CHB* II, pp. 492–505; Franz Bierlaire, *Erasme et Ses Colloques: Le livre d'une vie* (Geneva: Droz, 1977); Erika Rummel, *Erasmus' Annotations on the New Testament: From philologist to theologian* (Toronto and London: University of Toronto Press, 1986).
28. Quotations from *CHB* III, pp. 12, 23.
29. Dryden, *The Hind and the Panther*, quoted in *CHB* II, p. 179. See John Bossy, *Christianity in the West 1400–1700* (n. 25 above).
30. *CHB* II, p. 8.
31. Francis Turretin, *The Doctrine of Scripture*, ed. and trans. John W. Beardslee III (Grand Rapids: Baker House, 1981), pp. 57–70.
32. *CHB* III, pp. 194–5, 218–21.

33. Turretin, *Doctrine of Scripture* (n. 31, above), p. 129.
34. Hans W. Frei, *The Eclipse of Biblical Narrative* (New Haven and London: Yale UP, 1974). See also Stephen Prickett, *Words and 'The Word': Language, poetics and biblical interpretation* (Cambridge: Cambridge UP, 1986). Frei's unease with modern hermeneutics, and his desire to present 'a wide, though not of course unanimous, traditional consensus among Christians in the West on the primacy of the literal reading of the Bible' (p. 36) are well expressed in 'The "literal reading" of biblical narrative in the Christian tradition: Does it stretch or will it break?' in *The Bible and the Narrative Tradition*, ed. McConnell (n. 1, above), pp. 36–77. Frei's definition of 'literal', however, seems to me wisely and generously allegorical: certainly (p. 39), it is grounded in typology.
35. *Philo* (n. 14 above), III, pp. 394–5 (*De Ebrietate* 143).
36. *CHB* III, p. 244.
37. Grollenberg, (n. 4, above), pp. 29–30; F. Delitzsch, *Lese- und schreibefehler im Alte Testament . . .* (Berlin: de Gruyter, 1920).
38. *CHB* III, p. 242: closer, that is, in date – since modern scholarship dates the Pentateuch in its current form to about the time of Ezekiel.
39. *CHB* III, 269–71; Grollenberg (n. 4, above), pp. 11–12.
40. Julius Wellhausen, *Prologemena to the History of Ancient Israel* (1878; Cleveland and New York: Meridian, 1965); *CHB* III, pp. 287–90; Grollenberg (n. 4, above), pp. 15–23; *Semeia* 25 (1982). See also G. von Rad, *Theology of the Old Testament*, trans. D. M. G. Stalker, 2 volumes (New York: Harper and Row, 1962–5); Otto Kaiser, *Introduction to the Old Testament* (Minneapolis: Angsbury, 1975); Martin Noth, *A History of Pentateuchal Traditions* (Englewood Cliffs, NJ: Prentice Hall, 1972); David Robertson, *The Old Testament and the Literary Critic* (Philadelphia: Fortress Press, 1977); Robert Polzin, *Moses and the Deuteronomist* (New York: Seabury, 1980), pp. 1–24; Otto Eissfeldt, *The Old Testament: An Introduction*, trans. Peter R. Ackroyd (New York: Harper and Row, 1972).
41. This is argued by James D. G. Dunn, *Unity and Diversity in the New Testament* (n. 9, above).
42. Strauss, *Leben Jesu*, quoted in *CHB* III, pp. 275–6.
43. *CHB* III, p. 326.
44. See E. A. Speiser, *Genesis*, The Anchor Bible (Garden City, New York: Doubleday, 1964).
45. Klaus Koch, *The Growth of the Biblical Tradition: The form-critical method*, trans. S. M. Cupitt (London: A & C Black, 1969), pp. 59–61. See also James Barr, *Old and New Testament Interpretation* (London: SCM

50

Press, 1973). There is a good discussion of modes of literary analysis in chapter 1 of Lyle M. Eslinger, *Kingship of God in Crisis* (Sheffield: Almond, 1985), pp. 11–42, and of Wellhausen, von Rad and Noth in Part III of Robert M. Polzin, *Biblical Structuralism: Method and subjectivity in the study of ancient texts* (Philadelphia: Fortress Press, 1977), pp. 126–202.

46. Francis Landy, 'The case of Kugel: Do we find ourselves when we lose ourselves in the text?', *Comparative Criticism* 5, ed. E. S. Shaffer (Cambridge: Cambridge UP, 1983). pp. 305–16; p. 313. For some other modern approaches, see *Semeia* 40 (1987) – deconstruction, and 41 (1988) – speech act theory and narrative hermeneutics.

CHAPTER 3

The Bible in English

Translation and interpretation

We are used to free access to the Bible. The Bible is freely and cheaply available in bookshops, and indeed appears free of charge, wanted or not, in hotel rooms. However extraordinary it must seem to us, access to the whole text of the Bible was closely and jealously guarded in English history from the eleventh to the sixteenth centuries, so much so that in the fifteenth century to be found in the possession of an English Bible was an offence punishable by death. The King James Bible comes at the end of more than 500 years of debate about who should be allowed to read the Bible, and about what extracts from the Bible, in what reworked form, should be divulged to common or 'illiterate' people. Throughout that period of 500 years, one biblical phrase appears again and again to summarise the reaction of the learned to giving vernacular scriptures to the common people: the phrase is 'casting pearls before swine'.

On the eve of the great efflorescence of Bible translation, in the 1520s, Sir Thomas More wrote a treatise on the subject in which he took up an advanced humanist Catholic position. More himself experimented with Bible translation; but even he could not envisage free access by all to an English Bible.[1] Until More's day, the attitude of the English medieval church had grown increasingly restrictive and intolerant towards the notion of vernacular scriptures. There were several attempts at biblical paraphrase, and one or two at actual translation undertaken, albeit with misgivings, in the Anglo-Saxon period. There were to be no more for 300 years. This is no doubt partly due to the Norman Conquest, which downgraded the status of the English language itself – to a poor third after Latin and French – and it was not used for any official purpose until the late fourteenth century. Moreover, the Normans instituted sweeping reforms in the English Church, and their new Archbishops dismissed many saintly leading figures in the Saxon church as 'illiterate'. The word 'illiterate' was not used in the medieval period to mean 'unable to read'. Many who could read English were still classed as illiterate. Illiterate meant unable to read Latin; and by that standard probably the majority of the English parish clergy were, and remained, illiterate. There were embarrassing stories of English medieval clerics, some quite senior, making error after error in the language of the Mass and obviously in the dark as to the meaning of the words they attempted to speak. In some circumstances, illiteracy of priests might have been an argument in favour of translation, not against it; but how could a congregation be trusted with an English Bible when their priests were regarded as incompetent to explain it to them? The orthodox prohibition of an English Bible was rigorous, and remained so.[2]

Strangely, there was no uniformity about such prohibition across Europe. In England, the cause of vernacular Bible translation was fought and lost in the fourteenth century, and the orthodox position became harder and harder until the English Reformation. Indeed, there was never at any time in the international Church an official prohibition of Bible translation, though the attitude of some Popes came close to it. Consequently, even in England, the situation varies from one period to another. The English followers of John Wycliff in the late fourteenth century, called by their enemies 'Lollards', were perceived, correctly, as a political and social threat. In 1401 therefore a statute was passed that convicted Lollards were heretics and were to be burned at the stake; by 1407 this policy was being enthusiastically promulgated. Proof of guilt was the possession of the Wycliffite Bible. On the other hand, there is the story that in the 1390s the same Archbishop who conducted that witchhunt, Archbishop Arundel, had approved for the use of the Queen of Richard II, Anne of Bohemia, the use of a glossed English Bible which was apparently a Wycliffite Bible. Historians are unsure what to make of this story: it might be a later Lollard forgery interpolated into official history. Yet what seems to have mattered is not what was read (the Lollard Bible), but who read it. In the period before 1401 many of Wycliff's supporters were gentlefolk, courtiers, clerics or renegade academics, and the support of many of these was no longer so evident after the Statute of 1401. In any case, by 1401 it was clear that the Lollards were gaining popular support among shopkeepers, tradesmen and artisans; and there developed a serious revolt in 1413. It would be a mistake to overemphasise the difference between the learned and the unlearned arms of English Lollardy. But political circumstances vary, and with them attitudes to Bible translation. In the fifteenth century the repression grew so severe that when the unfortunate Bishop of Chichester, Reginald Pecock, wrote a long treatise against Lollards, he devoted so much space to the subject of Bible translation that he was stripped of his bishopric and thrown into prison.[3]

Strangely, too, the countries in which the cause of the vernacular Bible translations was won early or never became a major issue – France, Italy, Spain – are still Catholic countries; the countries in which it was lost until the sixteenth century – England, most of Germany – went Protestant. In the Reformation what was the connection between Bible translation, which seems on the face of it harmless enough, and political revolt? It is probably wise to think of Protestantism as reaction against an international establishment, the Church, which lays down the law in Latin, and which claims, in Latin, to be the ultimate authority – spiritual, moral, political and intellectual. (Latin was the language of the universities, and throughout the medieval period in order to attend university one had first to take minor holy orders.) Revolt against such an all-encompassing authority, and soon revolt against any authority at all (such as a king), will stress whatever may be used as counter-authority, and is at the same time open to individual interpretation. What more natural rallying point for such political opposition than the call for a vernacular Bible? In the first place this sort of radical demand is not likely to occur at the bottom of the social ladder, among the proletarian classes who would have been illiterate by the twentieth-century definition of the term, but rather half way up the social ladder, among the middle classes who were illiterate only by the medieval definition. The pressure for Bible translation occurs like most radical political movements at times of prosperity and upward social mobility. It is by no means accidental that the late fourteenth-century English Bible translation happens at a time when the English language and literature in English are also undergoing a great revival: some of

Chaucer's best friends were Lollards. An upwardly mobile middle class wanted a greater political say and a quality literature in their own language, both secular (Chaucer, and many other fine poets of the late fourteenth century) and religious: an English Bible.

Why did the Church oppose it? One very clear reason is that Bible translation raises theological issues. Sir Thomas More objected very strongly to Tyndale's translation of the words to be translated in the King James Bible as 'priest' and 'Church'. For 'priest' Tyndale translated 'senior' or 'elder'; for 'Church', he translated 'congregation': the changes were regarded as a theological and an institutional, threat.[4] And the theology of the established Church, as well as its authority, was vested in the Latin Vulgate. The Vulgate was *authorised*, and even after all the renaissance study of Hebrew and Greek the Counter-Reformation Council of Trent in 1546 simply restated this position. When English Catholics finally got around to producing their own Bible translation, completed in 1609, the Rhemes-Douai Bible, they based the translation on the Latin Vulgate, and went so far as to describe it, on the title page, as 'Faithfully Translated into English out of the Authentical Latin'. The translation is horribly wooden, literal and unidiomatic – again for theological reasons. The translators explained: 'We presume not in high places to mollify the speeches or phrases, but . . . keep them word for word, and point for point, for fear of missing, or restraining the sense of the Holy Ghost to our fantasy' ('fantasy' here means something more like 'fancy').[5] Now the point is not by any means that the Catholic Church failed to recognise that Jerome's Vulgate was translated from the Greek Septuagint, and that its text was in turn based on antecedent Hebrew and Greek versions. It is rather that doctrinal arguments in the Catholic Church were to be settled from the Vulgate and only from the Vulgate; in that sense it is 'authentic' or 'authorised'; and it is in just that sense too, as a final court of appeal for doctrinal dispute, that for the Anglican Church the King James Bible became the authorised version. For the medieval Catholic Church, the Book of Authority is a Latin book, and the Church's authority cannot be translated into English. Truth is Latin, not English.

Moreover, and crucially, the history of Bible translation cannot be separated from the history of biblical interpretation. Indeed, the original meaning of 'interpret' in English is 'to translate'. I have referred to the

view of medieval exegetes that interpretation requires specialised understanding, training, and is for adepts only. There was never any idea in the
medieval period that the text of the Bible could stand alone, without
critical interpretation, the gloss. Medieval Bible manuscripts almost
habitually contained texts together with gloss – almost like a parody of
modern scholarly editions, with a few lines of text on the page and the
majority of the page taken up with footnotes. An essential aspect of Bible
translation was therefore glossing. And since one was likely to be out of
sympathy with orthodox Catholicism to be translating the Bible into
English at all, the glosses in such translations were likely to be nothing
short of doctrinal scandals. It was Tyndale's marginal glosses even more
than his text that created controversy: and they were, in fact, highly
provocative. Here is Tyndale's gloss on Abraham's sacrifice of Isaac from
Genesis 22, and it blows aways centuries of allegorical exegesis:

> Jacob robbed Laban his uncle: Moses robbed the Egyptians: And Abraham is
> about to slay and burn his own son: And all are holy works, because they were
> wrought in favour at God's command. To steal, rob and murder are no holy
> works before worldly people: but unto them that have their trust in God: they are
> holy when God commandeth them.[6]

Wycliffite glosses, a century and a half earlier, were equally subversive. In fact, the issue of glosses became so troublesome in the sixteenth
century that one of the stipulations on the Authorised Version was that,
while running titles at the top of each page were in order, marginal
glosses were banned; but this step itself depends on a certain Protestant
confidence in the text on its own. Medieval Catholicism had no such
confidence, and it is hard to know whether outrage or incredulity
predominates in one medieval's chronicler's description of what Wycliff
and his followers were up to:

> This Master John Wycliff had translated from Latin into English the Gospel that
> Christ gave to the clergy and doctors of the Church . . . so that by his means what
> formerly belonged to those clergy who were sufficiently learned and intelligent,
> was made available to any lay person who knew how to read. And so the pearl of
> the Gospel is scattered abroad and trodden underfoot by swine.[7]

Not all medieval churchmen would have been quite so dismissive; but, significantly, the strongest statement of reverence for the Bible I have found comes from a scholar contemporary with this in Prague, which was to be the home of many exiled Lollards and was about to erupt in the proto-Protestant movement of John Hus. On the whole, however, the English medieval situation forms an absolute contrast to that in the sixteenth and seventeenth century described by Thomas Hobbes:

> After the Bible was translated . . . every man, every boy and wench that could read English, thought they spoke with God Almighty and understood what he said when by a certain number of chapters a day they had read the Scriptures once or twice over.[8]

There is very little distance here between political opposition and reading. The fear of both underlies medieval resistance to medieval Bible translation.

The last factor in such resistance was no doubt sheer conservatism. The Bible is old; truth is old; God is old; and so is Latin, whereas English is newfangled. This is the sort of conservatism that led medieval monks to make painstaking manuscript copies of early printed books because printing was merely a passing fad with no hope of survival; and it is articulated in 1547 by a bishop of Henry VIII's new Church of England, Stephen Gardiner.

> Religion has continued in Latin fifteen hundred years. But as for the English tongue, itself has not continued in one form of understanding two hundred years; and without God's work and special miracle it shall hardly contain religion long, when it cannot last itself.[9]

How then, did ordinary medieval Christians learn when they were denied access to the Bible in their own language? The prescription had already come from St Paul in Romans 10:17: 'Faith comes by hearing'. Public Bible readings were common, with the cleric translating or paraphrasing simultaneously and adding or interweaving comments or exhortations. Such readings were normally integrated into the liturgy, and survive to this day in religious services: in medieval Latin usage, the verb 'to read' is synonymous with the verb 'to sing'. Sermons in the medieval period were a popular pastime, and the preacher who taught for less than three hours or so was likely to disappoint his audience.

Certain parts of the Bible were frequently translated as extracts, in the service books, or in full, particularly the Psalter. The most important Middle English translation of the Psalter is that by the Yorkshire hermit Richard Rolle, who died in 1349, and Rolle's explanation of the character of his translation stresses two things: excessive literalism, arising from an anxiety to be as close as possible to the Latin and expressed in the stiff and awkward English style and thoroughly unidiomatic word order, and the integration in the translation of the standard glosses:

> In this werk I seke no strange Inglis, bot lightest and comunest and swilke that es mast like vnto the Latyn, so that thai that knawes noght Latyn, be the Inglis may cum tille many Latyn wordes. In the translacioun I follow the letter als mekil als I may, and thare I fynde na propir Inglys I follow the witte of the word, so that thai that sal rede it, tham thar noght dred errynge. In expounynge I folew haly doctours, for it may cum into sum envyouse mans hand that knawys noght what he suld say, that wille say that I wist noght what I sayde, and so do harme tille hym and tille other if he despise the werk that es prophetabil tille hym and other.[10]

If listening was one way for 'lewed folk' to learn, the other was looking; and religion throughout the medieval period – in Psalters, in Book of Hours, in altarpieces, in wood, in stone, on ceilings, on floors, and in books, especially Bible picture books, which omitted the text and supplied pictures instead – fulfils its dual purpose: it instructs people and glorifies God. To mention this kind of undeniable creativity is also to gain some insight into English (and indeed much European) medieval literature. The absence of Bible translation in the vernacular fulfils a creative function: it generates a whole vernacular literature that offers itself to 'lewed folk' as a kind of imaginative substitute for the English Bible that they are denied. The word 'imaginative' is perhaps an overstatement in face of much of this material: huge verse lives of Christ and the saints, biblical paraphases, enormous and enormously popular treatises with titles like *The Prick of Conscience* (or, the title favoured by James Joyce, *The Ayenbite of Inwit*) or *Cursor Mundi*, which by modern critical standards would be judged somewhat dull. But from this impulse arises too the best of Middle English poetry, excluding Chaucer; and much of the best of medieval English poetry offering itself as a kind of imaginative substitute for an absent Bible is alliterative poetry. The most famous example of the fourteenth century is the alliterative poem *Piers Plowman*, which proceeds by offering an extended English gloss on frequently quoted Latin texts.[11] It is at least possible that the verse form used, which employs the strong rhythms of the English language rather than any artificial device such as rhyme, itself contributes to the development of a style suitable for vernacular Bible translation two centuries later. In addition, the development of drama in England as in the so-called mystery cycles, is in direct response in the need to teach 'lewed folk' the outlines of 'salvation history', that is, biblical narrative.

Certain pressures arise from the withholding of a vernacular Bible in the medieval period. First, there developed an obvious disparity between theology, the Christianity of the learned who have Bibles, and the popular religion of the 'lewed folk', who have not. Some popular religion never loses aspects of practice and belief that are folkloric. There is little in the Bible or medieval Catholic theology, for instance, to explain the cult of the Virgin Mary as it is practised at a popular level in certain parts of Europe; and some of the practices of heretical sects, as examined by Le Roy Ladurie in *Montaillou*, seem to derive their strength from folk practices and beliefs rather than, and in the absence of, a Bible.[12] Secondly, the withholding of the vernacular Bible in England also ensures that the subject of Bible translation becomes politicised. Religious rebels will propose Bible translation as a direct challenge to the structure of the established Church, and they will make deliberate play out of the obvious question: 'What are they hiding?'. The Lollards refer to the Bible in a cult phrase or private formula as 'Goddis lawe' or 'Christis lawe', and they oppose it to the Church.[13] Christ was poor, the Church was rich; the Church must therefore be anti-Christ. Commitment to the notion of an English Bible is a political programme directed against the status quo, in the Lollard case, as a domestic opposition and in the time of Henry VIII as a useful tool of national opposition to the international Church. Thirdly, the longer the Bible is withheld, the more chance of an extremely literal response to it when it falls into the hands of ordinary people, and the more outlandish may be some of the interpretations proposed. If the Church is anti-Christ it must be Antichrist, and so on. And the less chance of reconciliation with orthodoxy. Therefore the English Bible lobby retains its association with social dissent and political radicalism, as in the Civil War and English Puritanism.

Marginalia of the Geneva Bible have been seen as anti-hierarchical, or anti-monarchical (as they were by James I). Certainly they implied a political right to resist. As the Duke of Newcastle put it of the 1640s, 'the Bible in English under every weaver and chambermaid's arm hath done us much hurt'.[4]

There is some evidence of a correlation between political opposition and good vernacular translation. Lollardy made its appeal in the late fourteeth century. If the appeal had succeeded, England would have had its 'authorised' vernacular Bible 200 years earlier than it did. For there are still in existence over 200 manuscripts of the Wycliffite Bible. Wycliff, an Oxford academic who enjoyed in his lifetime the protection of John of Gaunt, was condemned as a heretic after his death in 1384. As an academic, he wrote theological treatises in Latin, but the distance between Latin and vernacular Wycliffite writings is now seen as smaller than it has been for a very long time. Wycliff may have been involved in some way in vernacular Bible translation. The authorship of the Lollard Bible, once attributed to Wycliff's one-time secretary John Purvey, remains unknown and mysterious. What is known is that in the 1380s and 1390s the Lollards produced two complete versions of the Bible. The first, written in the time when Lollards were hopeful that their views might prevail in the English Church, is painfully literal and contorts the English language beyond its limit in order to preserve the word order of the Latin. This was surely some attempt to defer to the 'authority' of the Vulgate, to stay within the pale. The second translation was made after this hope had failed. The Lollards had enjoyed reasonable toleration in the reign of Richard II, and had hoped for more from his Lancastrian successor, Henry IV, who was the son of John of Gaunt. Henry IV, however, having deposed a rightful king, needed the sanction of the established Church if he was to hold his position against internal challenge, and he had to demonstrate therefore that he was impeccably orthodox. Lollards found themselves persecuted as traitors. The second translation, after all was lost, is freer, more confident, more idiomatic, doctrinally more contentious in its glosses, and less faithful to the Latin: for there was no longer any reason to defer to the received text of the Vulgate.

The moral here may be that excessive respect for any source impedes good translation. And the second translation is good translation, introduced by a General Prologue the last chapter of which discusses the four stages of the work: first, scholarly work to get a decent Latin text; secondly, work on the gloss; thirdly, general discussion on the linguistic and theological problems of translation; and fourthly, a translation which is based on the meaning of the Latin, not a faithful reproduction of the Latin word by word, which is therefore 'free' translation rather than 'stencil' translation. The recommendation of 'free' rather than 'stencil' translation in the second Wycliffite version is a great breakthrough in English Bible translation, one followed by all the sixteenth-century translators except, for doctrinal reasons, the translators of the Rhemes-Douai Bible. Only a free translation can be good English prose, though there are those who have thought that Tyndale took his freedom too far by including in his translation of the Old Testament colloquial phrases like 'babble too much', 'Shire town' and 'Easter holidays'.[15] One of the ironies of some modern revisions of the Bible is the return to stencil translation and pedantic fidelity to the 'original text'. Now, as is the fourteenth century, the result tends to be bad prose.

Did the Wycliffite version of the Bible, so viciously persecuted, have any influence on Tyndale? The standard answer has been that it did not. This needs to be revised: there are significant, though infrequent, parallels. Over 200 Wycliffite manuscripts survive, many in de luxe condition, and oddly, given the legal sanctions, most of these were made in England during the fifteenth century, at the same time as poor people were being incarcerated or being put to death for possessing a copy. It appears that those punished were nearly all of the lower classes. The evidence suggests that socially higher classes were able to persuade the authorities to turn a blind eye not only to their manuscript ownership but also to their manuscript production. Once again, it seems that it is not a question of what is read but of who does the reading. Furthermore, these Bibles did not identify themselves as proscribed Lollard Bibles. Sir Thomas More maintained that he knew of other early translations than the Lollard one, and possessed one. On being challenged, he failed to substantiate his claim. It is probable that this great Catholic, who was to accept martyrdom for his faith, owned and read a Wycliffite Bible. There were many copies around, and Tyndale denies so emphatically that he had consulted any earlier English version that it is plausible to infer the opposite.

William Tyndale was born in 1484. He is by far the greatest of all English Bible translators, and if any one man deserves the title of 'only begetter of English prose', it is Tyndale. He was of humble birth and went to Oxford then Cambridge where he studied Hebrew and Greek and made the famous vow to a clergyman: 'If God spare my life, ere many years I will cause a boy that driveth the plough should know more of the scriptures than thou dost'. He tried to interest the Bishop of London in his project for a Bible translation from Hebrew and Greek and came to a very practical conclusion: 'I understood at the last not only that there was no room in my Lord of London's palace to translate the New Testament, but also that there was no place to do it in all England'.[16]

Tyndale left for Europe, and arrived in Germany in time to fall under the spell of Martin Luther, whose magnificent translation of the Bible was already in print. To the end of his life, by strangulation and burning in 1535 after being betrayed, with English collusion, into the hands of agents of the Catholic emperor Charles V, Tyndale worked on his complete New Testament in English (published in 1525/6), and on an unfinished Old Testament on which he was working to the end of his life. In his valuable book *English Biblical Translation*, A. C. Partridge has summarised Tyndale's principles as being four-fold: fidelity to the Greek and Hebrew texts; relative impartiality in interpreting Christian doctrine; an attempt to match the language of translation to that of the times (so that Tyndale's idiom is directed at ordinary lay people and his style is modern, clear and strong); and the desire to produce a version suitable for reading aloud. This last is a totally new concept in English translations. It introduces considerations of prose rhythm that are to be of vital significance to the King James Bible. In England, Tyndale's translations were suppressed and met fierce resistance, even after the so-called Reformation of Henry VIII. For Henry VIII still was not committed to full scale Protestantism; at first he desired to head an English Catholic Church. Tyndale's translations were Lutheran in tone (using 'congregation' rather than 'Church'), in their glosses, and in their layout, typography and other format.

The political inability to embrace Tyndale's translations represented bad luck for Henry's new Church of England, which after marching out of the now Roman Catholic Church in supremely nationalistic gesture could hardly continue to resist the pressure for an English translation of the Scriptures – for which, in fact, the Convocation of Canterbury petitioned in 1534, the year before Tyndale's death. Miles Coverdale was commissioned to produce one, and he produced an eclectic first version based on the Latin Vulgate, on Tyndale's New Testament, on Luther's German Bible and on Zwingli's Zurich Bible of 1531. Coverdale also produced the official Great Bible of 1539 and its revised second edition in 1540. He was also in Geneva in 1558, and contributed in some way to the Geneva Bible of 1560. The Psalms as they appear in the Book of Common Prayer are in Coverdale's translation. After Coverdale's first version, the floodgates of English Bible translation were thrown wide open. The so-called Mathew Bible of 1537 was a covert English version of Tyndale and appeared more popular than Coverdale's first version. It had fiercely Protestant notes, which is why Coverdale was commissioned to revise it for use as an authorised Bible in English churches. His revision was the Great Bible of 1539, censored by the English Bishops, and this became the prototype for all subsequent official authorised English Bibles including the Bishops' Bible of 1556. Much of Coverdale's work was based closely on Tyndale, even though Tyndale's version was still banned. So it is really Tyndale who lies at the root of the English Bible.

There is an irony here, for the history of English biblical versions from Tyndale to the King James Bible is that of the struggle between full-blooded Protestant versions in the style of Tyndale and versions put out by the established church in some attempt to tame the Protestant tiger. The first type, like Tyndale's, were pioneering and creative; the second tended to be committee efforts, their brief being to censor and tidy up the more radical versions. The instructions given to the committee of the Bishops' Bible of 1556 were not to make any controversial notes and 'to follow the common English translation used in the churches and not to recede from it but where it varies manifestly' from the Hebrew or Greek original.[17] It was handsomely produced, with illustrations including maps of the Holy Land and portraits of Elizabeth, Leicester and Burghley; unedifying passages were marked 'that the reader may eschew them in his public reading', a mode of advertisement which may have struck later generations as an unwise procedure. The Bishops' Bible was meant to replace, and failed to replace, the most popular of all

Protestant Bibles, the Geneva Bible, published in 1560. This was prepared in the late 1550s by a group of exiles headed by William Whittingham, a Protestant cleric in exile from the Catholic reign of Queen Mary. Whittingham had sought refuge in Geneva, the city he called 'the store of heavenly learning and judgement, the place where God has appointed us to dwell.'[18] The Geneva Bible is based, yet again, on Tyndale. It set several precedents for the English Bible. For the first time, additional words required by English idiom were printed in italics; and chapters are divided into verses to facilitate the use of concordances. These features were simply reproduced in the King James Bible. The Geneva Bible is a superb production in the tradition of Tyndale. It was overwhelmingly popular. The figures, as presented by Richard L. Greaves, speak for themselves:

> By the time the King James Bible was published in 1611 more than 120 editions of the Geneva Bible had been issued. Although Archbishop William Laud subsequently proceeded to ban its publication in England, the number of editions climbed to nearly 200 by the outbreak of the Civil War. More people, therefore, came into contact with this book than any other until well into the seventeenth century.[19]

The Geneva Bible was also probably the single most important English Bible. As Peter Levi attests:

> It was the Bible of Shakespeare from about 1596 and the Bible of Milton, it survived well into the mid-century as the popular Bible of Scotland and took root in America with the Pilgrim Fathers in 1620. It was a source of the Soldiers Pocket Bible, which was sixteen pages of fighting texts which Oliver Cromwell printed for the army in 1643. It was naturally Bunyan's Bible. The reason why it ceased to be printed after about 1644 and almost ceased to be remembered after about 1700 is political and social: it was identified with forces in English society which were stifled in those years.[20]

The King James Bible became the great Bible of English literature after 1700. But it is the Geneva Bible that inspired two of the greatest English poets and the English Revolution. We should study it far more than we do. The King James Bible, by contrast, is the last and the greatest of the offical committee Bibles, and was intended to counter the popularity of the Geneva – whose notes were far too Calvinist and

Puritan for King James I. Seizing on a Puritan proposal for new translation, which was perhaps a criticism of the Prayer Book and perhaps too an expression of frustration at using one Bible in church and another at home, James in 1604 set up a committee of fifty-four people, in six companies working at Westminster, Cambridge and Oxford. It was only to be another revision, not a new translation; it was supposed to be a revision of the Bishops' Bible, with reference also to Tyndale, Mathew, Coverdale, The Great Bible and Geneva 'when they agree better with the text than the Bishops' Bible'. In other words the King James Bible is yet another cleaned up version of Tyndale, appearing almost 100 years after Tyndale's translation.

If the test were to be a simple word count, very little in the King James Bible would be seen as original. But the committee for the authorised version, unlike most committees, had an unerring instinct for prose style. This has been described many times, lately and best by Gerald Hammond.[21] To take just one phrase, 'whited sepulchres' (Matthew 23:27): Tyndale had 'paynted tombes'; Coverdale had 'paynted sepulchres', as did the Bishops' Bible and the Great Bible; Geneva, realising that Palestinian tombs were whitewashed but preferring the monosyllable 'tombes' to the Latin 'sepulchres', gave 'whited tombes'. The King James Bible grafts nearly a century of growth to give, for the first time, 'whited sepulchres'; and I do not think it is just familiarity that makes this the most satisfying version. Likewise it is King James Bible that for the first time gives for Elijah to hear 'a still, small voice'. Other versions come close, sometimes infuriatingly so: Geneva has a 'small, still voice'. Why is a 'still, small voice' better than a 'small, still voice'? Because lexical properties of stillness and smallness are better served by having a shorter vowel of 'still' precede the longer vowel of 'small', and the quieter dental /st/ of 'still' before the labial /sm/ of small. The phonetic qualities assist the sense, and this is part of the rhythmic and semantic sophistication of the King James Bible. Yet good style does not exist in an ideological vacuum, and judgements about what constitutes quality in English Bible translation require slightly more extensive treatment.

The King James Bible is perhaps the first great English Bible translation that is not aligned with a radical political or doctrinal movement. For all that, it is nevertheless the last wave of a movement for social change: the change from the medieval situation in which vernacular Bibles were unavailable, to the modern situation in which access is free. One sort of freedom may encourage others. *The Cambridge History of the Bible* tells the story of William Maldon, whose father in 1538 objected to his attendance at Bible readings: 'then thought I, I will learn to read English, and then will I have the New Testament and read thereon myself . . . The Maytide following I and my father's prentice, Thomas Jeffrey, laid our money together and bought the New Testament in English, and hid it in our bedstraw and so exercised it at convenient times'.[22] Access to an English Bible is a major change, and its social consequences were profound.

Style and transparency in English Bible translation

Most readers, including myself, make judgements about the quality of various English Bible translations. These judgements are often offered in terms of prose style. Yet quite often they have no direct reference to the source or to questions of the fidelity of a given translation. Nor, given the fact that they are liable to be expressed with some moral indignation, is it more than possible that they are merely aesthetic judgements.[23] This discussion focuses on questions of prose style, particularly with reference to the King James Bible. But it also looks at the questions of what value is put upon prose style, and where such value is located.

In spite of what I have just written, it may be as well to begin such a study by looking at what the English Bible translators of the sixteenth century were translating from. One point must be made immediately. Very little expertise in biblical languages is required to see that there is an enormous difference, in linguistic and stylistic terms, both within the Old Testament and the New Testament taken individually and, more, between the Hebrew of the Old and the Greek of the New. Any translation into one language makes more of a coherent book of the Bible than it can possibly appear in its original form containing both Hebrew and Greek. Any English translation, therefore, serves the Christian desire to see the Bible defined as Old and New Testaments in a canonical whole. Furthermore, unless the style with which individual books of the Bible are to be translated is singularly variable, even in translation of books in the same language a greater appearance of homogeneity is likely to arise from the very act of translation.

Historically, a good point at which to begin this study would be with Tyndale, for every subsequent translation using the Greek of the New Testament and the Hebrew of the Old is using Tyndale as an intermediary whether translators know it or not, for the rhythms of Tyndale are simply a part of their cultural heritage. Very early in Tyndale's career as the first English translator from both Greek and Hebrew, Tyndale speaks of an exciting pair of discoveries – one about New Testament Greek and one about Old Testament Hebrew. He realises that the Latin Vulgate of St Jerome, which is a gravely elegant piece of Ciceronian prose thoughout, fails to capture the essential quality of either language; it is too solemn and sonorous for the Greek, and insufficiently so for the Hebrew. For the Greek of the New Testament is not all of a piece: St Paul in his Epistles is, at times and for the most part, a decent prose stylist; the Greek of the Gospels by contrast, is distinctly odd Greek, even, not to put too fine a point on it, rather bad Greek. And Tyndale also realises why: he realises that the Greek of the Gospels may be based on the Aramaic that Jesus and his original followers spoke; it is rough-hewn Greek written by foreigners. The translators of the New English Bible capture this quality well, if accidentally, on the many occasions when their prose suggests that they learnt English by correspondence course and have not yet mastered its idioms. Tyndale concludes that the English language is in a far better position than Jerome's polished Latin to capture the quality of New Testament Greek. If this is the position with Greek, Tyndale goes on: 'the Hebrew tongue agreeth a thousand times more with the English than with the Latin'.[24]

This is an important point, and one that has been much repeated by writers on the English Bible – who have been particularly generous in their praise of the King James Bible and of Tyndale. While in one sense I can merely echo it, having little Hebrew, the grounds for it must be enumerated since they have a major bearing on persistent arguments for the primacy of the King James Bible and, more generally, of Tyndale-derived translations over more modern efforts. Again and again, it is the dramatic quality of Hebrew to which commentators draw our attention. English translators have much work to do in the unscrambling of the very simple Hebrew syntax. Frequent co-ordination is a characteristic of the Hebrew Bible, which eschews subordination and is very poor, unlike Greek, in connective particles: one particle, *waw*, serves for all co-ordination, and English translations that translate this with anything but 'and' are making judgements about the logical connection between statements which is at most implicit in the Hebrew. Greek on the other hand is rich in such particles – words like 'for', 'therefore', 'because' – and the explicit logical relations between clauses that they set up. Hebrew enjoys partial repetition with variation, and is able to direct emphasis by means of it; and it prefers direct speech to indirect speech, so that we might say that Hebrew narrative prose is starkly dramatic. It seems that the intensity of these qualities in Hebrew is virtually untranslatable into English, and English translations judged by these criteria will be judged in terms of relative failure. The King James Bible is then the smallest failure. James G. Williams gives the example of a proverb that has received its standard English form from the King James Bible:

> Pride goeth before destruction,
> And a haughty spirit before a fall.
> (Proverbs 16:18)

He feels that 'even when the effect in English is pleasing the Hebrew poetry may not be adequately conveyed', and offers a literal rendering of the proverb:

> Before breaking [is] pride,
> and before falling [is] haughtiness of mind.

Williams then compares the two versions, varying his translation as he does so:

What gives this proverb its punch in Hebrew is a quick juxtaposition of images, an almost stroboscopic effect. First there is a rapid flash of words; 'before breaking' followed by 'pride' without a verb; then a second phrase flashes: 'before stumbling' (or 'reeling'), followed by 'haughtiness of mind' (or 'spirit'). The King James Bible version is not bad, though it misses the total effect. But some of the modern translations merely compound the boredom readers may feel for the commonplace and their resistance to it when it is associated with the voice of authority.[25]

It is as if the syntactic effects of Hebrew occur faster than the eye may follow, whereas in English such effects may be imitated plausibly but more slowly, more formally, more self-consciously. Hebrew dances where English walks.

Lexically, Hebrew is a highly concrete language and avoids abstraction. Partridge quotes A.S. Cook:

> Nearly every word presents a concrete meaning, clearly visible even through a figurative use. Many of its roots are verbal, and the physical activity underlying each word is felt through all its special applications . . . everywhere we are face to face with motion, activity, life. Of the Hebrew words for pride, one presents the notion of mounting up, one of strutting, and one of seething, as a boiling pot. What fundamental ideas of similar concreteness does the English word 'pride' suggest?[26]

It would follow from this that almost any English translation, in a language of infinitely greater lexical variation, will be less physical and less figurative than the Hebrew. A last point is that biblical Hebrew has a very small vocabulary, of fewer than eight thousand words, and the symbolic connotations of this small word-stock are therefore very important. These points refer to biblical rather than colloquial Hebrew. Narrative may be close to colloquial utterance, but many other passages of the Old Testament are not, and are written in a distinctly literary language and style. While such writing, formal and highly wrought, may occur in any genre, including narrative, it is particularly prevalent in Psalms, or Proverbs, or anything that could be described as lyrical. Here the style of biblical Hebrew is in some sense poetic.[27]

It has been a commonplace of Old Testament scholarship for more than two hundred years that many parts of the Old Testament are actually poetry.[28] The view has recently been challenged by an American scholar, James L. Kugel, who insists that there is no poetry in the Bible, and that modern translations which quote the Psalms and many passages of other books, like the Book of Job, in verse lines are quite mistaken. Kugel's attitude would appear to resemble that of Tyndale and the translators of the King James Bible, who normalise everything in prose format. However, as Kugel also shows, the idea of biblical poetry occurs at least as early as St Jerome. Jerome saw holy books as a literature, parallel to and opposed to secular literature: 'the psalms were metrical because Horace was, and the psalms were to replace Horace'.[29] This is the inverse of what has been until lately an almost universal tendency: use of the King James Bible to bring the Bible into Engish literature, and with it the notion of canonicity. This 'metrical thesis', according to Kugel, stems in the first instance from Philo, and here again translation and interpretation run hand in hand: 'Philo, the first person known to have described Hebrew writing in the terminology of Greek meters, was also a consistent allegorizer of the Biblical text, and these are not unrelated facts'.[30] In other words, the desire to find poetry in the Bible is associated with the desire for interpretative openness. Hence it is not surprising that Kugel, after attempting to demolish 'the idea of biblical poetry', should conclude his book with an attack on literary approaches to biblical criticism. This is not the gratuitous afterthought that it has been taken to be. Kugel fears secularisation of the Bible, and he fears what he sees as its trivialisation as and into literature. There is a conflict here central to the history of Bible translation and interpretation, to which I shall have occasion to return.

From the more narrowly stylistic viewpoint, however, this interesting debate makes little difference. Such passages, whether formally poetry or not, are poetic: that is, as Kugel would concede, they are highly formal, or formalisations of the patterns of colloquial utterance. They have two distinct features, rhythm and parallelism (though one must understand parallelism with Robert Alter's sense that it does not always imply synonymity) and the third, which follows in their train, variation, encompassing some repetition.[31]

A good example would be the first eight verses of the eighth chapter of the Book of Proverbs:

1 Doth not wisdom cry? and understanding put forth her voice?
2 She standeth in the top of high places, by the way in the places of the paths.
3 She crieth at the gates, at the entry of the city, at the coming in at the doors:
4 Unto you, O men, I call: and my voice is to the sons of man.
5 O ye simple, understand wisdom: and, ye fools, be ye of an understanding heart.
6 Hear; for I will speak of excellent things; and the opening of my lips shall be right things.

7 For my mouth shall speak truth; and wickedness is an abomination to my lips.
8 All the words of my mouth are in righteousness; there is nothing froward or perverse in them.

The English translation of the King James Bible is regarded by most scholars as an uncannily excellent equivalent of the Hebrew. Each verse divides into two or three parts of roughly equal length, each part consisting of two or three stress phrases. There is a parallelism of statement: each idea is presented incrementally two or three times, in different words and from a slightly different viewpoint, either by contrast (as in verse 7), or by variation involving a certain amount of verbal redundancy: there is little extra information in verse 3 to distinguish 'the coming in of the doors' from 'the gates', or in verse 6 between 'speaking' and 'opening of the lips', or between 'excellent things' and 'right things'. This sort of literature lends itself to drastic paraphrase, but paraphrase is exactly what is not wanted. The power comes from extension of the statement and verbal amplification, and would be destroyed by compression. Sense does not come by direct statement, as it were in one hit, but in a cumulative unfolding. The King James version reflects this well, except once more that it is slightly too leisurely to capture what Robert Alter describes as the 'dynamic movement' within the line in the Hebrew and, in the movement from line to line, the sense of biblical poetry as 'the dynamic shaping instrument' through which 'the religious perceptions of the biblical writers' are not merely heightened or dramatised but rather discovered and made real.[32]

If in its English version it is to be seen as poetry, it is not a poetry that behaves according to complex standards. One does not count feet or syllables, nor make rhymes, nor impose any artifical formal restraint other than the parallelism of the statement and the accumulation of roughly balanced phrases, with skilful variation, in each verse. There is no need even to worry about secondary stress, as with iambic pentameter; one merely counts the primary stress of each stressed word. The English language is ideally suited to this, as Tyndale realised. For English is an accentual language. Primary stress is natural to English, secondary stress is not: that is, every word has its main stress and if we get that right, we will pronounce the word intelligibly. The English language also combines two and three stress phrases. These form units that support and follow sense. The sort of composition we find in the passage from Proverbs quoted above is therefore a powerful resource both in sound and sense; rhythm corroborates meaning. And it is this stylistic resource that Tyndale brings to English biblical translation, together with his shrewd understanding of Hebrew parallelism.

I have emphasised rhythm in this account so far because that is crucial to the style, to the sound and sense, of the English Bible in and after Tyndale. In another way, however, rhythm is a secondary consideration: secondary, that is, to the problems of all translation, and the specific problems of Bible translation: textual, theological and linguistic.

I need simply note the textual problem. Accurate translation cannot be made from a bad source text, and Renaissance humanists, like modern Bible scholars, had much work to do in this respect. What is interesting is that modern readers tend to take the accuracy of the scholarship in Bible translation for granted. Translators must also, of course, translate correctly. In medieval art, Moses is frequently depicted as a venerable and patriarchal figure with two horns projecting from his head. There is nothing to suggest horns in the Biblical narrative as it appears in English versions. Where then do they come from? They come in fact from a mistranslation in St Jerome's Vulgate. Hebrew as a written language omits all vowels, and frequently different words can be made by supplying different vowels for the consonants that are in fact written. Jerome simply supplied the vowels which turned the consonants q, b, n into 'horns' rather than a verb of perception. Nevertheless, the horns became part of any reader's experience of the Bible if that reader was reading Jerome's Vulgate.[33] One such reader, of course, was Michelangelo, whose horned Moses guards the tomb of Pope Julius II in San Pietro of Vinculi, Rome.

The theological problem grows out of such factors. How, for instance, to translate the Greek word *ecclesia* which simply means an 'assembly of people'? On this rock, says Jesus to Peter, will I build my *ecclesia*. The official Catholic translation, naturally, is 'Church'; Tyndale's Protestant translation, denounced by More, was 'congregation'. Beneath this disagreement, of course, lurks a much larger question: did Jesus mean his followers to set up a church? An equally famous example is the variant translations possible for the Greek '*metanoiete*' in Matthew 3:2. Jerome translated this as '*penitentiam agite*', 'do penance', and therefore assimilated it to the sacramental life of the Church. Erasmus led the way for Luther and Protestant reformers by suggesting for his version Latin equivalents of the Greek meaning 'change of mind' or 'reconsider'.

The most constant problems however, are linguistic ones. There are, for example, many words in Greek and Hebrew for which there is simply no English equivalent. There is a Greek noun *skandalon* used by St Paul to describe the impact of Christ's crucifixion: hence the term 'the scandal of the Cross'. The English words 'scandal' and 'slander' both derive from this Greek word. The basic concept is that of a physical block ('*skandalon*'), which impedes right progress or understanding and causes diversion into wrong courses, sin, or error, or at least causes difficulty. There is no one English word to translate it, or the associated verb *skandalizo*, which a modern translator translates variously: 'make it difficult' (Mark 6:3), 'make you go amiss' (Matt. 5:29), 'does not stand fast' (13:21), 'objected' (15:12), 'put me off' (16:23), 'cause trouble' (17:27) 'made to fail me' (26:31). The King James Bible on the other hand translates it consistently by one word, to 'offend'.[34] This is the regular King James Bible procedure, where possible to translate formula by formula, and is true to the usage of the Greek; but it fails to convey the many nuances of the term in Greek. On the other hand, modern translators find other words in the Greek or Hebrew for which the King James Bible gives up to fourteen synonyms, thus concealing connections in the original text. There seems no answer to this difficulty, unless we are to accept footnotes – or, in the medieval term, glosses; and there were doctrinal objections to this. To explore these problems is to see that no translation can fully reflect the original – and for translators to accept this is in fact the precondition of a literary production in the new language.

So it was with the two Wycliffite versions of the Bible, one painfully literal and the second less so, with the preface that put forward the notion of translating not word for word but sense for sense. That second version is a breakthrough; it makes an English Bible instead of a laboured crib, and Tyndale follows this lead. He accepts the necessary independence even of a faithful translation. It is the precondition of a decent prose style; and that, allied to his insistence that the Bible be suited for reading aloud, explains the paramount importance of rhythm in Tyndale's and all subsequent translations. The compilers of the King James Bible built on the work of Tyndale and all the subsequent English versions between his and theirs; they devoted two whole years to literary effect alone. Theirs is a triumph of rhythm, and it is rhythm to which they gave their special attention. Again, linguistic factors lead back to rhythm. But the emphasis on rhythm produces less an English *Bible* than an *English* Bible.

Rhythm or, better, cadence is everything in the King James Bible. That cadence captures the parallelism of Hebrew poetry, and it builds on nearly a century of English cadence-making. Examples abound and are examined in the many books on the making of the English Bible. Cadence and syntactic balance go hand in hand. I present an annotated passage from Job 7:1–3:

1 Is there not an appointed time to man upon earth? are not his days also like the days of an hireling?
2 As a servant earnestly desireth the shadow, and as an hireling looketh for the reward of his work:
3 So am I made to possess months of vanity, and wearisome nights are appointed to me.

PROSE RHYTHM

1	a. Is there nót an appóinted tíme/to mán upon eárth?	3:2
	b. are not his dáys/álso like the dáys of an hireling?	2:3
2	a. As a sérvant/eárnestly desíreth the shádow,	1:3
	b. and as an híreling/lóoketh for the rewárd of his wórk:	1:3
3	a. So am I made to possess/months of vanity,	3:2
	b. and wearisome nights/are appointed to me.	2:2

Nominal sets:
man on earth = Job = a servant, 'an hireling'
time, days months nights (shadow in 2a = nightfall: see 3b)
Lexical sets: desire (2a,2b); compulsion (1a,3a,3b)

All that is necessary to see the superb co-ordination of cadence and sense is to set out the phrases as I have, and to divide them into their component two- and three-stress phrases. At once it is evident that Job's complaint here is an envelope structure, opened and closed by the one repeated word, 'appointed'. The two outside sentences make the connection between Job and 'man upon earth' as Job presents himself as the type of all men. There are two major lexical sets in the nouns of the complaint: one is man on earth who is correlated with Job and with a servant, a hireling; the other is time, days, months, nights ('the shadow' in verse 2 is nightfall, an association made clear by 'wearisome nights' in verse 3). There is parallelism with variation here, and also contrast: the servant desires nightfall because that marks the end of the work, but Job even has to suffer 'wearisome nights'. Each half-verse links the two lexical sets, except significantly, 2b, to which I will return. Where a pattern is established, what deviates from that pattern is often the core of the sense. Elsewhere the half-verses are of roughly equal proportions: the 3:2 stress division of 1a are elegantly reversed in 1b, which brings the two lexical sets together. The shortest half-verse is 3b (2:2), in which Job relapses into gloomy contemplation of his state. One could go further: the balance of 2a and 2b is achieved by exact parallelism in the first half of each half-verse ('as a servant', 'as an hireling'), an elegant variation in the second – a verb in each belonging to the same lexical set, indicating desire, and a noun indicating the object of desire, but of unequal weight ('the shadow' does not adequately balance 'the reward of his work', hence the addition in 2a of the adverb 'earnestly'). That phrase, 'the reward of his work', is highlighted by the whole structure; it is the only noun set that does not apparently belong to either of the two other nominal sets (man and time), and actually belongs to both. The incongruity highlights the phrase, and thus the meaning of the complaint. Job is the servant who requires 'the reward of his work', a reward not of money but of time – or rather, an end of time. Instead of the 'wearisome nights' appointed in 3b, Job seeks the 'appointed time' of 1a: that is, death. The balance points to contrasts: it is achieved by grammar, by lexis, and is marked beautifully by the rhythm.

This sort of balance, then, highlights paradox, and it is used extensively for this purpose in the New Testament. An example would be the Gospel of John 12:44–50:

44 Jesus cried and said, He that believeth on me, believeth not on me, but on him that sent me.

45 And he that seeth me seeth him that sent me.

46 I am come a light into the world, that whosoever believeth on me should not abide in darkness.

47 And if any man hear my words, and believe not, I judge him not: for I came not to judge the world, but to save the world.

48 He that rejecteth me, and receiveth not my words, hath one that judgeth him: the word that I have spoken, the same shall judge him in the last day.

49 For I have not spoken of myself; but the Father which sent me, he gave me a commandment, what I should say, and what I should speak.

50 And I know that his commandment is life everlasting: whatsoever I speak therefore, even as the Father said unto me, so I speak.

This could be set out in much the same way as the example in Job, and analysed in the same way for the interplay of its lexical sets and its rhythms: it contains both balance and contrast; parallelism operates by thesis ('I am God', suggested in verse 45), antithesis ('I am not God', verse 44, 49), and synthesis ('even as the Father said unto me, so I speak', verse 50). The contrast directs us away from questions of *identity* ('is Jesus the same as God?') to the key lexical set of *speech*: to hear is to believe, and the person of Jesus – as John tells us in his first chapter – is not God but the Word of God. The balance makes the *non sequiturs* all the more apparent, and challenges us to resolve them in the paradox enunciated at the very beginning of John's Gospel.[35]

The history of English biblical translation from the King James Bible onwards is one of progressive weakening of this power that comes from the pressure of rhythm. There is no need to concentrate one's attack on twentieth-century versions. We can go back to the eighteenth century, to Dr Edward Harwood's *Liberal Translation of the New Testament*, the aim of which was 'to clothe the ideas of the Apostles with propriety and perspicuity', and replace the 'bald and barbarous language of the old vulgar version with the elegance of modern English'. Harwood's translation of John 1 was quoted in Chapter 1. *The Cambridge History of the Bible* compares his version with *A New and Corrected Version of the New Testament* by Rodolphus Dickinson (Boston, 1833):

The author condemns the 'quaint monotony and affected solemnity' of the King James version, with its 'frequently rude and occasionally barbarous attire'; and he declares his purpose to adorn the Scriptures with 'a splendid and sweetly flowing diction' suited to the use of 'accomplished and refined persons'. Examples are:

'When Elizabeth heard the salutation of Mary, the embryo was joyfully agitated' (Luke i. 41). 'Festus declared with a loud voice, Paul, you are insane! Multiplied research drives you to distraction' (Acts xxvi. 24).[36]

To modern readers both no doubt seem inane. But why do both concur in calling the style of the King James Bible 'barbarous'?

The answer is twofold. First, the eighteenth century loved long words, and that love of long words is what wreaks such havoc in both versions on the rhythm of the King James Bible. The simple fact is that in the King James Bible monosyllables outnumber words of two syllables or more, not counting proper names, by two and half times to one. The slow and majestical liturgical cadence of the King James Bible depends on this huge proportion of monosyllables; it is artfully varied, and relieved from the danger of tedium, by occasional well-placed polysyllables. This exploits a distinctive feature of the English language: no strongly inflected language can have any such preponderance of monosyllables, nor any such impressive sustained cadence. In that sense, Tyndale was right: 'the Hebrew tongue agreeth a thousand times more with the English than with the Latin'. And this holds true too for the second ground on which later meddlers have found the style of the King James Bible 'barbarous'. It is based squarely on the oldest tradition of English writing: alliterative writing, from the Anglo-Saxon period through to later Middle English in such texts as *Piers Plowman*. Here are the first two lines of *Piers Plowman*:

> In a sómer sésoun   whan sófte was the sónne
> I shóp me into shróudes   as I a shép wére . . .

The alliteration is very obvious but its major function is to signal stress. The line divides into two half lines, generally of two stresses, sometimes of three; the last stress of the b verse is generally without alliteration in order to speed the rhythm of one line into the next. Parallelism is frequent, and also involves artful variation and some verbal redundancy; the b verse is often an artful repetition or variation of the a verse; contrast is constantly exploited; there is no rhyme nor syllable count, but rather a succession of two and three stress phrases.[37] In short, England, uniquely, retained until the fifteenth century a form which perfectly reproduced the conditions of Hebrew 'poetry'; and this form was in the later medieval period a kind of halfway house between poetry and prose, passing in and out of both – like the Hebrew of the Old Testament, according to most scholars. It is this form, not any exotic Latin models, which gives English prose of sixteenth-century Bible translations and the King James Bible its thew and sinew, with the accentual patterns remaining and the alliteration dropping out. Strikingly, the Bibles of Tyndale and Coverdale contain much more alliteration than the King James Bible; it is as if English prose had to generate the confidence to drop the alliteration, to conceal the ancient and historical national matrix of the style.

It is not altogether surprising to see a great prose style develop out of a loosely poetic tradition. There is a tendency, whenever a prose writer stretches for the highly wrought effect, for prose to begin to imitate verse: the well-known instances where Dickens more or less accidentally composes blank verse are classic demonstrations. Something comparable happens in the sixteenth century when Tyndale searches for a style strong yet muscular enough for this matter. It was with this same alliterative poetic tradition in mind that Hopkins in the nineteenth century produced the concept of 'Instress' for Christian poetry, where the stress pattern of the writing corroborates and evokes the inner, spiritual stress in its writer and readers. Hopkins did not invent instress; he rediscovered it. The cadence of the King James Bible is, precisely, instress: for its balance and contrast is both rhythmical and logical; it ensures that meaning is always moving; that what is dictated and enforced by the stress patterns are patterns of *semantic relations*. And in this instress, where cadence and meaning go hand in hand, we find, though never in a form that defeats analysis, the strongest possible Englishing of the language of faith. If for T. S. Eliot poetry aspires to the condition of music, for English Bible translators from Tyndale onwards prose aspires to the condition of poetry. When we call the King James Bible 'a great masterpiece of English prose', we really mean that it is all but a great masterpiece of English poetry. And we claim for it the literary quality, and the interpretative openness, that so disturbs Kugel in *The Idea of Biblical Poetry*.

The copies of the King James Bible that we now possess are very different from the original production. For one thing, they are free of mistakes: the first century or two of the book's production were notorious for major printer's errors, the most unfortunate being in the so-called Wicked Bible of the seventeenth century, so called because of the singular omission which made the seventh Commandment read 'Thou shalt commit adultery'. For another thing, the spelling was modernised in two eighteenth-century revisions which have given us the King James Bible as the Authorised Version in its current state, and a full account of the language of the King James Bible would probably begin with its original spelling: 'he' sometimes spelt 'hee', *u* for *v*, *i* for *j* and vice versa, and the like. Oddly, to see the original spelling discourages one from a common misconception about its language, that in 1611 it was already archaic.

This is not really true, at least on the level of lexis: one can comb the Oxford English Dictionary for a long time before finding any word used in the 1611 Bible that was archaic in 1611; and one also finds in the Authorised Version, compared to Tyndale or the Geneva Bible, that there is a greater use of words derived not from the Anglo-Saxon tradition but from Latin and the Romance languages. These words tend to be polysyllabic. They are introduced, generally not for the sake of archaism or even formality, but again for the sake of amplifying the rhythm. They are used with great restraint, a restraint testifying to the translators' conception of 'Biblical English' as a language different from their own. This difference can be gauged quite clearly from their preface:

It is not onely an armour, but also a whole armorie of weapons, both offensiue, and defensiue; whereby we may saue our selues and put the enemie to flight. It is not an herbe, but a tree, or rather a whole paradise of trees of life, which bring foorth fruit euery moneth, and the fruit thereof is for meate, and the leaues for medicine. It is not a pot of Manna, or a cruse of oyle, which were for memorie only, or for a meales meate or two, but as it were a showre of heauenly bread sufficient for a whole host, be it neuer so great; and as it were a whole cellar full of oyle vessels; whereby all our necessities may be prouided for, and our debts discharged. In a word, it is a Panary of holesome foode, . . . a Pandect of profitable lawes, against rebellious spirits; a treasurie of most costly jewels, against beggarly rudiments; Finally a fountaine of pure water springing vp into euerlasting life.[38]

We have some reason to be glad that the translators stuck to the different style of 'Biblical English', which is meant less to appear archaic than it is to sound timeless.

How then can this style be characterised, if not as archaic? In syntax, it follows the English tradition of imitating Hebrew and Greek: 'and' is the most frequent conjunction in the Old Testament, but there are relatively more subordinate constructions in St Paul's Epistles. The habit of Hebrew parallelism, once acquired in English in the English version of the Old Testament, continues into, and colours, the New Testament; and this means that there are no 'sentences' as long and florid as the example quoted above the preface. Again rhythm is the major factor. So is there any sign, if not of archaism, then of conservatism? In one area there certainly is, again conditioned by rhythm. The inflexions of Tyndale's English are retained, particularly the third person singular of the present tense ending in -*eth* rather than -*s*: *He followeth, She loveth, God commandeth*, and so on. The King James Bible retains this ending at a time when it was breaking down, and had become, in the literature of the day, more of a metrical convenience than a spoken norm. Portia's famous courtroom speech in *The Merchant of Venice* (Act IV scene 1) uses both: 'it blesseth him that gives and him that takes'. Shakespeare was equally at home in the old form and the new, using the old perhaps more liberally in the courtroom scene to give a biblical resonance to Portia's Christian appeal against Shylock. By contrast, the King James Bible sticks to the old -*eth* form which was Tyndale's form; and equally significantly, it follows Tyndale's form in addressing God as 'thou'. This does not arise, needless to say, because God is regarded as a social inferior; it is because *thou* is the *marked* form of address indicating a special relationship. Or rather, this was the case when Tyndale was writing. Once, as occurred in the late fifteenth century, the historically plural 'ye' becomes the polite form for polite address to a single person, its use inevitably snowballed and was becoming standard at the time of the King James Bible. What the King James Bible does is simply retain the forms that were standard in Tyndale's translation because they were standard in Tyndale's day.

Hence the fugitive impression of archaism in the King James Bible – its language, following Tyndale, is almost 100 years older than the King James Bible itself. There is an important historical irony here: Tyndale, Coverdale and the translators of the Geneva Bible after him believed that the language of English Bible translation should be strong and *colloquial*. But Tyndale also believed that the translation should be satisfying to read aloud – in other words, that it should be *rhythmical*. Tyndale did his job too well. His rhythms, especially as incorporated in the Geneva Bible of 1560, became standard, and so well loved and familiar that the idea of substantial change had become inconceivable by the time of the King James Bible in 1611. The inflexions, the use of 'thou', are the features of Tyndale's language that had ceased in the process of time to be the common colloquial usage they had once been: all these contributed to the rhythmical effect. Moreover, this rhythmical effect was now *liturgical* rather than colloquial: Coverdale's Psalms and other biblical translations, themselves based on Tyndale, had been incorporated in the Church of England Book of Common Prayer (1549–52); and the language of worship is slow, incantory and hieratic – rather than colloquial. The colloquial in Tyndale's original programme had been well and truly killed off by the rhythmical; and the King James Bible buried it. As an extreme Lutheran, believing in extremely simple church services, Tyndale had seen no conflict between the colloquial and the liturgical. But the new Anglican Church kept its bishops, its vestments, its music and its elegant services, and it maintained this position against Puritans who continued to argue vehemently for colloquial simplicity in worship and Bible translation alike. The style of the King James Bible was meant to align the reading of the Bible with the worship of the Church of England; and its slightly old-fashioned language was meant to express the great antiquity of that Church. It marked a decisive shift in register from the colloquial to the liturgical.

'If ever successful establishment prose existed, this is it.'[39] Peter Levi's judgement on the King James Bible is eminently just, and it directs attention to the important connection between the King James Bible's great prose and its institutional nature. It is doubly surprising, therefore, that Gerald Hammond's praise of the King James Bible in very different terms may also appear to have at least some justice:

> At its best, which means often, the Authorized Version has the kind of transparency which makes it possible for the reader to see the original clearly. It lacks the narrow interpretive bias of modern versions, and is the stronger for it

> . . . Through its transparency, the reader of the Authorized Version not only sees
> the original but also learns how to read it.[40]

Whether or not Hammond's emphasis on accuracy to the original is
warranted (and I would argue that for most readers it is beside the
point), there seems little doubt that we must grant to the King James
Bible qualities of transparency and interpretative openness that may be
the last things we expect from institutional prose. But the 'successful
establishment prose' of the King James Bible is open by design.

The comparison with the Geneva Bible is instructive. Geneva is
designed for private and household reading as a complete behavioural
guide, and is often bound with the Prayer Book or the Psalms to make
a complete way of salvation for the Protestant reader. Its marginal
glosses are extensive and unashamedly partisan. The compilers, whose
translations are never dishonest in the name of party, build a vision of a
Protestant national destiny that is narrowly deuteronomic and broadly
allegorical, in interpreting the Book of Revelation in the closed manner
typical of sectarian readings. No interpretative stone is to be left
unturned, no textual crux unresolved. Whittingham's preface for the
New Testament translation set out a very clear programme: 'To my
knollage I have omitted nothing unexpounded, wherby he that is
anything exercised in the Scriptures of God might iustely complayn of
hardenes'. The book itself, as a foundation of the spiritual Temple, is
an institution in its own right.[41] Whereas in the King James Bible there
are no marginal glosses, by an instruction that goes back to Archbishop
Parker's prescription for openness in the Bishops' Bible: 'Item: to make
no bitter notis uppon any text or yet to set downe any determinacion in
places of controversie'.[42] Not only were interpretative aids to be
eschewed, but textual cruces themselves were to be left unresolved. In
the first place, this makes political sense in a Church divided into
interpretative factions: its vital text represents what all can accept
before divisive interpretation takes place. Of even greater importance,
however, is that such a Bible leaves a primary role for the Church, the
traditional role of teaching and preaching. The text is open to
institutional mediation. More than any other text, the King James
Bible best captures the circumscribed and paradoxical nature of English
freedom.

It is a complex series of institutional demands then, that leads the King James Bible to provide a text so open that it behaves like its great contemporary, Shakespearian literature, resonant with its thrilling ambiguities, a text that is supremely open to interpretation. It is a text ever likely to win approval in another latitudinarian institution, the modern university, where it is assimilated into a literary canon that it helps construct, and in which the secular teacher assumes the interpretative role formerly accorded to the cleric. Such a claim can be traced in the critical writing of Coleridge and Matthew Arnold through to Eliot and perhaps Frye. It is in that institution that the King James Bible is valued as 'a masterpiece of English prose'. For sectarian readers, by contrast, in the sixteenth century as now, openness and transparency have little to commend them as primary features of English biblical translation. In both cases, the Bible that readers prefer is the Bible they wish (or wish not) to believe.

Notes

1. Sir Thomas More, *Dialogue Concerning Heresies* (1528/9), provoked Tyndale's *Answer* of 1530, and More's *Confutation of Tyndale's Answer* (1532-3) and *Apology* (1533): *CHB* III (Chapter 1, note 6, above), pp. 153-5, and A.C. Partridge, *English Biblical Translation* (London: André Deutsch, 1973), pp. 40-6.
2. *CHB* II, pp. 362-87.
3. The authoritative work on Lollardy is that of Anne Hudson, *The Premature Reformation: Wycliffite texts and Lollard history* (Oxford: Clarendon, 1988); *Lollards and their Books* (London: Hambledon, 1985); and her edition of *Selections from English Wycliffite Writings* (Cambridge: Cambridge UP, 1978). See also M. Deanesly, *The Lollard Bible and other Medieval Biblical Versions* (Cambridge: Cambridge UP, 1920); and *CHB* II, pp. 387-415. The best discussion of the meanings of 'loller' (Lollard) in Middle English is that of Wendy Scase, *'Piers Plowman' and the New Anticlericalism* (Cambridge: Cambridge UP, 1989), pp. 150-7.
4. *CHB* III, p. 11, where such translation changes are put in context: 'Translation was itself exegesis'.
5. Partridge (n.1. above), p. 96. He comments, p. 97: 'The undisguised

purpose of this account was to teach Protestant paraphrasers a lesson in literalness'.

6. *CHB* III, p. 146.

7. *CHB* II, p. 388.

8. Quoted by Maurice S. Betteridge, 'The bitter notes: The Geneva Bible and its annotations', *Sixteenth Century Journal* 14 (1983), 41–62.

9. *CHB* III, 205.

10. *The English Works of Richard Rolle*, ed. Hope Emily Allen (Oxford: Clarendon, 1931), p. 7; see Partridge (n.1. above), p. 20.

11. See *A Companion to 'Piers Plowman'*, ed. John A. Alford (Berkeley, Los Angeles, London: University of California Press, 1988); John A. Alford, 'The role of the quotations in *Piers Plowman*', *Speculum* 52 (1977), 80–99.

12. E. Le Roy Ladurie, *Montaillou: Cathars and Catholics in a French village 1294–1324*, trans. Barbara Bray (London: Scolar Press and New York: Braziller, 1978).

13. Anne Hudson, 'A Lollard sect vocabulary?', in *Lollards and their Books* (n. 3, above), pp. 165–80.

14 Quoted by Betteridge (n.8, above), p. 62, and in L. Stone, 'Communication on *The Alienated Intellectuals in Early Stuart England*', *Past and Present* 24 (1963), 101.

15. Partridge (n.1, above), pp. 33–59; *CHB* III, p. 145; on 'free' versus 'stencil' translation, Samuel K. Workman, *Fifteenth Century Translation as an influence on English Prose* (Princeton: Princeton UP, 1940).

16. *CHB* III, p. 141; Charles C. Butterworth, *The Literary Lineage of the King James Bible 1340–1611* (Philadelphia: University of Pennsylvania Press, 1941) p. 57. This is an excellent account, recently supplemented by Gerald Hammond, *The Making of the English Bible* (Manchester: Carcanet, 1982), with its fine analysis of translators' methods.

17. *CHB* III, pp. 159–60; Butterworth (n.16. above), pp. 173–91.

18. *CHB* III, p. 156; Partridge (n.1. above), pp. 75–86.

19. Richard L. Greaves, 'The nature and intellectual milieu of the political principles in the Geneva Bible marginalia', *Journal of Church and State* 22 (1980), 223–49; p. 233.

20. *The English Bible 1534–1859* (London: Constable, 1974), pp. 27–8.

21. See note 16 for Hammond, and also Butterworth. See also Ward Allen, ed. and trans., *Translating for King James: Notes made by a translator of King James Bible* (Nashville: University of Tennessee Press, 1969).

22. *CHB* III, pp. 491–2.

23 .T.S Eliot's judgement of the New English Bible was that 'it astounds in its combination of the vulgar and pedantic.'

24. Quoted by Partridge (n.1., above), p. 37.

25. James G Williams, 'Proverbs and Ecclesiastes', in *Literary Guide* (Chapter 1, note 5, above), pp. 263–83: p. 269.

26. A.S. Cook, quoted in Partridge (n.1, above), p. 114. See G.B. Caird, *The Language and Imagery of the Bible* (London: Duckworth, 1980).

27. See Robert Alter, 'The characteristics of ancient Hebrew poetry', in *Literary Guide*, pp. 611–24.

28. Since Robert Lowth, *Lectures on the Sacred Poetry of the Hebrews* (London, 1753).

29. James L. Kugel, *The Idea of Biblical Poetry: Parallelism and its history* (New Haven and London: Yale UP, 1981): discussing Jerome, p. 152.

30. *ibid*, p. 135. See also Kugel's 'On the Bible and literary criticim', *Prooftexts* 1 (1981), 217–36; Adele Berlin, *The Dynamics of Biblical Parallelism* (Bloomington and London: Indiana UP, 1985); and Francis Landy's 'The case of Kugel: Do we find ourselves when we lose ourselves in the text?', *Comparative Criticism*, 5, ed. E.S. Shaffer (Cambridge; Cambridge UP, 1983).

31. Alter (n. 27, above), Robert ap Roberts, 'Old Testament Poetry: The translatable structure', *PMLA* 92 (1971), 978–1004.

32. Alter 'Ancient Hebrew poetry', in *Literary Guide*, p. 623.

33. *CHB* III, p. 301. See Eugene A. Nida and C. Taber, *The Theory and Pratice of Translation* (London: E.J. Brill, 1969); Werner Schwartz, *Principles and Problems of Biblical Translation* (Cambridge: Cambridge UP, 1955); H.W. Robinson (ed.) *The Bible in its Ancient and Modern Versions* (Oxford: Oxford UP, 1940).

34. Richmond Lattimore, trans., *The Four Gospels and Revelation, newly translated from the Greek* (London: Hutchinson, 1980), p. 294.

35. For a discussion of the opening of John, see above Chapter 1., pp 7–9.

36. *CHB* III, pp. 354–5.

37. See David Lawton, 'Alliterative style', in *A Companion to 'Piers Plowman'* (n.11, above), pp. 223–49.

38. Quoted in Butterworth (n.16, above), p. 19. For the style of the King James Bible, see Partridge (n.1, above), pp. 105–58. There is a good brief discussion in Barbara M.H. Strang, *A History of English* (London and New York: Methuen, 1974), p. 146.

39. Levi, *The English Bible* (n.20, above), p. 194.

40. Gerald Hammond, 'English translations of the Bible', in *Literary Guide*, pp. 647–66: p. 664.

41. On the Geneva Bible, see *CHB* III, Butterworth, Partridge, Levi, Hammond, already cited, as well as Betteridge (n.8, above: Whittingham is quoted from p. 42), Greaves (n.19, above), Dan G. Danner, 'The contribution of the Geneva Bible of 1560 to the English Protestant tradition', *Sixteenth Century Journal* 12 (1981), 5–18, and 'Marian exiles and the English Protestant tradition', *Studies in Medieval Culture* 13 (1978), 93–101; Hardin Craig, 'The Geneva Bible as a political document', *Pacific Historical Review* 7 (1938), 40–9; Richard L. Greaves, 'Traditionalism and the seeds of revolution in the social principles of the Geneva Bible', *Sixteenth Century Journal* 7 (1976), 94–109; Stanley Morison, *La Bible Anglaise de Genève* (Paris: Diffusion, 1972).

42. A.W. Pollard, *Records of the English Bible* (1911; London: Dawsons, 1974), p. 297.

CHAPTER 4

Narrative structures in the Old Testament

In my accounts of biblical interpretation and translation I presented what is in effect the hermeneutic circle. However much we know, however informed our reading, we cannot ultimately break out of subjectivity or break free from prejudice. I use the word 'prejudice' quite neutrally to mean beliefs, structural expectations, that we take for granted. Our reading is shaped at least in part by unseen determinations, what future historians will see and we do not. A text belongs to the past, a reader to the present; in that sense, they exist in a diachronic, syntagmatic relationship. We certainly need to have the gap bridged between the text's past and our present; that is what biblical criticism tries to do. Yet it must not ignore the vital fact that when we enter into dialogue with the text, however old, we make it our contemporary. Our reading sets us in a paradigmatic, synchronic relationship with it. We question its prejudices; it interrogates ours. We read it; it reads us. That reading process is never truly direct but always circular, extending into the text's past and our world's future. Moreover, text and reader, past and future: none of these is a fixed point. All exist in a mobile and fluid interrelation, somewhere on or near the hermeneutic circle.[1]

I shall make no further attempt to break into the circle by theological discussion. I shall simply try to show how as readers we can and do move around and within the circle – around or within, that is, the orbit of the text – at the prompting of the thematic and stylistic modes, the narrative structures, of the text. How do we accommodate biblical narrative with our own structural and ideological presuppositions? To ask this question is to question both the nature of biblical narrative and the nature of our own presuppositions. Work on the Bible in the historically changing medium of the English language and work on the Bible's historical significance, its power to signify, have in different ways underscored the challenge that the Bible presents to our reading. What begins here is an attempt to read afresh selected books of the Bible, with certain modern theoretical, structural and linguistic approaches to aid the reading. This chapter is concerned with the Old Testament, the next chapter with the New. In the first half of this chapter I shall look in detail at two stories: Cain and Abel, Abraham and Isaac; and compare them with a third, Jacob's fight with the Angel.

Narrative structures in Genesis

Abram is first mentioned in Genesis 11, in the generation of Shem, the favoured son of Noah. Born in Ur of the Chaldees, Abram was taken by his father to live in Haran, and in Genesis 12 receives a peremptory command from God:

> Now the Lord had said unto Abram, Get thee out of thy country, and from thy kindred, and from thy father's house, unto a land that I shall shew thee:
>
> And I will make of thee a great nation, and I will bless thee, and make thy name great; and thou shalt be a blessing:
>
> And I will bless them that bless thee, and curse him that curseth thee; and in thee shall all families of the earth be blessed.
>
> So Abram departed as the Lord had spoken unto him; and Lot went with him; and Abram was seventy and five years old when he departed out of Haran.

First he goes to Canaan, then to Egypt, then back to Bethel. The key note of his life is in Genesis 12:9: 'And Abram journeyed, going on still towards the south.' Abram is a wanderer, a nomad: his 'house' (Genesis 18:1) is a tent. Childless by his wife Sarai, Abram is given by Sarai herself his wife's maid Hagar, on whom he begets a son, Ishmael. God summons Abram to circumcision (Genesis 17), and renames him Abraham, Sarai Sarah; and God promises that the barren Sarah, at the age of ninety, will conceive a son, Isaac, with whom God will establish his covenant. Several chapters and several incidents later, and despite Sarah's incredulity, Isaac is born: Abraham's first-born by Sarah, but his second son if Ishmael is taken into account. Sarah insists that he should not be: she insists that her servant Hagar and Hagar's son Ishmael be cast out. Hagar departs (Genesis 21:14); God comforts her, and she and Ishmael dwell in the wilderness: 'And God was with the lad; and he grew, and dwelt in the wilderness, and became an archer' (Genesis 21:20).

By Genesis 22, then, Isaac is the living proof of God's favour to Abraham, and the covenant God has promised to make Abraham's life of exile dynastically worthwhile.[2] There follows this extraordinary episode:

> And it came to pass after these things, that God did tempt Abraham, and said unto him, Abraham: and he said, Behold, here I am.
>
> And he said, Take now thy son, thine only son Isaac, whom thou lovest, and get thee into the land of Moriah; and offer him there for a burnt offering upon one of the mountains which I will tell thee of.
>
> And Abraham rose up early in the morning, and saddled his ass, and took two of his young men with him, and Isaac his son, and clave the wood for the burnt offering, and rose up, and went unto the place of which God had told him.
>
> Then on the third day Abraham lifted up his eyes, and saw the place afar off.
>
> And Abraham said unto his young men, Abide ye here with the ass; and I and the lad will go yonder and worship, and come again to you.
>
> And Abraham took the wood of the burnt offering, and laid it upon Isaac his son; and he took the fire in his hand, and a knife; and they went both of them together.
>
> And Isaac spake unto Abraham his father, and said, My father: and he said, Here am I, my son. And he said, Behold the fire and the wood: but where is the lamb for a burnt offering?
>
> And Abraham said, My son, God will provide himself a lamb for a burnt offering: so they went both of them together.
>
> And they came to the place which God had told him of; and Abraham built an altar there, and laid the wood in order, and bound Isaac his son, and laid him on the altar upon the wood.
>
> And Abraham stretched forth his hand, and took the knife to slay his son.
>
> And the angel of the Lord called unto him out of heaven, and said, Abraham, Abraham: and he said, Here am I.
>
> And he said, Lay not thine hand upon the lad, neither do thou any thing unto him: for now I know that thou fearest God, seeing thou has not withheld thy son, thine only son from me.
>
> And Abraham lifted up his eyes, and looked, and behold behind him a ram caught in a thicket by his horns: and Abraham went and took the ram, and offered him up for a burnt offering in the stead of his son.

> And Abraham called the name of that place Jehovahjireh: as it is said to this day, In the mount of the Lord it shall be seen.
>
> And the angel of the Lord called unto Abraham out of heaven the second time,
>
> And said, By myself have I sworn, said the Lord, for because thou hast done this thing, and hast not withheld thy son, thine only son:
>
> That in blessing I will bless thee, and in multiplying I will multiply thy seed as the stars in the heaven, and as the sand which is upon the sea shore; and thy seed shall possess the gate of his enemies;
>
> And in thy seed shall all the nations of the earth be blessed; because thou hast obeyed my voice. (Genesis 22:1–18)

This passage has gripped the imagination of students of narrative. The most brilliant discussion of its narrative qualities is in the first chapter of Eric Auerbach's work, *Mimesis: The representation of reality in Western literature*. This is a classic book, and its examination of Genesis 22 is also classic. Auerbach first notes the lack of context and setting. Where is Abraham? Where is God? All we learn is: 'Here I am!', and in this, Auerbach notes, we hear the quiet statement of a tie, a relation rather than a geographical placement. Secondly, Isaac lacks complements, attributes, adjectives. He is just young, and dearly beloved: 'Only what we need to know about him as a personage in the action is illuminated, so that it may become apparent how terrible Abraham's temptation is, and that God is fully aware of it.'[3] There is a similar lack of detail in the journeys. Auerbach's discussion is so fine and influential that it demands hefty quotation:

> After this opening, God gives his command, and the story itself begins: everyone knows it; it unrolls with no episodes in a few independent sentences whose syntactical connection is of the most rudimentary sort. In this atmosphere it is unthinkable that an implement, a landscape through which the travellers passed, the serving-men, or the ass, should be described, that their origin or descent or material or appearance or usefulness should be set forth in terms of praise; they do not even admit an adjective: they are serving-men, ass, wood, and knife, and nothing else, without an epithet; they are there to serve the end which God has commanded; what in other respects they were, or will be, remains in darkness. A journey is made, because God has designated the place where the sacrifice is to be performed; but we are told nothing about the journey except that it took three days.[4]

Direct speech does not exist to externalise thoughts, and is merely 'an interruption of the heavy silence' as we reach the end of the journey in which 'everything remains unexpressed'. Auerbach's purpose in this chapter is achieved by comparing the style of Genesis with that of Homer: in the case of Homer everything is expressed and clarified; in the case of Genesis:

> the externalisation of only so much of the phenomena as is necessary for the purpose of the narrative, all else left in obscurity; the decisive points of the narrative alone are emphasised, what lies between is non-existent; time and place are undefined and call for interpretation; thoughts and feeling remain unexpressed, are only suggested by the silence of the fragmentary speeches; the whole, permeated with the most unrelieved suspense and directed towards a single goal (and to that extent far more of a unity), remains mysterious and 'fraught with background'.[5]

'Fraught with background': this marvellous phrase adequately represents the challenge of the story for the reader. The silences of the story are fraught with significance; and it is the silences that the reader must articulate in order to understand the story. But how can we articulate what is not there? It is as if, as readers, we are in the position of Isaac: disoriented, taken on a long journey to an unfamiliar place, aware of a terrible and terrifying significance yet totally blind to the true destiny of the narrative whose steps we trace. Auerbach chose this passage, I think, because he was aware of the book-length discussion of it by the great nineteenth-century Christian existentialist, Søren Kierkegaard: in a book appropriately named *Fear and Trembling*, obsessed with the unimaginable nature of Abraham's faith as manifested in the readiness to sacrifice Isaac, with the difference between our reading of the story and the agonising slowness of the process it describes:

> We mount a winged horse, and in the same instant we are on Mount Moriah, in the same instant we see the ram. We forget that Abraham only rode an ass, which trudges along the road, that he had a journey of three days, that he needed some time to chop the firewood, to find Isaac, and to sharpen the knife.[6]

Kierkegaard also takes an important step when he points out why

91

Abraham cannot speak. It is a condition of the test that he cannot explain it. It is therefore faith that impedes dialogue and explanation:

> At every moment, Abraham can stop; he can repent that the whole thing is a spiritual trial; then he can speak out, and everybody will be able to understand him – but then he is no longer Abraham.
>
> Abraham *cannot* speak because he cannot say that which would explain everything (that is, so it is understandable).[7]

And Kierkegaard offers four alternative versions of the episode in which something different happens. In the most shocking of these, Abraham tries gently to comfort and explain to young Isaac, who cannot understand and begs for his love:

> Then Abraham turned away from him for a moment, but when Isaac saw Abraham's face again, it had changed: his gaze was wild, his whole being was sheer terror. He seized Isaac by the chest, threw him to the ground, and said: 'Stupid boy, do you think I am your father? I am an idolater. Do you think it is God's command? No, it is my desire.'
>
> Then Isaac trembled and cried out in his anguish: 'God in heaven, have mercy on me, God of Abraham, have mercy on me: if I have no father on earth, then you be my father.'
>
> But Abraham said softly to himself: 'Lord God in heaven, I thank you; it is better that he believes me a monster than that he should lose faith in you.'[8]

Kierkegaard's interference with the original story here is in part thematic: he has asked the question: 'What kind of God is this who demands, even in test, the life of a child?'. The question reverberates all the way to the Book of Job. But Kierkegaard's interference is also stylistic. He has filled the silence of the text with words; he has brought the background into focus; he has articulated the illusion of inner life, or individuality, specifically by postulating a breach between the will of God on the one hand and the will of Abraham and Isaac on the other – a breach that the Old Testament text will not permit.

We have then in the Old Testament account of this episode a terrible and startling narrative. Its style is typical of key episodes in biblical narratives: in giving little characterisation to the characters involved, so that what they think must be inferred from what they do; in giving very little detail of any kind, so that the few details that are given stand out all the more; and, in syntax, mainly avoiding any intrusive notion of causation. That happens and then this happens, one event after another. It is a style that cries out for interpretation.

One recourse for all readers is to turn to commentaries. There is a wide range of interpretation available ranging from the frankly affective, which take Abraham's faith to be exemplary in the eyes of the reader, to such readings as that of Walter Beltz in his work of popularisation, *God and the Gods: Myths of the Bible*. Beltz sees the motif of the sacrifice of the first-born male as crucial to the interpretation of the story (see, for example, Exodus 13:12–13, 22:29–30). He sees parallels in surrounding cultures, and suggests that in the story of the sacrifice of Isaac we find 'the reflection of extremely ancient myth' to do with 'the battle between two gods'.[9] For Beltz, therefore, the story is 'pure Middle Eastern mythology'. A particularly balanced commentary is offered by E.A. Speiser in *The Anchor Bible*, who seems to expand the meaning of the story beyond the exemplary nature of Abraham's obedience to God. He points out that Abraham's obedience has already been demonstrated. What is at stake here is in fact something more, the preparedness to see one's very ideals snuffed out; 'the fact is that short of such unswerving faith, the whole biblical process could not have survived the many trials that lay ahead'.[10] All commentaries seem to have one thing in common: the note of extreme confidence that the commentator understands all the elements of the episode, presented together with an interpretation that invariably emphasises some elements at the expense of others. Beltz, for example, sets a great deal of interpretative store by 'the original myth', which does not of course exist. Speiser marks the crucial step of his argument with a confident statement ('the fact is . . .'), at exactly the point where the step cannot be demonstrated. All interpretations raise interesting questions, particularly the themes of sacrifice of the first-born in that of Beltz, and the notion of wandering, a journey to historical destiny fulfilled through many generations in Speiser's. I shall enlarge on both. But no one commentator's interpretation, in total, can really be said to match up to the episode itself. It seems that the awe-inspiring silences of its telling both cry out for and defeat interpretation.

If in fact the text is inexhaustible and the commentaries here, valuable as they are, are relatively quickly spent, it may follow that we are asking the wrong question when we ask: 'What does this mean?'. In the words of Roland Barthes, the problem is not to reduce the text to a signified, but to maintain its open *significance*. The question is not 'What does this mean?', It is rather: 'What *can* this mean? How and where does the text challenge us to select and find meaning?'. And that question, not the other, is the key question for this book.[11]

I now turn to another famous episode involving sacrifice, in order to make a comparison:

> And Adam knew Eve his wife; and she conceived, and bare Cain, and said, I have gotten a man from the Lord.
>
> And she again bare his brother Abel. And Abel was a keeper of sheep, but Cain was a tiller of the ground.
>
> And in process of time it came to pass, that Cain brought of the fruit of the ground an offering unto the Lord.
>
> And Abel, he also brought of the firstlings of his flock and of the fat thereof. And the Lord had respect unto Abel and to his offering:
>
> But unto Cain and to his offering he had not respect. And Cain was very wroth, and his countenance fell.
>
> And the Lord said unto Cain, Why are thou wroth? and why is thy countenance fallen?
>
> If thou doest well, shalt thou not be accepted? and if thou does not well, sin lieth at the door. And unto thee shall be his desire, and thou shalt rule over him.
>
> And Cain talked with Abel his brother: and it came to pass, when they were in the field, that Cain rose up against Abel his brother, and slew him.
>
> And the Lord said unto Cain, Where is Abel thy brother? And he said, I know not: Am I my brother's keeper?
>
> And he said, What hast thou done? the voice of thy brother's blood crieth unto me from the ground.
>
> And now art thou cursed from the earth, which hath opened her mouth to receive thy brother's blood from thy hand:
>
> When thou tillest the earth, it shall not henceforth yield unto thee her strength; a fugitive and a vagabond shalt thou be in the earth.
>
> And Cain said unto the Lord, My punishment is greater than I can bear.
>
> Behold, thou hast driven me out this day from the face of the earth; and from thy face shall I be hid; and I shall be a fugitive and a vagabond in the earth; and it shall come to pass, that every one that findeth me shall slay me.
>
> And the Lord said unto him, Therefore whosoever slayeth Cain, vengeance shall be taken on him sevenfold. And the Lord set a mark upon Cain, lest any finding him should kill him.
>
> And Cain went out from the presence of the Lord, and dwelt in the land of Nod, on the east of Eden.
>
> And Cain knew his wife; and she conceived, and bare Enoch: and he builded a

city, and called the name of the city, after the name of his son, Enoch (Genesis 4:1–17)

There are many puzzles in this account. Why does God refuse Cain's offering? It must surely be more than an antipathy to vegetarianism. Why does Cain murder Abel? We may again notice how completely and barely sequential is the syntax of the summary narrative of verse 8 ('it came to pass'), how completely shorn of any notion of causation it is. Why, if Cain is cursed, does he receive a mark or stigma from God to protect him from human vengeance? And the style here is similar to the Abraham and Isaac episode: it provokes questions, not answers.

Suppose the emphasis of the account lies not on what Cain and Abel are, but on what they do. That, after all, is what we are told: 'Abel was a keeper of sheep, but Cain was a tiller of the ground'. These are two contrasting lifestyles: keepers of sheep are nomads; tillers of the ground, farmers, are not. A very suggestive gloss on this is provided by the modern French novelist Michel Tournier, in his book *The Erl–King* – whose hero is named Abel:

The same thing with my given name, Abel, which seemed just an accident to me until I came across the lines in the Bible telling of the first murder in human history. Abel was a keeper of sheep, Cain a tiller of the ground. That is, the first was a nomad and the second a sedentary. The quarrel of Cain and Abel has gone on from generation to generation, from the beginning of time down to our own day, as the atavistic opposition between nomads and sedentaries, or more exactly as the persistent persecution of the first by the second. And this hatred is far from extinct. It survives in the infamous and degrading regulations imposed on the gipsies, treated as if they were criminals, and flaunts itself on the outskirts of villages with the sign telling them to 'move on'.

True, Cain is cursed, and his punishment as well as his hatred for Abel is renewed from generation to generation . . . So Cain is sentenced to what he considers to be the worst possible punishment: he must become a nomad as Abel was. He greets his verdict with rebellious words and does not obey. He went out in the presence of the Lord and built a city, the first city, which he named Enoch.

Well, I maintain that this curse on farmers – who are still as hard as ever on their nomad brothers – can still be seen working today. Because the earth no longer feeds them, the peasants are obliged to pack up and leave. They wander in thousands from one region to another: and in the nineteenth century, when the right to vote was linked to a residential qualification, it was in the knowledge that this excluded a large and fluctuating mass of people, rootless and therefore not right-minded. Settling in towns, they form the proletariat of the great industrial cities.[12]

God wants nomads; he does not want sedentaries. Tournier's Abel possesses

> my soul in patience because I know the day will come when heaven will tire of the crimes of the sedentaries and rain down fire on their heads. Then, like Cain, they will be flung in disorder on the roads, fleeing madly from their accursed cities and the earth that refuses to nourish them.[13]

Is this preference the reason why God refuses Cain's offering? Yet human beings have this persistent hankering to be sedentary, to settle down, to build cities: and a great deal of divine energy in the Old Testament goes into destroying those human cities and settlements, and scattering their people over the face of the earth. The first of these is Noah's flood, God's answer to the children of Cain's attempts at town planning; and after the flood, Noah, who has been called out in his old age to an involuntary sea journey, tossed around at the divine will and set down far from home, finally settles down in retirement and takes up farming – whereupon he is immediately degraded:

> And Noah began to be an husbandman, and he planted a vineyard:
>   And he drank of the wine, and was drunken: and he was uncovered within his tent.
>   And Ham, the father of Canaan, saw the nakedness of his father, and told his two brethren without. (Genesis 9:20–2)

Farming is an unsafe profession, even for the righteous retired.

The next act of destruction is the Tower of Babel in Genesis 11, which receives a narrative gloss in the Old Testament itself because of the Hebrew sense of 'Babel' as like the related English word 'babble', a confusion of tongues. God would not let human beings speak the same language. What I would emphasise here, however, is simply the human urge to build a city and the divine impulse to stop it, to 'scatter' folk 'abroad upon the face of the earth':

> And it came to pass, as they journeyed from the east, that they found a plain in the land of Shinar; and they dwelt there.

And they said one to another, Go to, let us make brick, and burn them thoroughly. And they had brick for stone, and slime had they for mortar.

And they said, Go to, let us build a city and a tower, whose top may reach unto heaven; and let us make us a name, lest we be scattered abroad upon the face of the whole earth.

And the Lord came down to see the city and the tower, which the children of men builded . . .

So the Lord scattered them abroad from hence upon the face of the earth: and they left off to build the city. (Genesis 11:2–5, 8)

Next on the list is Sodom and Gomorrah; and the Old Testament list of cities destroyed by acts of God is long and impressive, from Jericho to Jerusalem. No wonder Jonah is to become angry when God resolves to spare Nineveh: precedent is solidly against such a reprieve. On the one hand, then, the sedentaries, their hatred of the nomads, whom they persecute; on the other hand, God's positive preference for the nomads, the vocation of wandering that is the lot of the chosen, the wilderness, exile, the abrupt command from God one day to get up, leave home forever, set out on a ceaseless journey, emigrate, that characterises not only the Abraham story but the whole of the Pentateuch; and the covenant between God and the nomads that is expressed above all in ritual sacrifice, as in the Abraham and Isaac story and as here.

But what is sacrificed here? And who is doing the sacrificing? In one sense the Cain and Abel story is the structural reverse of the Abraham and Isaac story: in the latter, the attempt to sacrifice a son leads to the sacrifice of a sheep; in the former, the sacrifice of a sheep leads to the sacrifice of one son by another. In both stories, there is a substitution: of Isaac by the sheep, and of the rejected first fruit of the ground – perhaps by Abel himself? This last is the suggestion put forward by Alan Aycock in *Structuralist Interpretations of Biblical Myth*. Aycock points out that the 'mark of Cain' – the mark Cain receives from God – is like a kind of brand, indicating ownership. Nobody is to touch Cain: he belongs to God – a God who tries to reconsecrate Cain by sentencing him to a life of wandering, the sentence which Cain is to disobey by building a city. In a paradoxical way, the mark of Cain is therefore both a judgement on his imperfections and a mark of divine favour; it protects him against human vengeance and guarantees his life (though in this too God's will ultimately fails, by the intervention of the blind archer Lamech). It is

97

therefore a stigma, a holy mark like those of the Christian tradition, the stigmata received, for example, by St Francis, universally regarded as a mark of divine favour and of sanctity. How can Cain be said to have achieved sanctity? By making, suggests Aycock, a successful sacrifice to make up for his unsuccessful one: that is, by sacrificing Abel. 'The murder of Abel is a direct solution to Cain's problem of sacrifice.'[14]

This deliberately shocking interpretation is itself imperfect: it leaves out elements that other interpretations explain, such as God's hearing the blood of Abel crying out for revenge. Aycock's co-editor, Sir Edmund Leach, will have nothing to do with it. But another question might be this. Does this interpretation, imperfect as it is, explain elements that other interpretations omit? I think that it does: it explains why God does not punish Cain with death, a life for a life. The first sentence ever passed for murder is not execution but transportation. Just as Isaac is incapable of withdrawing his blessing from Jacob when it was intended for Esau and obtained under false pretences – because a blessing once given is final; so, the argument would run, is God incapable of disallowing credit for a properly made sacrifice. Under what law is sacrifice of somebody's son a proper sacrifice? By the law of the Old Testament itself: the divinely ordained law of sacrifice, as laid down by God himself in, for example, Exodus 13:2 (repeated in Exodus 13:13 and 34:20): 'Sanctify unto me all the firstborn, whatsoever openeth the womb among the children of Israel, both of man and of beast: it is mine.' The first born, however, is redeemable:

> And every firstling of an ass thou shalt redeem with a lamb; and if thou wilt not redeem it, then thou shalt break his neck: And all the firstborn of man among thy children shalt thou redeem. (Exodus 13:13)

> But the firstling of an ass thou shalt redeem with a lamb: and if thou redeem him not, then thou shalt break his neck. All the firstborn of thy sons thou shalt redeem. (Exodus 34:20)

This commutation did not apply at the time of Cain and Abel or of Abraham and Isaac – though a lamb is provided. The firstborn should have been sacrificed. Later in the law, in Numbers 3:41 and 45, the tribe of the Levites become a sacrificial substitute for the children of Israel:

And the Lord said unto Moses, Number all the firstborn of the males of the children of Israel from a month old and upward, and take the number of their names.

And thou shalt take the Levites for me (I am the Lord) instead of all the firstborn among the children of Israel; and the cattle of the Levites instead of all the firstlings among the cattle of the children of Israel.

And Moses numbered, as the Lord commanded him, all the firstborn among the children of Israel.

And all the firstborn males by the number of names, from a month old and upward, of those that were numbered of them, were twenty and two thousand two hundred and threescore and thirteen.

And the Lord spake unto Moses, saying,

Take the Levites instead of all the firstborn among the children of Israel, and the cattle of the Levites instead of their cattle; and the Levites shall be mine: I am the Lord. (Numbers 3:40–5)

The Levites are therefore inferior to the children of Israel; but they are also the Lord's. They are set to work as Tabernacle servants and in due time become specially privileged as priests. Priests serve both their congregations and God, and by serving their congregations in the name of God become, in one sense, superior to those they serve. In Numbers 35, the Levites, as priest-class, gain a singular reward that returns readers to the story of Cain: they are given cities to live in. Cain, then, is the perverted prototype of a Levite, a priest *manqué.*

The prototype is perverted because Cain himself is the first-born son; by all rights he should himself have been the offering. In a manner which delighted Freud when he came to write about sibling rivalry, Cain offered his younger brother as a substitute for himself (again, a mirror image of Jacob who offers himself as a substitute for his older brother). Cain, like Jacob, is a trickster: he succeeds by transgressing the law of primogeniture.[15] And it is that same law of the first-born that compels Abraham to be prepared to sacrifice Isaac, in seeming refutation of God's promise. But there is some ambiguity in the Isaac story too, because of Ishmael, Abraham's son by Hagar. Is not Ishmael really Abraham's first-born? He is sacrificed by Abraham, though at the bidding of Sarah, not God. Ishmael's apparent death sentence is commuted by God, provided that Ishmael becomes a nomad and dwells in the wilderness. Ishmael then, is a type of Esau; Isaac, the second son made first, is a type of Jacob, and bound to succeed where Cain failed in maintaining God's blessing for his line, for he is willingly offered as a victim of sacrifice.

It would be difficult to exaggerate the significance of these structures for the New Testament. Jesus is the Son of God, the first son; yet he is preceded, in life and in annunciation, by John the Baptist, who wears the skins of animals (like Esau), dwells in the wilderness (like Cain) and, according to Mark's Gospel, passes the blessing of the Father unto the Son in the Jordan Baptism. According to Matthew's Gospel, the birth of Jesus is a cue for Herod blasphemously to reinstate the sacrifice eschewed by God in the Isaac episode, the massacre of the innocents. Jesus escapes this because by divine summons Joseph and Mary are called to a far place and journey (ironically) into Egypt, on whose first-born the slaughter is meted out by God in Exodus. There is no trace of this story in St Luke's Gospel, where instead Joseph and Mary travel to the temple of Jerusalem, to present the infant Jesus to the Lord in keeping with the law of the first-born (Luke 2:23), and to offer a substitutory sacrifice 'according to that which is said in the law of the Lord, A pair of turtledoves, or two young pigeons' (2:24). The episodes in Matthew and Luke are therefore mutually exclusive. They substitute for one another according to one's version of the law of sacrifice of the first-born: in Luke, dead turtledoves, and in Matthew, dead children. In adult life, unlike John the Baptist, who remains in the wilderness, Jesus is called to a life of holy wandering, as are his apostles. He is the son of God as Isaac is of Abraham: but for him there is no commutation of the death sentence as Jesus is himself also the substitute, the Lamb of God. Instead, the first-born of God is offered by his Father as the substitute victim for his brothers and sisters, the rest of humanity, and receives the stigma of the cross.

Returning to the Old Testament, and to the sequential analysis of these two episodes, the common themes and implications may be charted as shown in the table on page 101. (I have added a third episode).

It is time to consider that third episode, Jacob's fight with the Angel in Genesis 32:22–32. I have charted its sequence opposite. The context fits the pattern almost exactly. Having cheated Esau of his birthright of blessing, Jacob flees and stays long in the land of his father-in-law, Laban. In Genesis 32, he decides to return, but hears that Esau is coming

	Abraham and Isaac	Cain and Abel	Jacob and the Angel
Context	Journey from home (Canaan)	Journey from home (Eden)	Journey from home (Isaac; Laban)
	First-born/cadet	First-born/cadet	First-born/cadet
Episodes	Place apart (journey)	Place apart ('in the field')	Place apart (journey)
	Beginning of sacrifice	Beginning of sacrifice	Beginning of *conflict*
	Success/Substitution	?Success/Substitution	Stalemate/Success
	Blessing	?Blessing/(Curse)	Blessing
	Naming		Naming
		Marking/(Stigma)	Marking/(Stigma)

to meet him with a band of 400 men – hardly a peaceful delegation. Nevertheless, Jacob persists and goes to meet Esau. This is the night before their fatal meeting:

> And he rose up that night, and took his two wives, and his two womenservants, and his eleven sons, and passed over the ford Jabbok.
> And he took them, and sent them over the brook, and sent over that he had.
> And Jacob was left alone; and there wrestled a man with him until the breaking of day.
> And when he saw that he prevailed not against him, he touched the hollow of his thigh; and the hollow of Jacob's thigh was out of joint, as he wrestled with him.
> And he said, Let me go, for the day breaketh. And he said, I will not let thee go, except thou bless me.
> And he said unto him, What is thy name? And he said, Jacob.
> And he said, Thy name shall be called no more Jacob, but Israel: for as a prince hast thou power with God and with men, and hast prevailed.
> And Jacob asked him, and said, Tell me, I pray thee, thy name. And he said, Wherefore is it that thou dost ask after my name? And he blessed him there.
> And Jacob called the name of the place Peniel: for I have seen God face to face, and my life is preserved.
> And as he passed over Penuel the sun rose upon him, and he halted upon his thigh.

101

> Therefore the children of Israel eat not of the sinew which shrank, which is upon the hollow of the thigh, unto this day: because he touched the hollow of Jacob's thigh in the sinew that shrank. (Genesis 32:22–32)

This narrative follows and matches the pattern of the other two, with two striking variations: in the place of sacrifice there is conflict, and success is gained apparently by stalemate rather than by substitution. I would suggest that this variation gives an important structural clue to Genesis: both sacrifice and conflict are agonistic – that is, they involve a struggle, ambiguously violent and sympathetic, always heroic, between God and human beings. In both, God wants something, and he makes it hard for humans to provide it. He resists. Both sacrifice and conflict are tests; success in either is a rite of passage. Moreover, Abel and Esau stick to the rules – of sacrifice and of primogeniture respectively (Deuteronomy 21:16–17). To succeed, one must know when to be a rule-breaker, like Cain and Jacob, or have the rules broken for one, like Abraham with Isaac. God is both umpire and opponent. One must be able to give the rule-breaking blows, like Cain and the Angel, and be able to take them, like Jacob.

There is an excellent analysis of this last episode by Roland Barthes,[16] who thrives more methodically than Auerbach on the silences and ambiguities of the text. Barthes divides it into three sequences: the passage (verses 22–4); the fight (verses 24–7); and what he calls namings or changes (verses 28–32). Of the first, the passage, Barthes asks: does Jacob stay alone before crossing? In which case, the episode is to do with the overcoming of an obstacle, like a knight who must fight another before he can cross a ford. Or does Jacob cross at the ford Jabbok, and then go off by himself? In which case, Barthes says, the action loses structural finality and gains religious finality: Jacob marks himself for election by solitude. Of the second, the fight, Barthes speaks in terms of ambiguity. Who is the 'someone' 'A man', whom Jacob fights: God or an Angel, or perhaps the Angel of Death? We are not told. The account avoids names, and we have a highly confusing syntactic sequence in which, at first reading, it is hard to tell which 'he' is which. Then, in the logic of narrative, the expert foul, the divine *coup de grace*, should win: it must succeed, because it is a *coup de grace*. The opposite happens: the expert fouler does not win. Nor, actually, does he lose. He is defeated by a time limit, the breaking of the day: 'Let me go,' he says, 'before the day breaketh.' The weaker wins, in exchange for which he is marked. The imbalance in the fight, and the rupture of the logic of narrative, are parallel to the imbalance Jacob has created in his own family and to the law of the first-born: the cadet is marked by Isaac, not the oldest son, Esau; to hold his own in his meeting with Esau, Jacob must first hold his own with God, who 'substitutes' for Esau: so here again, after all, is the substitution pattern. Esau is a progenitor of the Edomites, Jacob of the Israelites. Jacob keeps his hold on Isaac's blessing, and so is renamed Israel. In return for his breach of the law, like Cain, he receives a mark, a stigma, which is both a judgement and a guarantee of survival, a mark of divine favour. There follows the namings or changes which lead Barthes to argue that the whole episode functions as the creation of a multiple trace: on the body of Jacob, on the order of the brothers, in the name of Jacob, in the name of the place, and in food – the creation of an alimentary taboo. The three actions are three homologous sequences, each itself a rite of passage and part of a larger rite of passage, each to do with rules and rule-breaking.

Why must God's chosen people be lawbreakers? Because they are chosen to be nomads – gypsies, vagrants, against whom every society of city-dwellers in the history of the world has legislated. They must be lawbreakers in order to be the keepers of the law, in order to remain God's chosen people: journeying constantly, never at rest, called from some far country in a protracted quest through many generations for an elusive Promised Land: a land where they may finally have a home and a city, Jerusalem; and until which time, their vocation – as in all these three stories – is to wander in the wilderness. That wilderness, in the Old Testament, is a literal wilderness, and Jerusalem a literal place. The advent of Christianity in the first century coincides with what seemed until modern times the final collapse of that promise: the total destruction of Jerusalem and its temple by the Romans in AD 71. All the Gospels and Revelation may postdate this event: and in the New Testament, certainly, the chosen people's true home is yet more inaccessible than in the Old Testament. It is the heavenly Jerusalem, the heavenly city; and the wilderness has become figurative, the wilderness of the world, the pilgrimage of human life from which there is no rest and in which there is no stasis.

103

Reading the Bible is to wander in the wilderness of interpretation in our quest for the Promised Land of meaning. The journey is both worthwhile and a struggle. I would add, simply, how well the style of the Bible – 'fraught with background', stark, sequential, one step after another, shorn of detail, with the occasional detail thereby thrown into towering relief – conforms with the image of that wilderness: and how helpfully and unexpectedly recurrent structures such as these allow us to begin to map its contours. The wilderness is a space for poetics.

Narrative as discourse: The Book of Ruth and the Book of Job

The Book of Ruth is a masterpiece, which appears at first sight too small, both in scale and concerns, to be a member of the biblical canon at all – rather like a Jane Austen novel interpolated into *King Lear*. Ruth is gentle, muted and understated, a tale of the most ordinary sorrows and joys; not at all what we might have expected to find in the middle of the Old Testament's prophetic storms and royal bloodbaths. It is not at all what we might expect to follow Judges.[17]

Ruth opens simply as the story of a migrant, set in the Biblical past when in the days 'when the Judges rule'; the migrant is Ruth's future mother-in-law, Naomi, who with her husband Elimelech and her two sons Mahlon and Chilion moved from their home in Bethlehem in Judah to the foreign country of Moab. The reason for their migration is a familiar Biblical and historical one: famine. The account in the first chapter in the Book of Ruth is already so marvellously condensed that no summary can approach its quality:

> And Elimelech Naomi's husband died; and she was left, and her two sons.
> And they took them wives of the women of Moab; the name of one was Orpah, and the name of the other Ruth: and they dwelled there about ten years.
> And Mahlon and Chilion died also both of them; and the woman was left of her two sons and her husband.
> Then she arose with her daughters in law, that she might return from the country of Moab: for she had heard in the country of Moab how that the Lord had visited his people in giving them bread.
> Wherefore she went forth out of the place where she was, and her two

daughters in law with her; and they went on the way to return unto the land of Judah.

And Naomi said unto her two daughters in law, Go, return each to her mother's house: the Lord deal kindly with you, as ye have dealt with the dead, and with me.

The Lord grant you that ye may find rest, each of you in the house of her husband. Then she kissed them; and they lifted up their voice, and wept.

And they said unto her, Surely we will return with thee unto thy people.

And Naomi said, Turn again, my daughters: why will ye go with me? are there yet any more sons in my womb, that they may be your husbands?

Turn again, my daughters, go your way; for I am too old to have an husband. If I should say, I have hope, if I should have a husband also tonight, and should also bear sons;

Would ye tarry for them till they were grown? would you stay for them from having husbands? nay, my daughters; for it grieveth me much for your sakes that the hand of the Lord is gone out against me.

And they lifted up their voice, and wept again: and Orpah kissed her mother in law; but Ruth clave unto her.

And she said, Behold, thy sister in law is gone back unto her people, and unto her gods: return thou after thy sister in law.

And Ruth said, Intreat me not to leave thee, or to return from following after thee; for whither thou goest, I will go; and where thou lodgest, I will lodge; thy people shall be my people, and thy God my God:

Where thou diest, will I die, and there will I be buried: the Lord do so to me, and more also, if ought but death part thee and me.

When she saw that she was steadfastly minded to go with her, then she left speaking unto her.

So they two went until they came to Bethlehem. And it came to pass, when they were come to Bethlehem, that all the city was moved about them, and they said, Is this Naomi?

And she said unto them, Call me not Naomi, call me Mara: for the Almighty hath dealt very bitterly with me.

I went out full, and the Lord hath brought me home again empty: why then call ye me Naomi, seeing the Lord hath testified against me, and the Almighty hath afflicted me?

So Naomi returned, and Ruth the Moabitess, her daughter in law, with her, which returned out of the country of Moab: and they came to Bethlehem in the beginning of the barley harvest. (Ruth 1:3–22)

The remaining three chapters deal with the restoration of Naomi's fortunes or hope through what must be called divine providence, though that gloss is much clumsier than the text itself, and through the agency of the ever faithful Ruth: who is sent by Naomi in a concerted, and in Chapter 3 a somewhat titillating, effort to win the help and hand of Elimelech's powerful and wealthy kinsmen, Boaz. Both Ruth and Boaz are utterly sensible of family ties and obligations and of the part these play in representing and imitating or enacting the Jewish people's covenant with God. It is because of this all-embracing family piety that Boaz finally consents to become the redeemer of Elimelech's family: the Hebrew word for redeemer is *go-el*, and it means advocate, powerful protector, and in the strict financial sense, therefore, redeemer, that is, buyer back of the family land, and restorer of the family fortunes. And the family fortunes, as Boaz interprets them, also include children – to carry on the line of Elimelech; he therefore takes in marriage Ruth, the only woman left of that line still capable of child-bearing:

> And Boaz said unto the elders, and unto all the people, Ye are witnesses this day, that I have bought all that was Elimelech's and all that was Chilion's and Mahlon's, of the hand of Naomi.
>
> Moreover, Ruth the Moabitess, the wife of Mahlon, have I purchased to be my wife, to raise up the name of the dead upon his inheritance, that the name of the dead be not cut off from among his brethren, and from the gate of his place: ye are witnesses this day.
>
> So Boaz took Ruth, and she was his wife: and when he went in unto her, the Lord gave her conception, and she bare a son.
>
> And the women said unto Naomi, Blessed be the Lord which hath not left thee this day without a kinsman, that his name may be famous in Israel.
>
> And he shall be unto thee a restorer of thy life, and a nourisher of thine old age: for thy daughter in law, which loveth thee, which is better to thee than seven sons, hath born him.
>
> And Naomi took the child, and laid it in her bosom, and became nurse unto it.
>
> And the women her neighbours gave it a name, saying, There is a son born to Naomi; and they called his name Obed: he is the father of Jesse, the father of David. (Ruth 4:9–10, 13–17)

In that last verse the reader sights the reason for this Book's canonical status, which may be part legend but may indeed be fact, that Ruth the Moabitess was the great-grandmother of King David. There is also an act of naming, which is the biblical equivalent of a registration of change, the mark of a new status quo (hence, earlier, Naomi's change to Mara); and the peculiar statement by Naomi's neighbours of Ruth's child: 'there is a son born to Naomi'. It is this last statement that I wish to bring together with the first chapter of the Book of Ruth in order to establish a complex of cultural attitudes, common to almost the whole Old Testament, without understanding which we cannot possibly read the Book of Job – or indeed, much of the Old Testament.

The Book of Ruth is by no means a misnomer: Ruth's role, both as a foreigner and as the type of dutiful daughter-in-law, is vital. But Ruth's role is defined by the person to whom she most closely relates, Naomi; and Naomi is the true focus of the book. The book concerns Naomi's loss – of husband and sons, of the hope of that family; Naomi's homecoming; Naomi's restoration and redemption.

Naomi's redemption from the state of which she complains in Chapter 1 is fully achieved in the prosperity of Ruth's marriage, in the act of the buying of the land, and – most – in fact that 'there is a son born to Naomi'. The name of the dead has been raised up upon his inheritance; all the losses are wholly compensated for in the continuation of the family line. The child is Naomi's because – and for various technical reasons of the law – Naomi is the head of the family of Elimelech: since the sons of Elimelech and Naomi died without issue, it is as if they had never been; and the child is regarded as the child of Naomi and the dead Elimelech, for whom his kinsman Boaz and his daughter-in-law Ruth act as surrogates.

What underlies this is an attitude that may startle. In the main body of the Old Testament, there is little or no trace of a belief in personal immortality, or of a belief in personal resurrection, or much more than a trace of belief in a glorious afterlife. When we are dead, we are gone: we are gone for good, to no heaven, but to a chilling version of the underworld, Sheol, to be less substantial than dust, shadows, phantoms of forever abandoned selves beyond the thought or the care of the living. This is the vision of Sheol as given in the Book of Job:

> For there is hope of a tree, if it be cut down, that it will sprout again, and that the tender branch thereof will not cease.
>
> Though the root thereof wax old in the earth, and the stock thereof die in the ground;
>
> Yet through the scent of water it will bud, and bring forth boughs like a plant.
>
> But man dieth, and wasteth away: yea, man giveth up the ghost, and where is he?
>
> As the waters fail from the sea, and the flood decayeth and drieth up;

> So man lieth down, and riseth not: till the heavens be no more, they shall not awake, nor be raised out of their sleep. (Job 14:7–12)

What lives on is the ultimate reduction of personality in language, the name. There are only two ways in which this name, however virtuous, endures: in one's children, and one's children's children, and in the material possessions which 'make their name'. It is these two things that Boaz and Naomi restore to Ruth: it is in the removal of these two that Naomi's complaint in Chapter 1 is centred. Naomi does not complain of the death of her husband and son; she does not grieve that they were unique human beings from whose loss she will never recover; she complains rather that she is too old to have another husband and, even if she did, to have more sons (verses 11–12). It is clear from verse 12 that what Naomi defines as hope is not the well-known theological virtue but this prospect of continuing the chain of the family through future generations:

> And Naomi said, Turn again, my daughters: why will ye go with me? are there yet any more sons in my womb, that they may be your husbands?
> Turn again, my daughters, go your way; for I am too old to have a husband. If I should say, I have hope, if I should have a husband also tonight, and should also bear sons;
> Would ye tarry for them till they were grown? would ye stay for them from having husbands?

Job says much the same when he loses his children and worldly goods (these are the words which haunted Blake): 'I have said to corruption, Thou art my father: to the worm, Thou art my mother, and my sister. And where is now my hope? as for my hope, who shall see it?' (Job 17:14–15). No major Old Testament figure grumbles about death or dying: they accept, without demur, a future of eternal annihilation, as does Naomi; but if they are righteous layfolk (not, that is, prophets or patriarchs) they appear to expect for themselves a reasonably long life – to die, like Job, 'old and full of days', in a degree of material prosperity, and with children to keep up the good name. Yet this does not always happen. Even the righteous fall on hard times. When they do, they want a Boaz, a *go-el*, a redeemer. In the Book of Ruth, God, as it were, connives with Naomi to find this redeemer; but the Book of Ruth is like a microcosm of the whole Old Testament, Naomi is a type of the Jewish people, and in the Old Testament it is generally God himself who is expected to provide the buying back – the substitution; God in the Old Testament is Boaz writ large.

What happens to the righteous when it looks as if no redemption will take place? They often do what Naomi does – they complain; that is, in quite legal terms, they utter a formal complaint as if in advocacy before a court. The problem here is that God is both judge in the court and a defendant in the case. Such a complaint dares to ask God to judge his own conduct; and it dares to enter into a dialogic relation with God. Something similar happens in Genesis 18. Normally, as a matter of fact, there is very little dialogue between God and the people of the Old Testament; God mandates, humans accept – or refuse and, unless they seek to escape like Jonah, face the consequences. Only Moses is in the habit of conversing with God on a regular basis. But the complaint is meant to force an answer; not necessarily in words, but, as here, in a change of circumstances. Such quasi-legal complaints are a regular feature of the Old Testament (from Job, but also from Jonah, Jeremiah, Elijah, often in the Psalms) and figure too in the New Testament, as in that most harrowing complaint from Jesus on the cross, quoting Psalm 22:1: 'My God, My God, why hast thou forsaken me?'. Such a complaint presents a formal case against God to God. It is the ultimate confrontation; and here we see a happy outcome of it. Naomi's complaint is a purely personal one; other examples such as Jeremiah's or some of the Psalms may be on behalf of an entire people: but they always have a deeply personal force. They are not theologically phrased, as in: 'where does the evil in the world come from?'. They are experiential, as in: 'why am I suffering? why should this happen to us?'. Again and again criticism strikes a false note, the theological note, abstract and conceptual, not this experiential quality of angry human grievance and distress.

Three further comments on the Book of Ruth may serve to introduce the Book of Job. First, what seems at first sight to be a rather unassuming narrative, a short story with almost mundane concerns, is really a short allegory of a central theme of the Old Testament: God's covenant with his people. The style is an index of this: a kind of Hebrew high style, with cadenced 'poetic' passages. As in personification allegory, the names are type-names: to quote the gloss of the Jerusalem Bible, the two sons, who die young, are Mahlon ('sickness') and Chilion ('pining away'): Orpah means 'she who turns away', Ruth 'the beloved', Naomi 'my fair one' – so that in Chapter 1 Naomi suggests that she be renamed 'Mara', which means 'the bitter one' – and Elimelech means what the book affirms: 'my God is king'.

Secondly, Ruth is a foreigner, not an Israelite. So is Job. This represents a kind of foreign contribution to Hebrew wisdom, but it also picks up on a motif popular in the Old Testament. Abraham is called from Canaan; people from afar enter and reinspire the chosen people. It is particularly significant that Job is a foreigner: he never refers to God as YHWH, but always as 'Shaddai', the only name by which, according to YHWH in Deuteronomy, God was known to all who came before Moses. Job, then, is a righteous outsider like Ruth; and in this respect is all the more of an example to the people of Israel, the chosen people: if foreigners can exhibit such faith, how can they not do so? Moreover, Ruth, as David's grandmother, has an extratextual life. So does Job – his name being already a byword for good faith and patience in Ezekiel.

Thirdly, what we find in the Book of Job is an epic treatment, on an epic scale, of the really all too ordinary human disasters and distress that we see in such briskly sympathetic treatment in Ruth; in disaster, Job responds like Ruth with a single-minded integrity: and like Naomi, with a formal complaint. The narrative structure of both books is in outline the same. Complaint leads to redemption in the literal sense outlined here. It is like the clearing of a bankruptcy. Nothing can annul the former loss; but Job, like Naomi, is enabled to buy back his shares in life.

In the first two chapters of Job, the prosperous Job is subjected to an almost black-comic mayhem: in rapid succession, he loses his oxen, his asses, his sheep and shepherds, his camels and camel drovers, his seven sons and his three daughters; and, if that were not enough, in Chapter 2 he is afflicted with 'sore boils from the sole of his foot and to his crown', and reduced to sitting among the ashes scraping his sores with a potsherd. All this, apparently, because God is a sport: twice he accepts a challenge from one of his sons, a heavenly messenger named 'Satan', to prove that his confidence in Job's integrity is not misplaced. Job does maintain his integrity; even in the face of boils, he does not complain. What auses him to crack is the visit he receives from his three friends, the 'Job's comforters', who are to take a supremely orthodox view of Job's misfortunes: that they must be his own fault, or at any rate for his own good. But Job explodes before they speak. He explodes after seven days of silence in which his friends sit with him upon the ground attempting to share his grief. Like so many people, Job can stand everything except his friends. Once he has cursed the day of his birth, once his friends have begun to remonstrate with him, Job issues his formal complaint:

My soul is weary of my life: I will leave my complaint upon myself; I will speak in the bitterness of my soul.

I will say unto God, Do no condemn me; show me wherefore thou contendest with me.

Is it good unto thee that thou shouldest oppress, that thou shouldest despise the work of thine hands, and shine upon the counsel of the wicked?

Hast thou eyes of flesh? Or seest thou as man seeth?

Are thy days as the days of man? are thy years as man's days,

That thou enquirest after mine iniquity, and searchest after my sin?

Thou knowest that I am not wicked; and there is none that can deliver out of thine hand.

Thine hands have made me and fashioned me together round about; yet thou dost destroy me.

Remember, I beseech thee, that thou hast made me as the clay; and wilt thou bring me into dust again?

. . . I am full of confusion; therefore see thou mine affliction;

For it increaseth. Thou huntest me as a fierce lion: and again thou showest thyself marvellous upon me.

Thou renewest thy witnesses against me, and increasest thine indignation upon me; changes and war are against me.

Wherefore then hast thou brought me forth out of the womb? Oh that I had given up the ghost, and no eye had seen me!

I should have been as though I had not been; I should have been carried from the womb to the grave.

Are not my days few? cease then, and let me alone, that I may take comfort a little,

Before I go whence I shall not return, even to the land of darkness and the shadow of death;

A land of darkness, as darkness itself; and of the shadow of death, without any order, and where the light is as darkness. (Job 10:1-9, 15-22)

It is significant, of course, that Job refers to himself as marked by God; his sorrows and boils alike are a type of stigma. The contrast throughout is between Job's utter weakness and God's absolute power; and, lastly, Job's one desire is for the suffering to be allowed to end. He actively desires death, the one thing that is not permitted by God in the conditions that God set Satan for the test: 'but save his life', orders God in 2:6, and in 1:12 'only upon himself put not forth thine hand'. The one thing Job desires is the one thing withheld from him.

With the exception of the greatest commentary of all, Gregory the Great's *Moralia in Job*, most of the literature written on Job would give the impression that this book deals with the problem of evil: how does evil exist in the world, and why does God allow it? Why do the evil thrive and the good suffer? This is an understandable Christian response to the book, but I am not convinced that it is the crucial issue for Job.[18] Job does consider it in Chapter 21. He asks: 'Wherefore do the wicked live, become old, yea, are mighty in power?'. But within ten verses he has answered his own question: 'How oft is the candle of the wicked put out! and how oft cometh their destruction upon them! God distributeth sorrows in his anger. They are as stubble before the wind, and as chaff that the storm carrieth away.' The problem may be an abstract one, but it is not quite this one; even though Job maintains his faith, and retains it against the urging of his friends, in himself and in his own righteousness. He knows therefore that he does not deserve the extent of his afflictions; he cannot bear the allegations of his friends that he might deserve them. And because he knows that he does not deserve them, he knows that God must have some other purpose – though nobody is close to realising the wager in heaven framework of Chapters 1 and 2 – and he realises that he deserves, at least, an answer. Job says the same to his friends as he says to God. To them (6:24): 'Teach me, and I will hold my tongue'; to God in Chapter 7, first, 'why hast thou set me as a mark against thee, so that I am a burden unto myself?', leading to the crucial intention of Chapter 13 – 'Surely I would speak to the Almighty, and I desire to reason with God' – expressed in the direct challenge of 13:22: 'Then call thou, and I will answer; or let me speak, and answer thou me'. The formal complaint of Chapter 14 follows directly, and is meant to force an answer: it is like a solicitor's letter or summons. God must either let Job die, or he must reply. God must justify himself.

Here is the measure of Job's extraordinary audacity. This man, sitting in ashes and scraping his boils, is one of the greatest heroes of the Bible. He forces God to speak. 'Oh that I knew where I might find him' (23:2). He actively seeks what other biblical figures avoid – direct contact with God:

> People often talk about 'finding God'. They should read the Bible. The average biblical character wants nothing to do with him. Jonah flees to Tarshish; Moses obdurately tries to refuse his mission; Jeremiah argues in vain against the Prophetic voice; even Adam hides in the bushes. The Psalmist in Psalm 39 says 'Look away from me, and I will smile, before I go and am not' . . . God is obviously terribly dangerous, but there is also fear of what he sees in man: it is his eyes that Job and the Psalmist cannot stand, his nakedness Adam tries to protect – and the universal sadness and indifference he personifies.[19]

Job responds to all this like a resolute shop steward. He says unequivocally that it is not good enough; and he demands a meeting with management. This in spite of his chilling foreboding in Chapter 23 verse 15: 'Therefore am I troubled at his presence; when I consider, I am afraid of him'. But we must set this against the praise of wisdom in Chapter 28 verse 28: 'Behold, the fear of the Lord, that is wisdom'.

Job is 'righteous in his own eyes' (32:1). He therefore resists the 'consolations' of his friends, which develop horribly from sympathy, in the first speech of Eliphaz, to implied criticism (Bildad in Chapter 8: God is just, therefore you are unjust, to which Job answers simply, 'how should man be just with God?'), to open criticism (Zophar in Chapter 11: 'oh that God would speak, and open his lips against thee', the idea that Job's suffering in view of his blasphemy is actually less than he deserves), and finally, malice, a curse on Job for his wickedness. All of these are good orthodox attitudes: healthy, pious, and normally authoritarian human responses. Job ignores the last speaker, Elihu, in Chapters 32–7. Elihu is thought by most modern scholars to be a later addition by pious editors who thought that Job fared too strongly: but this should not prevent modern readers from seeing how well Elihu fits into the only text we have. The pious editors, if they ever existed, made a strange job of it if their intention was as surmised. Elihu is a young man, full of himself; he attempts 'to justify the ways of God to man', or in Elihu's phrase rather than in Milton's, 'ascribe righteousness to my maker' (36:3). In effect, therefore, Elihu sets himself in the place of God. And he says as much (33:6): 'Behold, I am according to thy wish in God's stead'. The fact that God appears, that the theophany occurs as soon as Elihu has done speaking, is surely an indication that God has not seen fit to employ this particular attorney.

Job has his will. God appears in person. He tells Job that his words were without knowledge, and he attempts to reverse Job's challenge: 'Gird up now thy loins like a man; for I will demand of thee, and answer thou me.' This is not exactly a conversation. Rather, to quote Elihu from 37:5, 'God thundereth marvellously with his voice'. At last, however, Job has a chance to argue: for he has succeeded in calling God to account. What happens is profoundly unexpected. At first sight, Job crumbles. He withdraws the action: 'Then Job answered the Lord, and said, Behold, I am vile; what shall I answer thee? I will lay my hand upon my mouth. Once have I spoken; but I will not answer: yea, twice; but I will proceed no further' (Job 40:3–5). And again in 42:6: 'Wherefore I abhor myself, and repent in dust and ashes.' If this were a defamation action, Job would just have incurred punitive damages.

Has Job lost? By no means. For Job has nothing to lose but his boils. On the contrary, it is God who pays damages: seven new sons, three new daughters, and double everything else Job had lost. God is to Job as Boaz was to Ruth and Naomi: God is Job's *go-el*, his 'redeemer', just as Job must be *go-el* or redeemer for his friends:

> And it was so, that after the Lord has spoken these words unto Job, the Lord said to Eliphaz the Temanite, My wrath is kindled against thee, and against thy two friends: for ye have not spoken of me the thing that is right, as my servant Job hath.
>
> Therefore take unto you now seven bullocks and seven rams, and go to my servant Job, and offer up for yourselves a burnt offering; and my servant Job shall pray for you: for him will I accept: lest I deal with you after your folly, in that ye have not spoken of me the thing which is right, like my servant Job. (Job 42:7–8)

And Job, of course, has expected as much all along: modern readers now have a chance to see the original Jewish meaning of Job's statement in 19:25, so utterly transformed in sense by Christian exegesis and Handel's *Messiah*: 'I know that my redeemer liveth, and that he shall stand at the latter-day upon the earth'.

I now wish to draw two types of significance from the Book of Job, a book which is surely inexhaustible. Tennyson was hardly overstating when he called the Book of Job 'the greatest poem of ancient and modern times', nor Carlyle when he called it 'one of the grandest things ever written with a pen . . . there is nothing written, I think, in the Bible or out of it of equal literary merit'.[20]

The first type of significance is structural. The Book of Job can be seen as an amplification, and in some ways as an inverse, of the kind of structure proposed in the analysis of three episodes from Genesis. Those had to do with the tension between first-born and second-born, with sacrifice and conflict; with the sort of success that involves substitution; and with blessing, naming and marking. The whole of the Book of Job is a test of the naming of Job, for it is apparent that even at the time of the book's composition Job was a byword for patience and wisdom; and it is also a test of the blessing that God had already bestowed upon Job. The process of Job's degradation is achieved by the sacrifice of the first-born – Job's children who died, sacrificed by God for a wager; it has to do with stigma – here taking the unusual form of boils; with a curse – by Job on Job; and with a conflict, marked by Job's challenge to God, where the righteousness of the test is maintained by substitutes (Job's friends). The process of Job's improvement that marks the end of the book is achieved by success, though that takes the paradoxical form of defeat (the success of the theophany, followed by Job's: 'I am dust'); it leads to a renewed blessing (by Job on God), to renewed sacrifice (again involving substitution: Job atones for his friends) and by the conferment of more children on Job, which marks, as it were, the symbolic victory of the second-born over the first-born as well as the restoration of Job's (family) name. Moreover, though some scholarship supposes that the wager in heaven framework is an addition to an original structure for the Book of Job, some kind of test is absolutely integral to any conception of the plot: Job's challenge can only be upheld because Job is under test, and the challenge must be to the tester. The major point about the sequential analysis of Job can be tabulated quite simply:

Context Naming (Job: patience, wisdom)
           Blessing (by God on Job)
Episodes Loss of Children (First-born; ? Sacrifice)
           Stigma (boils)

Curse (by Job on Job)	Process of
Beginning of the Conflict (challenge to God)	Degrada-
Substitution (three friends; Elihu)	tion
Success/Defeat (Theophany; Job: 'I am dust')	
Blessing (by God on Job)	Process of
Sacrifice (substitution; Job atones for friends)	Improve-
	ment
More children &c (Second-born)	

One more point about the narrative structure should be made, because it leads into the second sort of significance to be drawn from this book, which is lexical or semantic. Job has quite clearly foreseen the result of God's response to his formal challenge. In Chapter 9: 'How much less shall I answer him, and choose out my words to reason with him?' (verse 14); 'For he is not a man, as I am, that I should answer him, and [i.e., if] we should come together in judgment' (verse 32). And in Chapter 23: 'Will he plead against me with his great power? No, but he would put strength in me' (verse 6); 'when he hath tried me, I shall come forth as gold' (verse 10). It is this power and strength of God to which Job happily testifies after the theophany: 'I know that thou canst do everything . . . therefore have I uttered that I understood not; things too wonderful for me, which I knew not' (42:2–3). It is this that his friends have forgotten: only God has strength and power, and only the possessor of strength and power can have knowledge. By claiming knowledge Job's friends are truly presumptuous: they put themselves in the place of God, and they oppress Job, as he says (19:5), 'magnifying' themselves against him. Humans cannot have knowledge; only the fear of God's power, that alone is wisdom. Wisdom is therefore faith, a substitute for knowledge: and this Job has.

The fundamental semantic opposition in the Book of Job is not between good and evil but rather that of power and weakness, God in the whirlwind and Job in the ashes. It is pervasive throughout the book: infants, prisoners, servants, 'Man that is born of a woman is of few days, and full of trouble' (14:1); 'men groan from out of the city' (24:12); 'What is my strength', asks Job, 'that I should hope? . . . Is my strength the strength of stones? or is my flesh of brass?' (6:11,12); and, to God, 'Thou art become cruel to me: with thy strong hand thou opposest thyself against me' (30:21). Both Eliphaz – whose very name

116

means 'My God is Strength' – and Job himself harp back to the days when Job was himself a strengthener of the weak, the bygone days, as Job says, 'when God preserved me' (29:2), and God's protection gave him power to be 'eyes to the blind', 'feet to the lame', 'a father to the poor'; days when his very speech was powerful, while now 'I cry unto thee, and thou dost not hear me' (30:20), 'Terrors are turned upon me: they pursue my soul as the wind: and my welfare passeth away as a cloud' (30:15), 'He breaketh me with breach upon breach, he runneth upon me like a giant' (16:14). Power and weakness correspond to knowledge and ignorance: Job finally admits that he cannot have thoughts that God does not know, while he cannot know God in any comparable way. The writer of the Book of Job apparently did not need Foucault, as we did, to teach him that power is knowledge and knowledge is power.

God's magnificent speeches in the theophany do not build verbal bridges between human weakness (and ignorance) and divine power (and knowledge): they exalt the difference. 'Where wast thou when I laid the foundations of the earth? declare, if thou hast understanding' (38:4). They belong to the genre of the boast. Most of all, in fact, God boasts of his mastery in the great and terrible creatures of the abyss, behemoth and leviathan: 'Behold now behemoth, which I made with thee; he eateth grass as an ox' (40:15); 'Canst thou draw out leviathan with an hook?' (41:1), or the following passage in which God exults – one might say amorally, beyond morality – in the strength he has given to all creatures:

Hast thou given the horse strength? hast thou clothed his neck with thunder?
 Canst thou make him afraid as a grashopper? the glory of his nostrils is terrible.
 He paweth in the valley, and rejoiceth in his strength: he goeth on to meet the armed men.
 He mocketh at fear, and is not affrighted; neither turneth he back from the sword.
 The quiver rattleth against him, the glittering spear and the shield.
 He swalloweth the ground with fierceness and rage: neither believeth he that it is the sound of the trumpet.
 He saith among the trumpets, Ha ha; and he smelleth the battle afar off, the thunder of the captains, and the shouting.
 Doth the hawk fly by thy wisdom, and stretch her wings toward the south?
 Doth the eagle mount up at thy command, and make her nest on high?
 She dwelleth and abideth on the rock, upon the crag of the rock, and the strong place.
 From thence she seeketh the prey, and her eyes behold afar off.

Her young ones also suck up blood: and where the slain are, there is she. (Job
39:19–30)

This with a vengeance is the God of the Old Testament, a God like the
eaglets with the smell of blood among his intuitions. But it is not an
adequate response to this passage, in praise of which no superlative
would reach far enough: this is the quintessence of power and strength,
and it is the ultimate argument with which to silence a scratching human
being. Power and strength cannot be innocent. Creation is not innocent:

> Tyger! Tyger! burning bright
> In the forests of the night,
> What immortal hand or eye
> Can frame thy fearful symmetry?[21]

Blake's poem reaches to the very core of the Book of Job, and its last
line, 'Did he who made the lamb make thee?', is based on Job 31:15,
'Did not he that made me in the womb make him?'. Far from shying
away from an admission that this is indeed the case, God in the Book of
Job, like the warhorse, 'rejoices in his strength'. He does not try to pass
on the blame to Satan, or to a generalised evil. He accepts all the
responsibility for all the deaths and disaster and misery in the world.

The result is a consummate narrative paradox. God is all powerful;
humanity is all-feeble. Job wins the only possible victory against total
power: he wins because he submits. Job's victory is defeat; domination
and submission become equivalent. 'Gird up now thy loins like a man':
it is the total powerlessness, the humiliation, above all the mortality of
humankind that confer an unlikely dignity – and heroic stature on one
who dares to complain. 'I know that my redeemer liveth': in the next
chapter we shall see how this narrative paradox is converted into a
theological one.[22]

Notes

1. See the references to Paul Ricoeur (Chapter 1, note 1, above), to Hans Frei
   (Chapter 2, note 34, above); Robert Funk, *Language, Hermeneutic and the
   Word of God* (New York: Harper and Row, 1966): for the hermeneutic

circle, H. G. Gadamer, *Truth and Method* (New York: Seabury Press, 1975); Richard E. Palmer, *Hermeneutics: Interpretation theory in Schleiermacher, Dilthey, Heidegger and Gadamer* (Evanston Ill.: Northwestern UP, 1969); for versions of hermeneutic and reader response theory, Roman Ingarten, *Cognition of the Literary Work of Art* (Evanston, Ill.: Northwestern UP, 1973); Wolfgang Eiser, *The Act of Reading: A theory of aesthetic response* (Baltimore: John Hopkins UP, 1978); H.-R. Jauss, *Aesthetic Experience and Literary Hermeneutics* and also *Toward an Aesthetic of Reception* (both Minneapolis: University of Minnesota Press, 1982); Peter Stuhlmacher, *Historical Criticism and Theological Interpretation of the Scripture* (Philadelphia: Fortress Press, 1977); Umberto Eco, *The Role of the Reader* (Bloomington: Indiana UP, 1979); *Semeia* 31 (1985); Kathleen M. Wheeler (ed), *German Aesthetic and Literary Criticism* (Cambridge: Cambridge UP, 1984).

2. For commentary, see E. A. Speiser, *Genesis*, The Anchor Bible (Garden City, New York: Doubleday, 1964), pp. 85–182; John van Seter, *Abraham in History and Tradition* (New Haven and London: Yale UP, 1975).

3. Erich Auerbach, *Mimesis: The representation of reality in Western literature*, trans. Willard R. Trask (1964; Princeton, Princeton UP, 1968), pp. 10–11.

4. *ibid.*, p. 9.

5. *ibid.*, pp. 11–12.

6. Søren Kierkegaard, *Fear and Trembling* and *Repetition*, ed. and trans. H. V. and E. H. Hong (Princeton, Princeton UP, 1983), p.52.

7. *ibid.*, p. 115.

8. *ibid.*, pp. 10–11.

9. Walter Beltz, *God and the Gods: Myths and the Bible*, trans. Peter Heinegg (Harmondsworth: Penguin, 1983), pp. 54–5.

10. Speiser, *Genesis*, The Anchor Bible (n.2 above), p. 166.

11. Roland Barthes, essay on Genesis 32 in 'La lutte avec l'ange', in *Analyse structurale et exégèse biblique*, ed. F. Bovon (Neuchâtel: Delachaux et Niestle, 1971): English translation in *Image/Music/Text*, trans. Stephen Heath (London: Collins, 1977), pp. 125–41. See also Robert M. Polzin, *Biblical Structuralism: Method and subjectivity in the study of ancient texts* (Philadelphia: Fortress Press, 1977); *Semeia* 10 (1977); Jean Calloud, *Structural Analysis of Narrative*, trans. Daniel Patte (Philadelphia: Fortress Press, 1976); Claude Chabrol and Louis Marin, *Sémiotique narrative: Récits bibliques* (Paris: Seuil, 1974); Daniel Patte, *What is Structural Exegesis?* (Philadelphia: Fortress Press, 1976); Adele Berlin, *Poetics and Interpretation of Biblical Narrative* (Sheffield, Almond Press, 1983); J. P.

Fokkelman, *Narrative Art in Genesis: Specimens of stylistic and structural analysis* (Amsterdam: Van Gorum, 1975), especially pp. 11–45 (Tower of Babel) and 208–23 (Jacob and the Angel); David Jobling, *The Sense of Biblical Narrative*, 2nd edn (Sheffield: JSOT Press, 1986); *Ways of Reading the Bible*, ed. Michael Wadsworth (Hemel Hempstead: Harvester Wheatsheaf, 1981), especially Gabriel Josipovici, 'The Bible: Dialogue and distance', pp. 133–53. Generally helpful are Shlomith Rimmon-Kenan, *Narrative Fiction: Contemporary poetics* (London and New York: Methuen, 1983); Tzvetan Todorov, *The Poetics of Prose* (Oxford: Blackwell, 1977) and *Introduction to Poetics* (Manchester: Manchester UP, 1981).

12. Michel Tournier, *The Erl King*, trans Barbara Bray (London: Methuen, 1972), p. 34.

13. *ibid.*, p. 35. For Cain as the founder of cities (pp. 5–6), and the important qualification that the nomadic type is that of the shepherd, see Herbert N. Schneidau, *Sacred Discontent: The Bible and Western tradition* (Berkeley: Los Angeles and London: University of California Press, 1976).

14. D. Alan Aycock, 'The Mark of Cain', in *Structuralist Interpretation of Biblical Myth*, ed. Edmund Leach and Aycock (Cambridge: Cambridge University Press, 1983), pp. 120–7.

15. On the notion of the biblical trickster, see Barthes (n. 11 above); Harold Bloom 'Wrestling Sigmund', *The Breaking of the Vessels* (Chicago and London: University of Chicago Press, 1982), pp. 47–60 (Jacob and the Angel); and *Semeia* 42 (1988). On Jacob, see Thomas L. Thompson, 'Conflict of themes in the Jacob narratives', *Semeia* 15 (1978), 5–26.

16. See note 11 above.

17. On Ruth, see Lucas Grollenberg, *Rediscovering the Bible*, (London: SCM Press, 1978), pp. 139–42; Robert Alter, *The Art of Biblical Narrative* (New York: Basic Books, 1981), pp. 58–60; Edward F. Campbell Jr, *Ruth*, The Anchor Bible (Garden City, New York: Doubleday, 1975); Jack M. Sasson's essay in *Literary Guide* (Chapter 1, note 5, above), pp. 320–8; D. F. Rauben, 'Literary values in the Bible: The Book of Ruth', *Journal of Biblical Literature* 89 (1970), 27–37; and Berlin, *Poetics and Interpretation* (n. 11, above), pp. 83–110.

18. Marvin H. Pope, *Job*, The Anchor Bible (Garden City, New York: Doubleday, 1965); *Semeia* 7 (1976); Richard B. Sewall, *The Vision of Tragedy*, 2nd edn (New Haven and London: Yale UP, 1980), pp. 9–24; Lawrence L. Besserman, *The Legend of Job in the Middle Ages* (Cambridge, Mass. and London: Harvard UP, 1979); Gregory the Great, *Morals on the Book of Job*, ed. Charles Marriott, 3 volumes (Oxford: Parker, 1848–50); Moshe Greenberg, 'Job', in *Literary Guide*, pp. 283–304; René Girard,

Job: The victim of his people, trans. Y. Feccero (London: Athlone, 1987); Polzin (n. 11, above), pp. 50–125; *Semeia* 33 (1985), pp. 13–43, 125–34; *Semeia* 19 (1980) is devoted to Paul Ricoeur's reading of Job and the issues it raises.

19. Francis Landy, 'The case of Kugel: Do we find ourselves when we lose ourselves in the text?', *Comparative Criticism* 5, ed. E. S. Shaffer (Cambridge: Cambridge UP, 1983).

20. Quoted by Grollenberg, (n.17 above), p. 242.

21. William Blake, *Complete Writings*, ed. Geoffrey Keynes (London: Oxford UP, 1969), p. 214.

22. René Girard (n. 18 above) writes, p. 162: 'The accounts of the Passion gather into one tight bundle all the threads of a structure scattered throughout Job'.

CHAPTER 5

A Gospel of signs

Belief and interpretation

In all the spheres so far examined in this book, questions of belief (Christian or Jewish), questions of narrative structure, questions of interpretation and questions of language are all interlinked: whether in persistently recurrent narrative structures in Genesis involving ritual sacrifice and naming or marking, in the controversy between Tyndale and More about the Greek word *ecclesia* that may be translated as 'Church' or 'congregation', or in the ancient and ongoing debate about the linguistic register of Bible translation. This chapter is concerned with the New Testament, again from the viewpoint of a student of language and narrative rather than, primarily, that of a student of theology. Its focus is again the interlinking of belief, language and interpretation. Its argument is that this interlinking is the key to the discourse of the Gospel. There is no belief that is innocent of language, nor any belief innocent of interpretation. Belief is an act of interpretation, and interpretation is an act of belief: the material medium of both is language. Considered as acts of language, belief and interpretation are equivalent. To believe and to interpret are the same act: in the case of the Gospel, an act of reading.[1]

A crucial word in the Hebrew Old Testament is *dabar*, the word for 'word'. It also means event or history and so, like the French word *histoire*, not recognising any difference between 'history' and 'fiction', it means narrative. The word brings the worlds of language and events into a common semantic universe. Words and events are signs in which we seek meaning; and that search for meaning in the signs both of language and of events is what we now call semiotics. A semiotic approach to the Old Testament is true to the range of the word *dabar*; a semiotic approach to the New Testament is true to the equivalent Greek word, of vital importance throughout the New Testament: *kerygma*. The word is sometimes translated, along with *evangelion* (gospel) as 'good news'. It is derived from another noun, *keryx*, a herald or someone who proclaims something, and a verb *keryssein*, to proclaim, declare or reveal. Again, it is both a speech-act and a 'real' act, an event. The word *kerygma* therefore means a proclamation or revelation, either by speech or by deed. The *kerygma* of Jesus is both verbal – his teaching and preaching – and actual, his life, his miracles, his death and resurrection. There is no separation between the two. Semiotically, and theologically, teaching and life are one *kerygma*.

The second section of this chapter looks at the narrative of the life of Jesus, and the third at the discourse of his teaching. The aim, however, is to show their underlying unity as narrative and discursive events, as one *kerygma*, one text. That text is constructed to express and inspire belief, and it is already an act of interpretation: not only in the *textual* sense (the life of Jesus is presented as having significance) but also in the *intertextual* sense (the network of relations between this text, the life and death of Jesus, and others). Specifically of course, the New Testament is constructed on the Old Testament; it cannot stand without it. The text, the *kerygma* of Jesus, is an interpretation of the Old Testament. Its intertextual relation is necessary to its meaning and to its narrative structure.

Before I begin to demonstrate this claim, however, I need to say a little more about the problems of the text, in order to indicate both the advantages and the explicit limits of a semiotic approach. There are many apparent differences and divergences within the New Testament itself, to such an extent that one might be led to ask whether 'orthodoxy' is a meaningful concept within the New Testament canon or the New Testament period. A mainly negative answer to this question comes, for example, from James Dunn in *Unity and Diversity in the New Testament*. Dunn distinguishes four different and incompatible types of *kerygma* within the New Testament. That of Jesus himself is to do with the imminent coming of the Kingdom, the *parousia*, and is summarised in statements like Mark 1:15, 'The Kingdom of God is at hand', 'The time is fulfilled' and the call, as in Mark 10:17, to 'Repent and believe in the gospel': that is, in the good news of the *parousia* that Jesus brings, though the words were very soon subject to quite another interpretation. The point is that Jesus is not the object of the faith he proclaims. In Acts, however, 'the proclaimer has become the proclaimed'. The *parousia* suddenly seems a more distant prospect; all the actions of Jesus are attributed to God; and the faith proclaimed is not in the ministry of the living Jesus but in the resurrection. The *kerygma* of Paul also proclaims Jesus, but hardly at all the historical Jesus: rather, the scandal of the Cross, the risen Jesus, and once again the imminent *parousia*. Dunn finds a fourth type of *kerygma* in John, which specifically proclaims Jesus as Christ, the Chosen One, the Son of God. Dunn asks: 'Can we discern sufficient continuity between Jesus the proclaimer and Jesus the proclaimed to enable us to affirm that the *kerygma* of Jesus and the *kerygma* of the first Christians are ultimately one and the same?'[2] A semiotic approach can shed no light whatever on such a question. But it can point to the way the question more or less has to be asked, and ask in turn which subject ('we') performs what type of act of 'discernment'. Any particular answer from any particular subject will be a reading: it will raise the same fundamental issue about the interlinking of belief and interpretation.

A second problem, of course, is that there are four 'Gospels', or rather four versions of the Gospel, not one. The point is developed by that subtle modern theologian Samuel Beckett, in *Waiting for Godot*: a play in which, for all Beckett's disclaimers that Godot has anything to do with God, Godot nevertheless sends his *keryx* each night to proclaim his *kerygma* (that he won't be coming today but may come tomorrow). 'And if he comes?' asks Estragon. 'We'll be saved,' replies Vladimir. They face up to the textual problem in their discussion of the two thieves 'crucified at the same time as our Saviour':

ESTRAGON: Our what?

VLADIMIR: Our Saviour. Two thieves. One is supposed to have been saved and the other . . . (*he searches for the contrary of saved*) . . . damned.

ESTRAGON: Saved from what?

124

VLADIMIR: Hell.

ESTRAGON: I'm going.

He does not move.

VLADIMIR: And yet . . . (*pause*) . . . how is it – this is not boring you I hope – how is it that of the four Evangelists only one speaks of a thief being saved. The four of them were there – or thereabouts – and only one speaks of a thief being saved. (*Pause.*) Come on, Gogo, return the ball, can't you, once in a way?

ESTRAGON: (*with exaggerated enthusiasm*). I find this really most extraordinarily interesting.

VLADIMIR: One out of four. Of the other three two don't mention any thieves at all and the third says that both of them abused him.

ESTRAGON: Who?

VLADIMIR: What?

ESTRAGON: What's all this about? Abused who?

VLADIMIR: The Saviour.

ESTRAGON: Why?

VLADIMIR: Because he wouldn't save them.

ESTRAGON: From hell?

VLADIMIR: Imbecile! From death.

ESTRAGON: I thought you said hell.

VLADIMIR: From death, from death.

ESTRAGON: Well what of it?

VLADIMIR: Then the two of them must have been damned.

ESTRAGON: And why not?

VLADIMIR: But one of the four says that one of the two was saved.

ESTRAGON: Well? They don't agree, and that's all there is to it.

VLADIMIR: But all four were there. And only one speaks of a thief being saved. Why believe him rather than the others?

ESTRAGON: Who believes him?

VLADIMIR: Everybody. It's the only version they know.

ESTRAGON: People are bloody ignorant apes.[3]

'It's the only version they know': being, in that eloquent phrase, 'bloody ignorant apes', most of us have in our heads a single composite version of the life and death of Jesus. Such a composite version was well known to the early Christians and throughout the Middle Ages as a

Gospel harmony, though our present model was vigorously reassembled during the nineteenth century. The origin stories of the birth of Jesus which we celebrate at Christmas occur in one Gospel only, Luke: in Luke's Gospel, what we know as 'the Sermon on the Mount' (from Matthew) is preached quite specifically 'in the plain'; and there is in fact no end to the divergences and incompatibilities of detail, trivial and otherwise, among the four Gospels – so much so that we might wonder whether Gospel *harmony* is really a suitable description for any composite version.

And this, on the whole, is what preoccupies modern New Testament scholars. They debate which account is true, whether the Sermon on the Mount ever happened at all and if so whether on a mount or in a plain, the historicity of the virgin birth and the Resurrection, and so on. 'Liberal revisionists' fight 'conservative fundamentalists', but they are fighting on common ground: on the question of historical truth, whether events were actual, whether any of these things really happened.

The radical proposition inherent in my more semiotic approach is that one should have nothing whatever to do with such contests. Not only is the question of historical truth beyond the competence of students of language and literature: it is also well outside my area of professional interest, and even, one might think, antipathetic to it. For students of narrative, an event in a text is an event. It happened because it happens (and continues to happen) in a text. As for inconsistencies, they too are events in a text, and, more, events between texts: they are intertextual events.

It so happens that such radical modernity captures well, as I have tried to demonstrate, the approach of early Christian exegesis. The early Christians did not read or write like nineteenth or twentieth-century biblical scholars debating historical accuracy. Moreover, for nearly 100 years after the death of Jesus, many Christians may have lived without Gospels, perhaps with little knowledge of the 'events' of the life of Jesus, perhaps with only fragmentary collections of his 'sayings' (including many later discounted as apocryphal) – but with that adamantine faith expressed by Paul in the crucified and risen Christ and the scandal of the Cross.[4] For them and for later medieval readers, the passages in the Old Testament taken to be predictions of Jesus were just as real as any historically accurate record.

The life and death of Jesus

So it was too for the four Gospellers. What they wrote was in every case a narrative structure derived almost entirely from, and shaped by, those self-same Old Testament passages that Christians read (that is, believed to be and interpreted) as predictions of the life and death of Jesus. This is the intertextuality of the Gospel. Its traditional name is typology.

Some modern Christians sometimes seem embarassed by typology. It must seem to them, I think, that a clearly established pattern of literary relationship must challenge a claim to historical truth. The reaction rests on a very Platonic view of literature: authors tell lies. Surely it is misplaced. As C. S. Lewis urged, it seems a failure of belief to baulk at the notion that the God who made the world and died for it was also able to ensure that the life of Jesus conformed to the detail of Old Testament prophecies.[5] Certainly, the typology of the Bible was much enjoyed by early Christian and medieval commentators, who delighted in pointing it out. And theirs is the attitude of the evangelists.

It is in keeping with this attitude that we find in what is probably the first of the Gospels in order of composition, in Mark 1:2: 'As it is written in the prophets [the reference is to Isaiah], Behold, I send my messenger before thy face, which shall prepare thy way before thee.' Verse 3 continues to quote from Isaiah; verse 4 introduces John the Baptist, who in turn introduces Jesus, whose role is made clear at his baptism in verse 11 by the voice of God, who in his turn also quotes Isaiah: 'Thou art my beloved Son, in whom I am well pleased'. These are more than quotations: they are identifications. They do not just establish the credentials of John the Baptist and of Jesus; they also identify them as characters within an existing book. In verse 13 of the same chapter, Mark disposes quickly of the temptations in the wilderness: 'And he was there in the wilderness forty days, tempted of Satan; and was with the wild beasts; and the angels ministered unto him'. The reference here is to I Kings 19:8, in which Elijah is fed by angels in the wildnerness and so sustained for 'forty days and forty nights'.

The Elijah comparison recurs in Chapter 6, verse 15: Herod hears of Jesus and believes that John the Baptist, whom he has executed, has risen from the dead: 'Others said, That it is Elias' [Elijah]. In verse 34 of the same chapter, Jesus is moved to preach to the people 'because they were as sheep not having a shepherd' – a reference to Zechariah 13:7. In Chapter 7, verse 6, Jesus himself quotes Isaiah at the scribes and Pharisees, and the miracles with which the chapter ends lead people to say 'he maketh both the deaf to hear, and the dumb to speak' – another quotation from Isaiah. Chapter 9 contains the Transfiguration, in which Jesus is seen together with Elijah – who, we are told in verse 13, has already come in the form of John the Baptist – and Moses, whom Jesus now supersedes as the new Joshua (the names Jesus and Joshua are cognate). Chapter 10 provides another quotation from Isaiah; and in Chapter 11, Jesus enters Jerusalem on a donkey – fulfilling the prophecy in Zechariah 9:14 of the King who comes to Zion 'riding on a donkey' – and he drives the moneychangers from the temple, fulfilling the prophecy in Zechariah 14:21 that there will be no more traders in the temple of Yahweh. Jesus prophesies the immediate coming of the Kingdom in Mark 13 (especially verse 30), quoting, and citing, Daniel (in verse 14). The details of the Crucifixion are almost all intertextual references: the scourging, the crown of thorns, the vinegar Jesus is given to drink (Psalm 69:21); the sundown falling at noon (Amos 18:9–10), and the earthquake (Psalm 114). The account in Chapter 15 does not leave the intertextual allusions to chance: it is marked in verse 28, which alludes directly to Isaiah 53:12, 'And the scripture was fulfilled, which saith, And he was numbered with the transgressors'.

Mark is probably the earliest Gospel, the shortest and in many interesting ways – there is no pejorative element in this judgement – the crudest. In subsequent Gospels, the intertextual reference becomes more insistent and more precise. An example is the opening of Matthew, which is a genealogical table in Old Testament style tracing the ancestry of Jesus directly from Abraham through David to Joseph, 'husband of Mary'. One wonders why the author of Matthew's Gospel bothered with this grand attempt to give Jesus an Old Testament legitimacy, true or false, for he is about to give the world a new piece of doctrine, the Virgin Birth, which rather undoes his good efforts: since Joseph is not the father of Jesus. Why, then, does he introduce the Virgin Birth? For intertextual reference, as he emphasises in verses 22 and 23: 'Now all this was done, that it might be fulfilled which was spoken of the Lord by a prophet, saying, Behold, a virgin shall be with child, and shall bring forth a son, and they shall call his name Emmanuel, which being interpreted is, God with us'. As a matter of fact, the verse cited from Isaiah (7:14–15) says, in Hebrew, not 'virgin' but 'young girl'; but the author of Matthew did not read the Old Testament in Hebrew but in the Greek Septuagint, in which the word is translated 'parthenos', which can be understood as 'virgin'. This is the lexical basis of modern suggestions that the Virgin Birth is the greatest of translation errors; certainly, it is a palpable tribute to intertextuality.

In Chapter 2, Matthew says explicitly that Jesus' birthplace is Bethlehem in order to fulfil an Old Testament prophecy; that the massacre of the innocents is to fulfil Jeremiah's Lamentations (verse 18); and his dwelling place is Nazareth because of the Old Testament prophecy, 'He shall be called a Nazarene'. Chapter 3 has the obligatory references to Isaiah in the context of John the Baptist, and these are made explicit in verse 3, citing Isaiah 40:3. Jesus moves from Nazareth to Capernaum, again explicitly (4:14) to fulfil Isaiah. The first teachings by Jesus are given, in verse 17 of Chapter 8, an explicit gloss from Isaiah 53: 'himself took our infirmities, and bare our sicknesses', and in Chapter 12 verses 17 to 21 Matthew quotes the whole of a passage from Isaiah (examined below, page 131–2). This is to be compared with the quotation of another key passage from Isaiah in John 12:38–41. Jesus explains in the next chapter of Matthew (13:14,15) that he speaks in parables to fulfil the prophecy of Isaiah 6:9–10; the words of the Transfiguration in Chapter 17 are again from Isaiah; and so on.

Similar detail can be provided from Luke and John, but the point is already plain. John 12:41 makes it explicit: 'These things said Esaias, when he saw his glory, and spake of him'. Luke makes the intertextual reference, the link with Isaiah, almost outrageously clear in a scene unique to this gospel:

And he came to Nazareth, where he had been brought up: and, as his custom was, he went into the synagogue on the sabbath day, and stood up for to read.

And there was delivered unto him the book of the prophet Esaias. And when he had opened the book, he found the place where it was written,

The Spirit of the Lord is upon me, because he hath anointed me to preach the gospel to the poor; he hath sent me to heal the brokenhearted, to preach

> deliverance to the captives, and recovering of sight to the blind, to set at liberty
> them that are bruised,
> To preach the acceptable year of the Lord.
> And he closed the book, and he gave it again to the minister, and sat down.
> And the eyes of all them that were in the synagogue were fastened on him.
> And he began to say unto them, This day is this scripture fulfilled in your ears.
> (Luke 4:16–21).

What could be plainer? 'This day is this scripture fulfilled in your ears.' Jesus assumes, and appropriates, a role from the existing scriptures; he inserts himself as a character into an existing text. He performs the most radical possible act of interpretation: he lives the book. He brings the book to life in such a way that it is superseded. He lives the book, and he closes it. As he says in Luke 16:16: 'The law and the prophets were until John: since that time the kingdom of God is preached, and every man presseth into it'. By his reinterpretation, he makes redundant the professional interpreters of his day: the scribes and the Pharisees. No wonder that he invites their malice, and is made to defend his interpretation against them in almost every chapter of every Gospel. Jesus lives a book; he is persecuted and dies for the sake of an argument about interpretation of that book. If we fail to see the centrality of intertextual allusions in the Gospels, we fail to see what the Gospellers are about. They are about writing, or rewriting, the old book so that intertextual reference – reference from one book to another – becomes *intratextual* reference, within the same book, the Christian as opposed to the Jewish Bible. Their intention is never put more cogently than in John 20:30–1:

> And many other signs truly did Jesus in the presence of his disciples, which are not
> written in this book:
> But these are written that ye might believe that Jesus is the Christ, the Son of
> God; and that believing ye might have life through his name.

The implication is this: in order to believe, one must first read what is written. Again, since there is no reading without interpretation, belief and interpretation are synonymous. The proof that Jesus is the Christ will be found in reading the network of intertextual relation that is the life and ministry of Jesus.

'Jesus is the Christ, the Son of God', the anointed one, the Servant:

if there is one place in the Old Testament to which all the evangelists turn to substantiate this or some such claim, it is the work of the deutero-Isaiah, in Chapters 40 to 55 of the Book of Isaiah; more specifically, to four quite short passages within those chapters which are among the most mysterious in the entire Bible.[6] They are known collectively as the four Servant Songs, and were written during the time of the Babylonian captivity (*c.550–540* BCE) concerning a new Servant of God, a new Chosen One. Who is this chosen one? Early Christians and traditional Christian commentary agree: Christ ('the anointed one'). Such is the gist of running titles·in many editions of the King James Bible (I quote a modern one): over Isaiah 42, 'The Office of Christ'; over Isaiah 49, 'Christ sent to the Gentiles'; over Isaiah 50, 'Exhortations to trust in Christ'; over Isaiah 53, 'Benefit of Christ's Passion'. The consensus survived well beyond the medieval period, with rare dissenters such as Andrew of St Victor, who accepted the view of Jewish commentators that the suffering Servant is the type of the Jewish people. That was the traditional Jewish view, counterbalancing the traditional Christian one. In biblical studies of the nineteenth and twentieth centuries, Jewish and Christian, the traditions have to some extent broken down. But the identity of the Servant remains, more than ever, an enigma. The Anchor commentary denies that the passages are predictive prophecy (and denies too that any such thing exists in the Old Testament), suggesting instead that the Servant, rather than being Christ or the Jewish people, is 'an ideal person'. This does little to blow away the golden clouds that surround him.

The first Servant Song (Isaiah 42:1–4) begins with the words used in the New Testament by God at the baptism of Jesus: 'Behold my servant, whom I uphold; mine elect, in whom my soul delighteth'. This is the 1611 translators' version from the Hebrew, whereas that from the Greek in Mark 1:11 is 'Thou art my beloved Son, in whom I am well pleased'; but the New Testament Greek depends on its allusion to the Old Testament Hebrew, and it is meant to be recognised. The pleasure or delight indicates that the chosen one has been committed to a sacred mission to be mediator of the revelation of God, or, in the Old Testament phrase, to 'bring forth judgment to the Gentiles'. In the Servant Song, verse 2 emphasises secrecy, patience and stealth: 'He shall not cry, nor lift up, nor cause his voice to be heard in the street'. In the response of verses 5 to 9, the Servant is then called a covenant, a bond of union between the Lord and his people, a light of joy and deliverance. The response includes an affirmation of the divine name:

> I am the Lord: that is my name: and my glory will I not give to another, neither my praise to graven images.
>
> Behold, the former things are come to pass, and new things do I declare: before they spring forth I tell you of them. (Isaiah 42:8-9)

Here and in the rest of the chapter the Servant's role is seen in terms of freeing prisoners (verse 7), and healing the deaf and blind (verses 8,18). The second Song (Isaiah 49:1-6), presents the Servant as God's secret weapon, formed by the Lord 'from the womb' (verse 1), his major vocation expressed in verse 6: 'I will also give thee for a light to the Gentiles that thou mayest be my salvation unto the end of the earth'. The third Song (Isaiah 50:4-9) is rather badly translated in the King James version of verse 4, which in the original (and in the Septuagint and the Vulgate) contains not only the Servant's claim that God has divinely inspired him to speak 'the tongue of the learned' (as Jesus does when he disputes in the synagogue), but also mention God's order that the Servant should have disciples, students who commit the words of the teacher to memory. The Servant speaks of his voluntarily undergoing tortures (verse 6), with the strength of the Lord God (verses 8-9).

It is the fourth Servant Song, however, that has rightly won pride of place in the Christian tradition. Nobody with more than a cursory acquaintance with Christianity will have escaped the reverberations, of Isaiah 53:3-7:

> He is despised and rejected of men; a man of sorrows, and acquainted with grief: and we hid as it were our faces from him; he was despised, and we esteemed him not.
>
> Surely he hath borne our griefs, and carried our sorrows: yet we did esteem him stricken, smitten of God, and afflicted.
>
> But he was wounded for our transgressions, he was bruised for our iniquities: the chastisement of our peace was upon him; and with his stripes we are healed.
>
> All we like sheep have gone astray; we have turned every one to his own way; and the Lord hath laid on him the inquity of us all.
>
> He was oppressed, and he was afflicted, yet he opened not his mouth: he is

brought as a lamb to the slaughter, and as a sheep before her shearers is dumb, so
he openeth not his mouth.

The Servant is compared to the victim of an atonement sacrifice. He is
one who has been touched by the wrath of God (an apt comparison here
would be Job 19:1–22); he is cursed, but the curse does not belong to the
person who suffers but is transferred to him from others; and for those
others, the vicarious curse on the Servant is their blessing. This Song,
like Job, admits that the righteous may suffer; and the suffering of the
righteous becomes a medium of salvation to the community. Even
stranger than the apparent prophecy of Christ's Passion in verses 3 to 7
are verse 10 to 12 of Chapter 53, with God as the speaker of verses 11
and 12.

> Yet it pleased the Lord to bruise him; he hath put him to grief: when thou shalt
> make his soul an offering for sin, he shall see his seed, he shall prolong his days,
> and the pleasure of the Lord shall prosper in his hand.
> He shall see of the travail of his soul, and shall be satisfied: by his knowledge
> shall my righteous servant justify many; for he shall bear their iniquities.
> Therefore will I divide him a portion with the great, and he shall divide the
> spoil with the strong; because he hath poured out his soul unto death: and he was
> numbered with the transgressors; and he bare the sin of many, and made
> intercession for the transgressors.

The Servant has been put to death, and, in verse 9, 'made his grave
with the wicked'; then, in highly allusive terms in verses 11 and 12, God
promises him some sort of posthumous reward or regeneration, a
promise which can be interpreted as delivery from death. The Anchor
commentary notes simply that this promise is 'paradoxical in a poem
which is earlier than any attested belief in resurrection'. It is verse 12
that Mark cites during the account of the Crucifixion (Mark 15:28); the
first Servant Song is quoted in full in Matthew 12:17–21; and the fourth
and third are extracted in John 12:38–41.

These observations add up to a major insight into the narrative
structure of the Gospels. Only two of the four Gospels give Jesus a
childhood; all four, however, give him a baptism, and a baptism is an
act of *naming*. He is named, in all four Gospels, by a voice from Heaven
that applies to him the first verse of the first Servant Song in Isaiah 42.

This is the key intertextual reference: Jesus is named as the elect, the chosen one, of that Song: in Greek, as the anointed one, the Christ. He is identified as the Servant of the four Servant Songs in Isaiah. The narrative structure of the Gospel then follows the sequence of the four Songs. The life of Jesus is a gloss on Isaiah. 'These [signs] are written,' writes John, 'that ye might believe that Jesus is the Christ.' Jesus teaches, revealing the knowledge of Isaiah 53:12; he heals the sick, especially the blind and the deaf-mute; he works miracles, but tries to do so by stealth, as in Isaiah 42:2; he collects disciples, he suffers the torture and ignominious death prescribed in the third and fourth Servant Songs in order to 'bear the sin of man'; and he rises again, in fulfilment of the promise at the close of the fourth Song. He is, like the Servant, a new Moses and a new Elijah, the narrative transformation of which is enacted in the Transfiguration. As the second Moses, he brings a new law; as the second Joshua, he enters Zion; as the new Elijah, he establishes his credentials over life and death by doing what only Elijah and his disciple Elisha did in the Old Testament, raising the dead. The majority of these miracles, as in I Kings 17 (Elijah) and II Kings 4 (Elisha), are the raising of dead children. Only once, and in one Gospel only, does Jesus bring an adult back to life (Lazarus in John 11), the sole action which in these intertextual terms is aberrant. I can now put some flesh on the the claim that belief is interpretation and interpretation is belief: Christian belief – that is, belief in the life and salvific role of Jesus as structured in the Gospel – is an interpretation of the Servant Songs of Isaiah.

Those Servant Songs are in many respects a recrudescence, a distillation of the role of God's chosen in the Old Testament. I have tried to characterise that role in three ways: in terms of an ambivalence between first son and second son; in terms of the chosen one as lawbreaker (for which the supremely concrete and ironic image is that of Moses himself smashing the tablets of the Law he had just taken down at God's dictation – lawbreaking as lawgiving); and in terms of the chosen one as a nomad. Jesus completely fulfils these roles. He is lawbreaker both in political terms, to end up crucified, and in theological or ecclesiological ones, in his constant verbal overturning of the law of the scribes and Pharisees. He is a consummate nomad, forever moving from place to place. In the childhood-narrative of Luke he is taken from one place,

Nazareth, in the womb to another, Bethlehem, for the census, and flees for his life into Egypt before he is weaned; and in this, he is like a Jacob, or better – his father's namesake – a Joseph. And of his whole earthly ministry, the same applies, until the fateful entry into Jerusalem, which is the confrontation with death. Here too he is the transcendent nomad: dead, buried and risen again. What of the first son/second son ambivalence? It is there, at start and end. At the start, John the Baptist, 'clothed with camel's hair, and with a girdle of a skin about his loins', and a sedentary man (he goes to the wilderness by the Jordan and stays there), is the Esau to Jesus's Jacob. At the end, Pilate offers the mob the choice for reprieve between Jesus and the common murderer, Barabbas. They choose Barabbas, and the eldest son is saved from the ultimate journey: for the name Barabbas is hardly a name at all – it means simply 'son of the father'.

Moreover, the sequential structure I proposed as typical of the Old Testament is fulfilled in the Gospel, provided that one combines the patterns of conflict with that of sacrifice. The pattern of all four evangelists reveals the same sequence as shown in the following table:

Old Testament	New Testament
Journey from home	Origin (appearance of Jesus)
Naming	Baptism (as Servant)
Conflict (with authority; with doubt)	Ministry (Sayings; Miracles; Parables)
Blessing/curse/marking:	
Beginning of the sacrifice	Entry into Jerusalem
Resolution of Conflict	Betrayal and death
Successful sacrifice (substitution)	
Naming (justification)	Resurrection (and ? Ascension*)
Blessing	Reappearance/? disappearance of Jesus

*The Ascension is found in Luke 24:51 only; Mark 16:19 is probably a late addition. It fulfils the Old Testament pattern of Homecoming.

The correspondence is remarkably coherent. Jesus 'journeys from home' into the Virgin's womb. His ministry is a conflict with authority and with doubt, and its instrumentality is both verbal and actual, words and deeds. The resolution of the conflict is the beginning of the sacrifice to which it leads, and he proves his divine blessing by assuming the role of victim in the ultimate atonement sacrifice, whose stigma is the Cross and whose burden is the sin of humanity – for whom Jesus substitutes as innocent proxy. He is not saved by a substitute, like Isaac; he is himself the salvific substitute. His resurrection fulfils the blessing conferred on the Servant, and justifies the role of Jesus in a second naming, as the Christ. (The use of the name of God has been enough: so Matthew 20:30–4.) The first name of Jesus is the first verse of the first Servant Song ('my beloved son/servant'); that name has been justified at the end of the Gospel by the Resurrection, which fulfils the last verse of the last Servant Song and confers blessing. Luke's inclusion of the Ascension, as homecoming, fulfils the narrative typology of the Old Testament.

There is also a relation based on narrative paradox. The essential narrative paradox of the Gospel is also the essential spiritual paradox of the Christian faith: the Cross, the ultimate mark of weakness and shame, is the enduring source of power and glory. Jesus crucified is all weakness; the risen Christ is all power. This is probably all that many early Christians, of whom Paul was one, knew or needed to know. But when, later, it came to putting together the Gospel, turning the claim that the crucified Jesus is the risen Christ into biography, the evangelists may have had, say, three types of source: that knowledge itself, already presenting itself intertextually; a miracle source; and collections of the sayings of Jesus. They had to work out the theological paradox, weakness/power, as a narrative structure.

Weakness can only be salvific if the power is first established: hence the importance of miracles, and of teaching too. Sayings, miracles, parables are different types of signs, and they operate differently, but they have only one message: all are there to establish Jesus as the Servant. Just as in his teaching Jesus claims to supersede the law, of the book (the Old Testament), so in his life he takes over its existing main role in order to live the book. The most cursory examination of actantial roles would show that the evangelists exploit the paradox.[7] In his ministry Jesus is almost always subject, sender, helper: in his passion he is object, recipient, helpless before his opponents. In the ministry, his power –

whether of word or deed – seems inexhaustible. There is only one suggestion to the contrary, in Mark 5:30, when the woman with an issue of blood is healed by touching Jesus' garment and Jesus immediately knows 'that virtue had gone out of him'; and this hint of weakness is omitted from the later account in Matthew.

How, then, to modulate the narrative transition from total power to total weakness? By subtle gradation, by exploiting a further narrative paradox. The weakness of the crucified Jesus is a concealed power. Hence the irony of the crowd's mockery – if you are the son of God, step down from the Cross. Hence Pilate's surprise that Jesus has died so quickly – which is not to be interpreted as a sign of further weakness, but as a sign of the power of the divine will to die. In the same way, the power of Jesus' ministry must be a concealed power. Jesus steadfastly refuses to *give a sign* in response to public and open challenge; again and again we read that he instructs those he has cured to say nothing, again and again we see his determination to hide his light. This is true of his actual deeds, the miracles, and of his verbal deeds, the parables. Both are a form of necessary concealment. They are there, in their concealed form, not only to fulfil the intertextual suggestion, but also to fulfil the function of a text. They are there to challenge belief – that is, to demand interpretation.

Concealment and competence

If the New Testament is to be seen as the 'fulfilment' of the Old, it is important that the word 'fulfilment' should not retain here the sense of something inevitable. As far as the horizon of narrative expectation goes, the Gospel of Jesus proclaims a fulfilment of the Scriptures that is inevitable only in the light of a Christian typological reading. The scribes and Pharisees of the New Testament, representing an alternative school of interpretation, remain unconvinced. So do the Jewish people; so do other types of interpreters, among whom Nietzsche, for example, characterised the New Testament as a cruel and incongruous joke upon the Old. There is room here for a neutral literary judgement. The Bible of Judaism, the 'Old' Testament without the 'New', is self-evidently a very different book from the Christian Bible, which consists of the two

Testaments. The fulfilment offered by the Gospel, the meaning of the Gospel, is a difference.

I use the word 'difference' in two senses. The first is the normal sense, illustrated in continuity between Old and New Testaments that is nevertheless radically recontextualised in the New. Take, for example, the ambivalent relationship between first-born and cadet sons seen in Genesis in the relation of Cain and Abel, Ishmael and Isaac, Jacob and Esau. As already mentioned, this persists in the New Testament: in Christ's teaching, such as the Parable of the Prodigal Son, and in his life, in his relation with John the Baptist and then with the transparently named Barabbas, son of the father; and in larger terms, Jesus is presented as the New Adam, the second of the line. Yet Jesus is also the only Son of God; there seems to be an ambivalence here. He retains the privileged status of the Old Testament cadet, the lawbreaker, the nomad; yet his claims as first-born are equally stressed. In spite of the continuity from the Old Testament, there is here a major shift of emphasis; and I suggest that it reflects upon the major debate of early Christianity, between the Judaising school of Peter – which regarded Christianity as an exclusively Jewish sect – and the mission of Paul to the Gentiles, the 'people'. Paul prevailed, and Paul devoted an important chapter of his Epistle to the Romans (that is, to Peter's school) to this question of the first and second sons. He is troubled by the promise made to Rebecca when she was still carrying Isaac's two sons in her womb: 'It was said unto her, The elder shall serve the younger. As it is written, Jacob have I loved, but Esau have I hated. What shall we say then? Is there unrighteousness with God? God forbid' (Romans 9:12–14). Paul recognises the source of his ambivalence: the Israelites, the chosen ones, are the descendants of the second son, not the first son, Esau, forefather of the Gentiles whom Paul inclines to support. But Paul turns this problem to rhetorical advantage: he implies that the Jews of Rome are now behaving like the first-born of the Parable of the Prodigal son – they are casting the Gentiles in the role of second son, and attempting to exclude them from the good news.

That is an example of a difference in the normal sense. The second sense of 'difference' is that derived from structuralist and post-structuralist writing in the writing of Jacques Derrida, where it is spelt *différance*, to distinguish it from the usual word. English has not followed this spelling and the result is that the English word 'difference' can now be a synonym for *meaning*.[8] The usage is based on a Saussurean theory of perception and language: we see and name things not essentially but differentially, black as distinct from white, New from Old, and so on. In this use of 'difference' as 'meaning', however, there is another major sense adopted from French: that of *deferment*. Narrative exists through deferment. Otherwise novels need only be one or two sentences long; and the Gospel might read more like a creed than a narrative: 'Jesus was born of Mary, was the Son of God, was baptised by John the Baptist, taught, performed miracles, was betrayed, crucified, rose again and is the Christ.' From this viewpoint, it is not the plot or even the message that counts: the text is different from, is a deferment of the plot and even the message. Even though the Gospel is a fulfilment of the Scripture, the *kerygma* of Christ is a deferment, a difference: it is something that has not yet happened but is promised, the *parousia*, the coming of the Kingdom. Jesus prophesies the *parousia* when before the high priest he is asked: 'Art thou the Christ, the Son of the Blessed? And Jesus said: I am: and ye shall see the Son of man sitting on the right hand of power, and coming in the clouds of heaven' (Mark 14:61–2). There seems to be little doubt that Jesus expected this to be an imminent event: in Mark 9:1, he tells his disciples: 'Verily I say unto you, That there be some of them that stand here, which shall not taste of death, till they have seen the kingdom of God come with power'. To this extent, Jesus' teaching is apocalyptic, but it must be said that where apocalyptic expectations tend to be immediate, Jesus' apocalyptic tone is qualified.

None the less, the early Christians expected the coming of the Kingdom at any moment; and Christian faith, adapting itself in due course to God's more leisurely time-scale, makes a positive virtue of the future hope of the Kingdom. The intimate association of faith and hope is again Pauline, in a passage that hints at another kind of deferment/ difference: 'For we are saved by hope: but hope that is seen is not hope: for what a man seeth, why doth he yet hope for? But if we hope for that we see not, then do we with patience wait for it' (Romans 8:24–5). For Paul here, the meaning of the text that is Christ is deferment, hope; and in that sense the meaning of the text is left open, to interpretation, to faith. However, for Paul as for Jesus the meaning that is faith and hope, for that is to come, yield pride of place to the spiritual and ethical imperative of love, that is now. This whole passage from Romans 8 was a favourite of Tyndale's, and the Authorized Version preserves his fine translation of the last two verses: 'For I am persuaded, that neither death, nor life, nor angels, nor principalities, nor powers, nor things present, nor things to come, Nor height nor depth, nor any other creature, shall be able to separate us from the love of God, which is in Christ Jesus our Lord.' It is a *kerygma*, a proclamation of faith, that brings together then and now, what is to come with what must be done, word and deed; for Jesus and the early Christians, a speech-act was simply another deed, another *sign*.

Such a faith must stand up to the most rigorous test. It requires training, and the Gospel is designed to supply that training. The meaning of the Gospel is difference in all the senses so far used, and it is designed for a special kind of reader – a reader that can recognise almost immediately the intertextual relations that have occupied a good deal of this chapter, who can recognise at the same time the difference between Old Law and New, and a reader too who can profit equally from the narrative difference, the deferment of the plot, the discursive delays, the digressions which are an equal part of the meaning.

A good example of an explicit delay occurs in Mark 12. Already Jesus has incurred the bitter enmity of the chief priests, the scribes and the elders. He therefore tells a parable about an absentee lord of the vineyard who sends several servants to his husbandmen, all of whom the husbandmen kill. The Lord then decides to send his 'one son, his wellbeloved', reasoning 'they will reverence my son'. The husbandmen kill the son too. This is an unusually transparent parable, and it has an unusually direct effect: 'And they sought to lay hold on him, but feared the people: for they knew that he had spoken the parable against them: and they left him, and went their way'. What this parable does explicitly, all the events of Jesus' ministry do implicitly: they put off the fatal moment, they delay the end of narrative. The purpose of this delay is its meaning: it enables the reader to acquire a competence in belief in interpreting the diverse signs of the ministry of Jesus. These signs – sayings, miracles and parables – are all very alike, different in order but not in kind. Both verbal and actual signs are challenges to belief, constructing the interpretative competence of the reader.

The French *Groupe d'Entrevernes*, led by the semiotician A. J. Greimas, argue in their study *Signes et Paraboles* that the whole Gospel is structured according to values figured in the metaphor of 'the Kingdom of God'.[9] Miracles are bodily works, parables are speech works. Both demand interpretation of two types: practical (the way in which, and the competence with which, a musician 'interprets' a musical score by playing it); and cognitive (the way in which, and the competence with which, an observer interprets an event). Both are involved in a reader's reading of a text. The interpretative balance of parables inclines to the practical, that of miracles to the cognitive. The one is fictive, the other is historical, but the borders between fictive and historical are dissolved in the text, which passes freely from one to the other: narrative and discourse are thoroughly intertwined. Both miracle and parable are deliberately provocative, corresponding to Jesus' clear strategy to provoke confrontation: an example would be the scandal he deliberately creates at the beginning of Mark 3 by healing a man with a withered hand in public in the synagogue on the Sabbath. But the example is not quite typical. A miracle is an irruption of power, a proof that Jesus has the power to save. Jesus has to be persuaded to show this, and he must also be motivated: by faith. Blind men in Matthew 20 have only to call on him by the divine name, 'O Lord, thou Son of David,' for him to take compassion on them. In his own country, however, in Mark 6:5,6 'he could there do no mighty work . . . And he marvelled because of their unbelief'. In other words, a sort of contract is required, a contract of faith. If Jesus is to give this sign of his salvific competence, to proclaim *his* difference by miraculously subverting traditional commonsense values, he must first receive a pledge of answering competence in belief. The most poignant example occurs in Mark 9:23–4, when Jesus is asked by a father to cast out an evil spirit from his child: 'Jesus said unto him, If thou canst believe, all things are possible to him that believeth. And straightway the father of the child cried out, and said with tears, Lord, I believe; help thou mine unbelief.'

Whereas miracles require one sort of contract, of belief, parables require another, of interpretation; but belief and interpretation, as I have argued, are two different aspects of the one act. Parables are in fact the means by which competence in belief is acquired. The *Groupe d'Entrevernes* says that they perform practical transformations on their level of narrativity – a remark which I shall need most of the rest of this chapter to elucidate – and that they have no other consequences on their hearers, or readers, than to perform a transformation in recognition, in knowledge. They communicate knowledge; or, more precisely, they are an apprenticeship in an interpretative competence – of the order, adds the *Groupe*, of *savoir-faire*. What the *Groupe* points to here is an interesting paradox which shows the narrative and discursive complementarity of miracles and parables. Parables are fictive speech-acts which are meant to induce a specific *praxis*; miracles are 'real' actions which provoke the quest of a meaning. There is a curious crossplay here. The word demands an active interpretation – that is, a series of 'real' acts to show belief; the actions, based on a contract of belief, call for a cognitive interpretation. To put it as simply as possible: miracles are actions which demand interpretation; parables are interpretations which demand action. Both link knowledge and doing; and knowledge and doing make up the programme of signs required for Christian competence.

I have said that parables, like miracles, are concealed signs. They are concealed partly for narrative reasons, because they are, in the most serious sense, a kind of game, and games need competence if one is to play them. There are other reasons for the concealment; and I dissent here from the *Groupe de'Entrevernes*, who maintain that the function of parables is to shed light on the teaching of Jesus. Most of the parables do not shed light easily; most of them seem to be deliberately hard, like particularly testing examinations. The major reason for both the difficulty and the concealment goes back, once more, to Isaiah, this time to verses 8–10 of Chapter 6. This is a vision of the first Isaiah before the throne of God. Isaiah's lips are purified by seraphim, whereupon Isaiah volunteers to be God's messenger to the people: 'And [the Lord] said, Go, and tell this people, hear ye indeed, but understand not; and see ye indeed, but perceive not. Make the heart of this people fat, and make their ears heavy, and shut their eyes; lest they see with their eyes, and hear with their ears, and understand with their heart, and convert, and be healed.' These verses are quoted by Jesus in Mark 4:12, after he has explained to the disciples why he speaks to the crowd in parables: 'Unto you it is given to know the mystery of the kingdom of God: but unto them that are without, all these things are done in parables: That seeing they may see and not perceive; and hearing they may hear and not understand; lest at any time they should be converted, and their sins should be forgiven them.' There is an expanded version of this, typically citing the Isaiah source by name and quoting it in full, in Matthew 13; and in this chapter Jesus actually proceeds to give his disciples an exhaustive gloss on the allegorical parable of the sower. Again, in the same chapter, he proceeds to tell to the multitude the parable comparing the Kingdom of heaven, in an extended metaphor, to a man who sowed good seed in his field among which his enemy sowed tares; and again we are told (Matthew 13:34–5): 'All these things Jesus spake unto the multitude in parables; and without a parable spake he not unto them: That it might be fulfilled which was spoken by the prophet, saying, I will open my mouth in parables; I will utter things which have been kept secret from the foundation of the world.' And again, when 'the multitude' has departed, his disciples have to come asking for an explanation of this parable, a full gloss – which Jesus provides. Finally (verse 51), 'Jesus saith unto them, Have ye understood all these things? They say unto him, Yea, Lord.'

The disciples in Matthew act as stooges for the reader. They give the reader a chance to acquire parabolic competence. Parabolic competence is competence in *metaphor*: for only metaphor can describe what 'we see not'. The values of the Kingdom are in conflict with the world: the world is what we see, the values of the Kingdom are metaphor. Poetic truth is truer than reality. The poor disciples never quite grasp the skill of it. In Matthew 16:6, Jesus tells the disciples to beware the leaven of the Pharisees. They take this literally, and organise a kind of unofficial conference to thrash out why Jesus has called for a boycott on bread; and again Jesus wearily has to explain – 'the leaven of bread' was a metaphor for the doctrine of the Pharisees. Because they have failed to understand metaphor, he calls them, in the familiar phrase (v.8), 'O ye of little faith'. They have failed in interpretation; they have therefore failed in belief. For belief is metaphor. The competence they lack is the competence to understand parabolic discourse – which is metaphorical discourse, which is the language of the poetic. The competence they lack, the competence they need, is – in one word – reading.

A parable is anything from a cryptic saying (so used in Mark 3:23) to a short story with an allegorical meaning. So there is no effective demarcation between the parables and the rest of Christ's teaching. Indeed, in John 16:25 there is an interesting translation variant in the

English (reflecting the Greek). The Passion is about to commence; Judas and the officers are about to arrive; and Jesus tells his disciples: 'These things have I spoken unto you in proverbs, but the time cometh, when I shall no more speak unto you in proverbs, but I shall show you plainly of the Father'. The disciples, literalists to the end, are delighted (verses 29–30): 'His disciples said unto him, Lo, now thou speakest plainly, and speakest no proverb. *Now are we sure that thou knowest all things*' (my italics). At last, Jesus has started to speak plain Aramaic; at last, he has abandoned nasty, troublesome things like metaphor. The disciples never appear in danger of passing their examination in parabolic competence. There is, however, a further implication to the promise made by Jesus here. 'The time that cometh' is of course the coming of the Kingdom, which will be the climax, and so the end, of narrative. The first act of the Kingdom will be the abolition of metaphor: metaphor is the promise of the coming of the Kingdom.

There is also no effective demarcation between parables, speech-acts, and the behavioural signs of the life of Jesus: there is a semantic continuity between them. That is one reason why Jesus so often refers to the prophets. He is alluding to the profession of Old Testament prophets[10] – and the fact that it was a profession is clear, for instance, from the proud announcement by the prophet Amos that he is not a professional prophet. Prophets were organised into guilds, known as guilds of madmen – outcasts, holy fools: their profession was not to tell the future ('prophesy' does not mean 'foretell' but 'represent') but to speak for, or in place of, God. They often suited the action to the word, turning parable into play. None more so than Jeremiah: the Lord compares himself to a potter forming Israel in his hands like a clay pot (a parable): so Jeremiah marches out by the east gate of Jerusalem clutching a clay pot, and after the appropriate speech he smashes it. God inspires Jeremiah to preach submission to the Babylonian conquest and the yoke of Nebuchadnezzar, so Jeremiah actually marches around wearing a yoke and other miscellaneous bondage. There is a continuity between social behaviour and verbal acts, though Jesus manages it more subtly than this. And on the level of the text, parables slip and slide into sayings and into actions. For example, Jesus is made to curse a fig tree on his way into Jerusalem, and the tree withers and dies. This is uncharacteristically unecological behaviour: it looks very like a slippage into narrative from a parable, especially since figs are favourite parabolic fruit as far back as Jeremiah, who made great rhetorical play with a basket of what the Authorized Version calls 'very naughty figs'.

This sort of slippage is particularly evident in John's Gospel, probably the last-composed of the four, in which all the claims made by the early Christians for Jesus appear uniquely in his mouth in a chain of statements beginning 'I am . . .'. These 'I am' statements distinguish John from the three Synoptic Gospels. In John 10:1–18, a new parable is used merely as an excuse for the 'I am' statements that follow it: 'I am the door': 'I am the good shepherd . . . and I lay down my life for the sheep'. Running metaphors fuse together different genres of narrative and discourse (compare John 15:1–8). The raising of Lazarus from the dead is unique to John 11, but it is odd that so major an achievement finds no place in the other three Gospels. It is an eerie account: 'And he that was dead came forth, bound hand and foot with grave clothes: and his face was bound about with a napkin. Jesus saith unto them, Loose him, and let him go' (John 11:44). This scene gave lepers the name of lazars, the living dead. Some New Testament scholars have suggested that it is a fictive event developed out of the parable in Luke 16:19–31, the parable of Dives and Lazarus.[11] Lazarus is the beggar who dies at the gate of the rich man Dives; Lazarus 'was carried by the angels into Abraham's bosom', while the rich man dies and goes to hell, and pleads with Abraham at least to allow Lazarus to return to earth to warn the rich man's five brothers to repent, 'lest they also come unto this place of torment'. It is a deeply Christian request, but Abraham refuses with these words: 'If they hear not Moses and the prophets, neither will they be persuaded though one rose from the dead'. If the raising of Lazarus in John was narrative developed from this parable, it would be used as it is used, as the ultimate index of hard-heartedness, the blindness of the many who have seen Lazarus 'rise from the dead' and yet remain unpersuaded.

There is in fact a hard-heartedness in the Dives and Lazarus parable found in Luke which is typical of those longer parables relating the THEN rather than NOW, to the *parousia*, the coming of the Kingdom: parables such as the two or three on the subject of feasts – 'many were called and few were chosen' – and the cluster of harsh *parousia* parables in Matthew 22 and 25, which build up into Christ's account of the Last

Judgement and the separation of the sheep from the goats (25:31–46). The two parables which precede this, the parable of the talents, and the parable of the wise and foolish virgins, are both harsh and alien. The five wise virgins, for instance, who have trimmed their lamps and stocked up on oil for the bridegroom's arrival, appear priggish and un-Christian in their refusal to lend some of their oil to the five foolish virgins whose stocks have run out; so that when the bridegroom arrives, they alone enter into the feast and the bridegroom casts the five foolish virgins into the outer darkness to wail and gnash their teeth. Such harshness, however, is inevitable in *parousia* parables: the bridegroom is the kingdom, the oil is that same metaphorical competence discussed above, and the moral drawn by Jesus is unequivocal – 'Watch, therefore, for ye know neither the day nor the hour wherein the Son of Man cometh'. 'Those who are not for me are against me.' The values of the Kingdom are alien; they are a total overturning of normal values, including the values of love and compassion so pre-eminent in Jesus' own earthly ministry.

Love, compassion and hope for all are fully valorised in the other type of parable, the type relating to NOW.[12] One such parable is the Prodigal Son, in Luke 15. I have already noted its theme of sibling rivalry and its significance to the early Christians, and need add only a comment on the immediate purpose of the parable, which is to justify, in debate against the Pharisees and scribes, Jesus' habit of eating with publicans and sinners. This is a recurrent theme of the Gospel, first enunciated in Mark 2:17: 'I came not to call the righteous, but sinners to repentance'. The actantial roles of the parable cast a direct reflection on the actors in the framing debate. The Pharisees and scribes are guardians of the law, and they correspond to the elder son, who took offence at the forgiveness granted to the cadet; the publicans and sinners are the transgressors of the law, and they correspond to the Prodigal, who sins – as a sign of which he is made to engage in the taboo activity of feeding swine – and at his homecoming confesses his sin: 'Father, I have sinned against heaven, and in thy sight, and am no more worthy to be called thy son'. And Jesus corresponds to the father, who had compassion and, with all the Old Testament reverberations of ritual sacrifice, killed the fatted calf.

I will comment a little more closely on one more parable of the NOW type. It selects itself: the Parable of the Good Samaritan (Luke 10: 25–37):

25 And, behold, a certain lawyer stood up, and tempted him, saying, Master, what shall I do to inherit eternal life?

26 He said unto him, What is written in the law? how readest thou?

27 And he answering said, Thou shalt love the Lord thy God with all thy heart, and with all thy soul, and with all thy strength, and with all thy mind; and thy neighbour as thyself.

28 And he said unto him, Thou hast answered right: this do, and thou shalt live.

29 But he, willing to justify himself, said unto Jesus, And who is my neighbour?

30 And Jesus answering said, A certain man went down from Jerusalem to Jericho, and fell among thieves, which stripped him of his raiment, and wounded him, and departed, leaving him half dead.

31 And by chance there came down a certain priest that way: and when he saw him, he passed by on the other side.

32 And likewise a Levite, when he was at the place, came and looked on him, and passed by on the other side.

33 But a certain Samaritan, as he journeyed, came where he was: and when he saw him, he had compassion on him,

34 And went to him, and bound up his wounds, pouring oil and wine, and set him on his own beast, and brought him to an inn, and took care of him.

35 And on the morrow when he departed, he took out two pence, and gave them to the host, and said unto him, Take care of him; and whatsoever thou spendest more, when I come again, I will repay thee.

36 Which now of these three, thinkest thou, was neighbour unto him that fell among the thieves?

37 And he said, He that shewed mercy on him. Then said Jesus unto him, Go, and do thou likewise.

My comments are indebted to the *Groupe d'Entrevernes* to the extent that the account I present is largely theirs, with some simplification and alteration. Theirs is an excellent piece of semiotic interpretation, and the example activates many of the points made in this chapter.

The entry of the lawyer in verse 25, and his dismissal from the narrative by Jesus in verse 37, 'Go', mark the frontiers of a narrative that is easily extracted from its surrounding context. Formally, it has two sections, verses 25–8 and 29–37 respectively; each begins with a question from the lawyer and ends with an order from Jesus; in each case the order contains the word 'do'. The first section is a test of Jesus by the lawyer, the second his attempt to 'justify' himself. The first answer by the lawyer is based on the law (26; 'this do', v.28); the second has a direct bearing on the person of the lawyer himself ('Go and do thou likewise', v.37). This movement from abstract question to concrete choice marks the transformation worked by the parable. Moreover, the two orders issued by Jesus at the end of the two sections each follow an act of critical appraisal: in the first section, by Jesus, an appraisal of the lawyer's citation of the law ('Thou hast answered right'); and in the second section by the lawyer, an appraisal solicited by Jesus in response to the story he has just told ('He that shewed mercy on him'). Formally, then, we have a debate interrupted by a story which transforms the ground of the debate. It is a carefully patterned structure.

So, indeed, is the narrative of verses 30–5. Though it ostensibly deals with chance encounters – the man 'fell among' thieves, the priest came 'by chance' – the intricate game of resemblances and differences played among the actors of the story gives the lie to any impression of a fortuitous series of events. For example, it is very much part of the parable's meaning that the Samaritan is the reverse of the thieves – for he puts right what they have made wrong; at the same time, the Samaritan is also the reverse of the Levite and the priest, who do not put it right. By implication, therefore, the Levite and the priest are structurally equivalent to the thieves: priests and Levites, as it were, reduce people to the state of the man after the thieves have done with him. The priest, the Levite and the Samaritan all 'interpret' the state of the wounded man, but in the first two cases the narrative programme is aborted: their knowledge, unlike the Samaritan's, does not lead to action, to the desire to help, which is compassion or mercy. Pity, not knowledge – not the priestly and Levitical law which is the equivalent of the lawyer's first answer – achieves the programme of transformation. The Samaritan is the subject of that process of transformation: man is the recipient of his will to help; and his power to help is figured in the oil, the wine, the beast and the money. These inanimate objects fulfil the one actantial role of helper: they succeed in the narrative because they are drawn from the level of the language stock itself, both from colloquial use and from emotive biblical imagery. They come with connotations from previous discourses. The present discourse recontextualises and limits these other connotations: this is a matter of narrative focus. The thieves, for example, are defined solely by their attack on the traveller; there is less here about the innkeeper and innkeeping than there might be in other stories, though I suspect that there is further endorsement here of publicans; and, indeed, the focus is not on the restoration of the man, for we never learn how long he took to recover or whether or not he was grateful, but rather strictly on the role of the subject, the Samaritan.

'A certain man', the one who is transformed, is the only actor in the story not presented as being in a fixed category – though like everyone else in the story but the innkeeper, he is a wayfarer. The other wayfaring characters are, if anything, overdetermined. First, why does this story happen on the road from Jerusalem to Jericho? We are not told why the man makes the journey. Medieval exegetes had a good answer here: Jerusalem is the city of God and Jericho, destroyed by Joshua/Jesus, is the city of sin; the man's journey therefore represents the human condition, travelling confidently in the wrong direction and receiving the beating inevitable for all on such a route. The *Groupe d'Entrevernes* have another type of answer, equally plausible: the area from Jerusalem to Jericho is the Jewish space. The outsider in this space is the Samaritan. He is both a geographic outsider and a religious one: Samaritans are looked down upon by the orthodox, the Jews of the cult of the Temple of Jerusalem whose ministers were priests and Levites. Geographic and religious roles therefore intersect; so do social and professional roles. But the logic of the narrative – and I do mean logic, for, as the *Groupe* demonstrates, the narrative transformations in the parable correspond to the interplay of logical propositions in the surrounding discourse – is to strip away these overdetermined roles. The ministers of the religious cult are prepared to leave the wounded man, presumably one of their own, without help in their own geographical space (area of responsibility); it is left to the outsider to assume the truly religious role by showing mercy. The tale hinges on the classic Old Testament antithesis between the religious law of purification and ritual sacrifice on the one hand, and mercy on the other. We are forced to deny the religious and geographical overdeterminations in the tale – Jewishness versus Samaritanness – and to see the Samaritan in the same human terms as the wounded victim, as 'a man'.

Jesus uses this story to redefine the word 'neighbour' so that it is no longer geographical, opposed to 'outsider' or 'foreigner', but social. Which of these three, he asks, was the neighbour? The form of the answer is vital. The lawyer does not reply 'The Samaritan'; he replies, abandoning narrative detail for discursive relevance, 'he that shewed mercy on him'.

This is the transformation of the debate. Jesus has approved the knowledge of the lawyer in order to write into it a programme 'love'. He begins with the lawyer's knowledge as a cognitive state – to have knowledge, to be wise – and he forces this knowledge to undergo a practical transformation. Transformations are signalled by the word 'do', which is an actor both in the debate and the parable. Jesus gets the lawyer to acquire for himself, by the act of interpreting the parable of the Good Samaritan, the competence that leads from knowledge through desire to action, and produces the equivalence suggested by the parable itself. To Love equals To Do. In fact, the story goes so far with this equation that it requires a corrective, and the very next episode in Luke 10 supplies it – Jesus tells the caring, busy, active Martha ('cumbered about much serving') that her sister Mary's act of sitting at his feet is more important than Martha's selfless housework. At this moment, however, the practice of love is all important. Twice Jesus tries to lead the lawyer from a self-sufficient knowledge to the practice of love. He invites a lawyer who 'acts' like a 'priest' or a 'Levite' to 'act' like a Samaritan instead: 'Go and do thou likewise'. Jesus is to the lawyer as the Samaritan is to the wounded man.

The *Groupe d'Entrevernes* points out, lastly, that the narrative does not operate as an illustration of the commandment of the law; it only becomes an example to imitate if it is interpreted, in knowledge, then in practice (*praxis*) and in concrete circumstances different from those of the narrative. That is what the *Groupe d'Entrevernes* mean by *savoir-faire*: it is as if parables are a little like learning to drive in a simulator. One must be a Mary before one can be a successful Martha. For Mary knows the value of competence, and understands the difference. She believes because she interprets.

Notes

1. Semiotic approaches to the New Testament are found in Daniel Patte, *What is Structural Exegesis?* (Philadelphia: Fortress Press, 1976); Jean

Calloud, *Structural Analysis and Narrative* (Philadelphia: Fortress Press, 1976); Claude Chabrol and Louis Marin, *Sémiotique narrative: Récits bibliques* (Paris: Seuil, 1974); Dan O. Via, Jr, *Kerygma and Comedy in the New Testament, A Structuralist Approach to Hermeneutic* (Philadelphia: Fortress Press, 1975); Louis Marin, *Sémiotique de la Passion: Topiques et figures* (Paris: Aubier, 1971). Generally, see Roland Barthes, *The Pleasure of the Text* (New York: Hill and Wang, 1978).

2. James D.G. Dunn, *Unity and Diversity in the New Testament* (London: SCM Press, 1977), p. 31.

3. Samuel Beckett, *Waiting for Godot* (London: Faber and Faber, 1965), pp. 12–13.

4. This inference, once common, cannot be made confidently in the light of J.A.T. Robinson, *Redating the New Testament* (London: SCM Press, 1976); but Paul's writings certainly discourage the notion of a detailed canon circulating widely among the earliest Christian communities.

5. See *Ways of Reading the Bible*, (ed.) Michael Wadsworth (Hemel Hempstead: Harvester Wheatsheaf, 1981), pp. 55–78.

6. See John L. McKenzie, SJ, *Second Isaiah*, The Anchor Bible (Garden City, New York: Doubleday, 1968) for detailed commentary; also, M.D. Hooker, *Jesus and the Servant* (London: SPCK, 1959); Claus Westermann, *Isaiah 40–66* (SCM Press, 1969); Joseph Blenkinsopp, *A History of Prophecy in Israel* (Philadelphia: Westminster Press, 1983); Luis Alonso Schökel, 'Isaiah', in *Literary Guide* (Chapter 1, note 5, above), pp. 165–83; Gerald L. Bruns, 'Midrash and allegory', *ibid.*, pp. 625–46; and G. Vermes, *Jesus the Jew* (London: SCM Press, 1983). On New Testament narrative, especially Mark, see Q. Quesnell, *The Mind of Mark*, Analecta Biblica 38 (Rome: 1969); D.E. Nineham, *The Gospel of St Mark* (Harmondsworth: Penguin, 1963); James N. Robinson, 'The Gospel as narrative' in *The Bible and Narrative Tradition*, ed. Frank McConnell (New York and Oxford: Oxford UP, 1986), pp. 97–112; Elizabeth Struthers Malbon, 'Fallible followers: Women and men in the Gospel of Mark' *Semeia* 28 (1982), 29–48; Erhardt Güttgemanns, 'Narrative analysis of synoptic texts', *Semeia* 6 (1976), 127–80; Walter J. Ong, SJ, 'Text as interpretation: Mark and after', *Semeia* 39 (1987), 7–26, and Werner H. Kelber, 'Narrative as interpretation and interpretation as narrative', *ibid.*, 107–34. *Semeia* 43 (1988) contains several essays on Mark, Gospel narrative and discourse, and *Semeia* 16 (1979) was devoted to Mark.

7. See Shlomith Rimmon-Kenan, *Narrative Fiction: Contemporary poetics* (London and New York: Methuen, 1983), pp. 34–5; and A.J. Greimas, 'The interaction of semiotic constraints', *Yale French Studies* 41 (1969), 86–105.

151

'The interaction of semiotic constraints', *Yale French Studies* 41 (1969), 86–105.

8. The best discussions in this context are the essays on Derrida in *Semeia* 23 (1981) by Schneidau, Crossan and Leavey. See also *Semeia* 40 (1987). See, generally, Christopher Norris, *Deconstruction: Theory and practice* (London and New York: Methuen, 1982), pp. 24–32; Jacques Derrida, *Of Grammatology*, trans. with an introduction by Gayatri Chakravorty Spivak (Baltimore: Johns Hopkins UP 1978) and *Writing and Difference*, trans. Alan Bass (London: Routledge and Kegan Paul, 1978).

9. Groupe d'Entrevernes, *Signes et Paraboles* (Paris: Seuil, 1977).

10. On prophets, see Blenkinsopp (n. 6, above); Lucas Grollenberg, *Rediscovering the Bible* (London: SCM Press, 1978), pp. 157–80.

11. Frank Kermode, *The Genesis of Secrecy* (Cambridge, Mass. and London: Harvard UP, 1979) notes, however, the suggestion from the work of Morton Smith that Clement of Alexandria has a version of Mark that must have contained an episode like the raising of Lazarus (pp. 57–8).

12. On parables, see also C.H. Dodd, *The Parables of the Kingdom* (1935; New York: Harper and Row, 1981); Joachim Jeremias, *The Parables of Jesus*, trans. S.H. Hooke (London: SCM Press, 1954); Dan O. Via, Jr, *The Parables: Their literary and existential dimension* (Philadelphia: Fortress Press, 1967); John D. Crossan, *In Parables: The challenge of the historical Jesus* (New York: Harper and Row, 1973); John Drury, 'Origins of Mark's Parables', in *Ways of Reading the Bible* (n. 5, above), pp. 171–89, and Bernard Harrison, 'Parables and transcendence', *ibid.*, pp. 190–212; Daniel Patte (ed.), *Semiology and Parables* (Pittsburg: The Pickwick Press, 1975); on reader response criticism, Gary A. Phillips, 'History and text: The reader in context in Matthew's parables discourse', *Semeia* 31 (1985). *Semeia* 1 (1974) was devoted to parables, as was 2 (also 1974) and 9 (1977). J. Martin Soskice has a valuable study of *Metaphor and Religious Language* (Oxford: Oxford UP, 1985).

CHAPTER 6

Metaphor, text and belief

Difficulty and transference in the Song of Songs

O night, my guide!
O night more friendly than the dawn!
O tender night that tied
lover and the loved one,
loved one in the lover fused as one!

On my flowering breasts
which I had saved for him alone,
he slept and I caressed
and fondled him with love,
and cedars fanned the air above.

Wind from the castle wall
while my fingers played in his hair:
its hand serenely fell
wounding my neck, and there
my senses vanished in the air.

I lay. Forgot my being,
and on my love I leaned my face.
All ceased. I left my being,
leaving my cares to fade
among the lilies far away.[1]

The poem is called 'Black Night'. In it the poet tells of leaving home

153

unseen in darkness and going by a secret route, lit only by the fierce light of the heart, to where the loved one waits. The second part of the poem then celebrates the apparent union between lover and loved one. The poet's lover, identified by the male gender, sleeps on the poet's breast. The poet swoons with ecstasy, and lies leaning his face on his love in a state of total forgetfulness among the lilies.[2]

The gender of the poet is not marked. I have supplied it as masculine because that is the gender of the poet, St John of the Cross, writing in Spanish in the sixteenth century. Obviously, the poem is one interpretation, and one application, of the Song of Songs. It is obviously a love poem; just as obviously, it seems to be something more. I suspect that this would be evident whether or not we knew the identity of the writer: to know that its writer was male is not to make this poem a homosexual love poem, though its entire field of metaphor is homoerotic. That homoerotic field is determined not by the gender of the poet but by the gender of the love object. To know that the writer was a saint and a mystic only confirms an impression already redolent in the poem: of something supplementary, something beyond the natural. This fugitive sense, of something supernatural or possibly divine, is odd: because there is nothing at all in the code of the poem that is explicitly supernatural or divine. The code works by its very suggestiveness, as if everything in it is a portent of an unstated significance: night, disguise, secrecy, the flight from a house, imagery of light, fire and flowering limbs, union, utter forgetfulness and a sense of infinite distance – all is obscurity, all is implication. The key is cultural, in that we recognise the intertextual reference in John's poem: its entire field of reference is an extension of the Song of Songs. To recognise that reference is also to give the lie to the rather glib modern attitude one finds to the Song of Songs, in the Church and out of it: the notion that generations of blind and life-denying fathers of the Church have traditionally insisted on a spiritual interpretation for a poem that is in fact to do with erotic and orgasmic human passion. For in fact we accept as part of our reference for the Song of Songs precisely that spiritual dimension – or supernatural, or divine – that we sometimes pretend to have dismissed: the sense of an overwhelming otherness, of superabundant significance. So far as I can see, criticism and interpretation of the Song of Songs has always responded, as we still do, to that otherness and supplementarity. The

Song of Songs presents itself as a chain of metaphors which both invites interpretation and defeats it. It is a discourse which appears to state, and to be about to state, more than it actually states or can possibly state: for direct statement is not the nature of metaphor.

The subject of this discussion is the difficulty of the Song of Songs. A good reading of the Song must begin and end with its difficulty. For the Song is not a code to be broken, or a series of equations to be solved. It is not even a text to be understood. Like the Peace embedded in the names 'Solomon' ('the King who is peaceable') and 'Shulamite' ('she who has found peace'), it passes understanding. But it also challenges it. Its difficulty is greater than the sum of its component difficulties. It is the sum of its possible meanings, as attested by the multiplicity of different and conflicting interpretations that make up its literary history. Any modern reading of the Song of Songs must contain that literary history and respond to it; so once more, this study is concerned first and foremost with the power of the text to signify.

The poem 'Black Night' by St John of the Cross is one interpretation of the Song of Songs. Here are others, as samples of that power to signify. First, the Jewish rabbi Aqiba, defending the sanctity of the Song, its power to 'defile the hands':

> No man of Israel ever disputed about the Song of Songs, that it did not defile the hands. The whole world is not worth the day on which the Song of Songs was given to Israel, for all the Scriptures are holy, but the Song of Songs is the Holy of Holies.[3]

The same note is sounded in Christian exegesis by Origen: the Song of Songs is 'strong meat' which is 'for the perfect . . . who have their senses exercised to the discerning of good and evil'. Then there is the Jewish *Targum*, which turns the Song into historical allegory, a sequence of ten songs that cryptically re-enacts the entire biblical history of the Lord's love for Israel, his chosen Bride.[4]

Medieval Christian exegesis transferred the reference, as the running titles of the King James Bible show, to Christ and the Church. For St Athanasius, this is the jubilee song of the Church at the incarnation of Christ; for Gregory of Nyssa, it is rather the same in microcosm, the story and discourse of the soul's yearning for God. For Rupert of Deutz,

the Bride of the Song is the Virgin Mary, the mother of God.[5] Origen
again: 'this book must be understood in the spiritual sense, namely in the
sense of the union of the Church with Jesus Christ, under the names of
bride and groom, and of the union of the soul with the Divine Word'.[6]
As the contemporary of St John of the Cross, St Teresa noted: 'Do we
not unite ourselves with the Most Holy Sacrament?'.[7] And, together
with this traditional spiritual interpretation – to be found in early
Protestantism, though with slightly different emphases, as much as in
medieval exegesis, there are continued attempts to make the progress of
the lovers in the Song conform to various stages in world history. The
late medieval glossator, Nicholas of Lyra, produces a characteristically
humane reading of the Song, showing the spiritual kinship of the Jewish
and Christian communities: Martin Luther produces a distinctive
reading of the Song as celebrating the favourable political circumstances
of the reign of Solomon;[8] and the somewhat deranged eighteenth-
century English commentator, Brightman, converted the *Targum*,
making the Song an allegory of world history up to the year AD 1600.

Then, from the eighteenth century, the reaction, the swing of the
pendulum in favour of carnal love, and to what is now the normal
Protestant exegesis of the Song. In the words of two twentieth-century
Protestant exegetes:

> The Song does celebrate the dignity and purity of human love . . . the Song is
> *therefore* didactic and moral in its purpose.(my italics)

> It is a strange paradox that among those most vociferous about their belief in the
> Bible 'from cover to cover' is often found an attitude that sex is 'nasty' . . . the
> Bible should have given the lie to this kind of attitude. It is, to be sure, fully aware
> of lust and the misuse of sex, but at the same time is forthright in approving the
> wholesomeness of sex.[9]

Certainly, one cannot argue with the latter critic about forthrightness.
An example might be verses 4–5 of Chapter 5:

> My beloved put in his hand by the hole of the door, and my bowels were moved
> for him.
>   I rose up to open to my beloved; and my hands dripped with myrrh, and my
> fingers with sweet smelling myrrh, upon the handles of the lock.

This in fact seems considerably more forthright than the running title in my copy of the King James Bible: 'Christ awaketh the Church'. But one might well ask how in fact the Song proceeds to distinguish, like the theologians just quoted, between the wholesomeness of sex and its misuse. The fear that no such distinction is apparent in the Song is what may have led William Whiston in the eighteenth century to the unequivocal view that the Song of Songs is indeed *dirty*; it 'exhibits from the beginning to the end marks of folly, vanity and looseness. It was written by Solomon when He Was become Wicked and Foolish and Lascivious and Idolatrous'.[10]

The more explicit symbolism of the Song has caused problems of other kinds. For example, there is no mention of marriage in the Song: *therefore* (my italics), in the view of an eighteenth-century German scholar, 'the Song describes the chaste passion of conjugal and domestic love, the attachment of two delicate persons, who have been long united in the sacred bond'.[11] And a whole new narrative structure springs up in the nineteenth century to justify the idea of chastity. For Dr Samuel Davidson, in 1856, the Song:

> warns against impure love, encourages chastity, fidelity and virtue, by depicting the successful issue of sincere affection amid powerful temptations. *The innocent and virtuous maiden, true to her shepherd lover, risks the flatteries of a monarch and is allowed to return to her home.*[12] (my italics)

This is a symptom of an extraordinary fantasy about the Song which reaches its peak in the work of Christian D. Ginsberg in 1857, who contends that 'upon careful examination' the Song 'will be found to record an example of virtue in a young woman who encountered and conquered the greatest temptations, and was, eventually, rewarded'. Ginsberg then explains further 'the simple narrative . . . divested of its poetic form', offering in several paragraphs an impeccably detailed narrative paraphrase complete with brothers, shepherd, lover king, damsels, and even a widowed mother: the plot supplied by Ginsberg makes for the high moral ground by way of the pastoral genre and bourgeois melodrama.[13]

In 1973 at long last the Song received a feminist interpretation, from Professor Phyllis Trible, who points to the mutuality of the sexes in its

verses, in total contrast to sexual stereotyping. The woman, in fact, on
any count gets more verses to speak than the man. She is not, says Trible,
a wife, nor does her work involve procreation. She actively seeks and
desires her lover. 'Male dominance is totally alien to the Canticles. Can
it be that grace is also present?'[14] This is a splendid answer to some
nineteenth century clerics, such as the one who argued that the Song
could not conceivably be about human lovers on the ground that the
women appears to be making advances to the man: 'What writer, with
the feelings, or the reason, of a man, would begin a poem on his fair one
by describing her as courting him? . . . Never would human love speak
thus'.[15] Trible's point is well made, and it has been echoed on many
subsequent occasions. I am not sure that it entirely accommodates the
fact that the Song is largely, in the words of Roland Barthes, 'an episode
of language which stages the absence of the loved object . . . and
which tends to transform its absence into an ordeal of abandonment'.
As Barthes goes on to say, 'historically, the discourse of absence is carried on by the woman'.[16] (However, the point made by Barthes is
another way of restating the relevance of feminist interpretation of the
Song.)

Until recent feminist readings of the Song of Songs, what strikes one
most is the relative poverty of modern interpretations of the Song when
compared to more traditional ones. The recognition by theologians that
the love celebrated in the Song is carnal love was a belated recognition,
well beyond the Reformation: for this very suggestion Sebastian
Castellio was expelled from Calvin's Geneva.[17] But the recognition has
moved promptly to a *non sequitur*, the idea that the Song is about and
only about human sex. Sacred sex, to be sure, but nevertheless, sex. If, as
modern scholars contend, there was little excuse for overlooking the
highly sexual denotation of the Hebrew, there is less still for ignoring its
rich connotation. But traditional Christian exegesis, as in the case of
Origen, responded to that rich field of reference, to the metaphors of the
Song of Songs. The course of Jewish exegesis was set above all by certain
passages in Isaiah (Chapters 62 and 66) by the relation of a king to his
land (discussed by Northrop Frye as 'the royal metaphor'), so that the
land is married to its ruler, who is Israel.[18] Such interpretations are self-
consciously esoteric: in adding a further link to the metaphors of the
text, they are a response to metaphor. Compare the frequent efforts of
the last 200 years or so – bizarre fantasies demanding a Cecil B.de Mille

cast of king, shepherd, girl, little sister, king's mother, girl's mother, shepherd's mother, courtesans, Charlton Heston and all – to supply the Song with a coherent framing narrative that it all too plainly lacks. This is relentless literalism. Modern criticism, not traditional exegesis, fails to respond to the metaphors of this text. When Origen cautions that the text must be understood spiritually, he acknowledges that his reading is less than inevitable; he invokes not the text but the resonance of the text. Compare modern form-criticism, which informs us that the Song 'is' a collection of lyrics assembled for a cultic occasion such as a Wedding Week; or *is* this, or *is* that.[19] Not only is this less interesting than Origen's spiritual sense: it seems to me that it is also less reputable, at this historical remove just another bizarre fantasy of intelligibility.

Such criticism 'explains' the metaphorical level of the Song in the worst possible way – away. And it does so, happily announcing that the Song is this or that, without any awareness of the sort shown by traditional exegesis and articulated by Professor Frye, that there is nothing more metaphorical than the verb 'to be'. Or – contrariwise (the adverb is designed for those looking through a glass, darkly) – the insistent use of the copula in the Bible ('I am the Way, the Truth and the Life'; 'I am Alpha and Omega, the beginning and the end') is the constant index of metaphor, metaphor that (grammatically) invites and (conceptually) defeats direct statement.

I am not arguing that traditional exegesis is good and modern criticism is bad. What strikes me most is simply the multiplicity of interpretation. As literary critics, perhaps we accept it too easily: such diverse opinion about the nature of a whole book is unusual in biblical studies. Take, for example, the question of literary form. So much depends upon judgements on an often absent narrative structure. Who is speaking in a particular verse? How many speakers are there? To what genre of discourse does the Song belong? Every answer is a confident one, and no two answers are the same. On the one hand, an example would be Milton's assessment: 'The Scripture also affords us a Divine pastoral Drama in the Song of Songs, consisting of two persons, and a double Chorus, as Origen rightly judges.'[20] One has only to compare this with the large cast postulated by other readings to see how impossible it is from the text to ensure agreement on the number of characters. (Compare here the Jerusalem and the Good News Bibles, which mark speakers for all the world as if the casting were canonical, and conflict on several crucial occasions). On the other hand, there is Goethe's feeling of resignation: the Song of Songs, seen as a collection of songs, is the 'most tender and inimitable expression of passionate, yet graceful love that has come down to us', but unfortunately the songs 'cannot be fully enjoyed because they are fragmentary, telescoped or driven into one another, and mixed up'.[21]

Is it the Song or its interpreters that are 'mixed up'? One thing is sure: even if Goethe and many modern scholars are right, we cannot and will not refrain from interpreting the Song in just the form, and in whatever translation, we have it. All interpretations, however conflicting, have something in common. They try to meet the 'extra' significance by adding something in to their interpretation. Either the narrative structure is rationalised, however outrageously, or the metaphors are homogenised in a form of exegetical algebra, by which one set of metaphors, the interpreter's, is substituted for another, in the text. In this substitution we never escape metaphor. In the statement, say, that the Song treats of the union of Christ and the Church, or the soul, we cannot escape the word 'union', which remains a metaphor – not to mention the words 'Christ', 'Church' and 'soul' which are figurative in the Augustinian sense because they name invisible mysteries, not visible 'realities'. (For Boccaccio *figura* is a euphemism for fiction.[22]) Unless we have the genius and tact of St John of the Cross, we literalise metaphor at our peril. Indeed, we cannot: John too, in *'Noche oscura'* supplies a further metaphorical field in which that of the Song of Songs can function as a new series of combinations. He gives the Song a symbolic cohesion by arranging its diverse metaphors into a narrative structure that enables one to see them as one common semantic field.

I have stressed the role of metaphor in the Song. I believe, certainly, that a true narrative analysis would be an account of the way the metaphors of the Song behave. The important connection is made by Northrop Frye, in his distinction between the centripetal and centrifugal aspects of the Bible (and of all verbal structures). The centripetal 'arises simply from the interconnection of words'; the centrifugal comprehends 'secondary meaning . . . that may take the form of concepts, predictions, propositions, or a sequence of historical or biographical events, and that are always subordinate to the metaphorical meaning'. To quote Frye again: 'the primary and literal meaning of the Bible . . . is its centripetal or poetic meaning'. And 'this primary meaning . . . is the metaphorical meaning'.[23] Certainly, metaphor is the literal level of the Song of Songs. This is so because the Song of Songs is indeed, as Roland Barthes defines it, a lover's discourse:

> The lover's discourse exists only in outburts of language . . . These fragments of discourse can be called *figures* . . . The figure is the lover at work. Figures take shape insofar as we can recognise, in passing discourse, something that has been read, heard, felt . . . A figure is established if at least someone can say: *'That's so true! I recognise that scene of language'* . . . Ultimately it is unimportant whether the text's dispersion is rich here and poor there: there are nodes, blanks, many figures break off short; some, being hypostases of the whole of the lover's discourse, have just the rarity – the poverty of essences . . . Each of us can fill in this code according to his own history . . . In linguistic terms, one might say that the figures are distributional but not integrative; they always remain on the same level: the lover speaks in bundles of sentences but does not integrate these sentences on a higher level, into a work; his is a horizontal discourse: no transcendence, no deliverance, no novel (though a great deal of the fictive).[24]

It might be objected that I have taken the arguments of Frye and Barthes and applied them to the easiest, that is, the most metaphorical of the books of the Bible; but there is a complication.

This arises in the first place from the nature of metaphor in the Song. If we take the great 'I am' claims of St John's Gospel, we find a marked and known subject, Christ, and a series of familiar complements: Way, Truth, Life, Good Shepherd, and so on. Subject and complement elucidate one another. However metaphorical, these statements are brilliantly intelligible. Their function is to ideologise metaphors by arranging them on a given axis of typology. By contrast, the Song of Songs appears impenetrable. Chapter 2, verse 1, 'I am the rose of Sharon, and the lily of the valleys', does not explain roses or lilies, and it certainly does nothing to define 'I'. All is made mysterious, not plain. Since the verb 'to be' equates with two things, what goes before, the subject, becomes as problematic as what comes after, the complement. There is nothing simple about the 'she' who claims to be 'rose of Sharon'. To make matters more complex, the chain of metaphors whose movement is the Song proceeds metonymically: the person of each lover is never described, even in metaphor, directly or in whole, but in terms of emblems, like the rose and the lily, the fawn and the dove, or attributes

161

wherein the part stands for – or here, more often, hints at – the whole. The opening of the Song works like this:

> The song of songs, which is Solomon's.
>> Let him kiss me with the kisses of his mouth: for thy love is better than wine.
>> Because of the savour of thy good ointments thy name is as ointment poured forth, therefore do the virgins love thee.

We have a series of mutual identifications – song, love, four out of five senses (not sight), him, thee, Solomon; a pun in Hebrew, on kiss and drink, which links wine with love and song; a link between ointments and savour, as aphrodisiacs: but where is the Lover? He exists as two personal pronouns, He and Thou, but otherwise only as 'kisses', 'savour', 'ointment' and 'name'. Metaphor refracts the pronouns. Hence the need felt by all readers to give the pronouns of the Song a definite identity. The resource here is typology.

In a good reading of the Song of Songs, then, metaphor is uniquely intermixed with typology. This can be illustrated from traditional exegesis. As soon as we suggest a metaphorical identity between the Lover and God, or Christ, or between the Beloved and the Church, or the Promised Land, we take the first significant step in interpreting metaphor typologically, rather in the way that the Gospel compilers used the Old Testament. Here, as with Isaiah's Servant, we are supplying an identity, not merely a type: not A + B, but A = B. If, like St Athanasius, who viewed the Song as the jubilee song of the Church at the Incarnation, we propose a typological *occasion*, we take a second step. In the twelfth century, Christianity took a third, in the commentaries of Rupert of Deutz and William of Newburgh.[25] The Beloved is not only the Church and/or the soul but also the Blessed Virgin Mary. This identification of the Beloved, for the first time, with a specific New Testament character is a sudden development, corresponding to the quite sudden twelfth-century foregrounding of the Virgin to resolve a crisis in penitential theology. (It was mortally wounded last century, on equally dogmatic grounds: the promulgation by the first Vatican Council of the Immaculate Conception, whereas the Beloved of the Song is evidently born into sin.)

Yet there is a fourth, still more radical typological reading, representing an extreme of the type of reference that it would be hard to know whether to call intertextual, from one of the 'little books' to another, or, since it exists within a canon, intratextual. Most Christian exegesis of this kind is focused on the Book of Revelation, as the New Testament counterpart of the Song. In fact, there is only one Christian example applied to the Song, and it is eccentric: Thomas Brightman in the seventeenth century, who saw the Song as an allegory of world history from the Fall to the year AD1600 and found, for example, in one verse (5.14: 'His hands are as gold rings set with the beryl: his belly is as bright ivory overlaid with sapphires') allusions to Dante, William of Ockham, Edward III and John of Gaunt and John Wycliff. The Jewish example, however, is extremely central: the *Targum*. It too turns the Song into historical allegory, a sequence of ten songs that cryptically re-enacts the entire biblical history of the Lord's love for Israel. In this view of the Song, metaphor and typology converge to the point of identity. Language and history are one. Do they meet as myth? If so, this myth is irretrievably lyric: it is unable to unfold itself as narrative. It is myth without *mythos*. As Francis Landy puts it, the proposition is that 'every word (in the rest of the Bible) is the exoteric expression of that which is esoterically contained in the Song'.[26] This reading approaches the limit of what the Song of Songs can credibly be taken to signify. Such an alignment of metaphor and typology redefines both. It is like a new language, in which metaphor is syntagm and the whole sequence of biblical narration is paradigm. This is the difficulty of the Song of Songs, and I have called it transference.

First, the metaphors of the Song are transferable. The obvious comparison with the opening of Chapter 1 occurs in Chapter 4, verses 8–11, where there is a complete and pointed reversal: it is *her* love that is better than wine, her fragrance, her ointments, her lips. Other metaphors behave similarly: in Chapter 2:2, she is 'as the lily among thorns' and in 2:9, the man is 'like a roe': in 2:16 he feeds among the lilies; and in 1:15 he has doves' eyes. In Chapter 4:1–2, she is the one who has doves' eyes and in verse 5 her two breasts are 'like two young roes that are twins, which feed among the lilies': all the metaphors used of the male are transferred to the female. Chapter 5:2 makes the woman the dove again; by verse 12 of the same chapter, it is he who has doves' eyes and (verse 13) 'lips like lilies, dropping sweet smelling myrrh.' By Chapter 6:9 it is again she who is the dove. Another example would be the motif of the lover coming up out of the wilderness: in 3:6 she so describes his coming; in the matching 8:5, it is she who comes out of the wilderness, 'leaning upon her beloved'. Let these examples stand for all. No one metaphor is exclusively *his* or *hers*: whatever the one becomes, the other becomes the Other. The metaphors are also unstable. In 4:12–5:1, she is the enclosed garden (*gan*) but also the sealed spring (*gal*); yet streams in the garden flow from Lebanon, so she is also Lebanon, elsewhere than garden or spring. When in 6:11 the male 'went down into the garden of nuts to see the fruits of the valley' she is both the garden and elsewhere: for, as 6:13 makes evident ('Return, return, O Shulamite') she is no longer there. There is no fixed point of reference in the metaphors: except, taking metaphors to be complements of the verb 'to be', that she is the Shulamite and he is Solomon.

This relates, among other things, to the locales of the Song. There are two obvious ones: the city (Jerusalem) and the wilderness.[27] She is a foreigner, 'black and comely', who belongs to the wilderness (that is, the area outside the city), but appears to be resident in Jerusalem, while he is a king, a shepherd (like Solomon's father David or like Moses before they were called to lead the Israelites) and a soldier. He belongs to the city but appears often to be absent from it, for does he not 'come out of the wilderness'? The time of Solomon was the time of Jewish nationhood in a particular form, a sedentary kingdom based in Jerusalem (hence the celebration of the male lover in terms of Israel's military might in Chapter 3). Before then the Jewish life-style had been voluntarily or involuntarily nomadic, that is, based on the wilderness. The problem is to try to harmonise the newer, sedentary, political life of the city, with the traditional nomadic values of the wilderness. Where minor characters – the Daughters of Jerusalem, the watchman – are restricted to the city, both lovers occupy both spaces, city and wilderness, and these two spaces are the mainspring of the Song's metaphors. Love as lawbreaking forces a return to the wilderness, yet the celebration of that love as writing is a product of the city. The interplay of city and wilderness corresponds, unpredictably and unstably, to the dialogue between masculine and feminine, and also to the thematic debate between love and death. The Anchor commentary makes a fascinating suggestion that the 'banqueting hall' in which consummation keeps almost taking place – but for the fact that the male passes out – is, or is near to, a tomb; and that the orgies of these banquets are similar to those condemned by St Paul in 1 Corinthians 10–15 as Paul struggles to define Christian love or charity in the face of orgiastic love feasts for the dead.[28] Tombs are the product of a sedentary city civilisation; they are permanent monuments, whereas nomads dispose of their dead and move on. The notion of a joyous afterlife grows out of tombs; resurrection is an urban ideal, inspired in part by a fear of the earth foreign to nomads. The link between love and death is the self-conscious product of a city civilisation, which in turn produces its own form of gender stereotyping.

Secondly, the 'narrative' structure of the Song seems no more than an extension of the metaphorical field. I suggest, at least, that character roles are as transferable as the metaphors; and in this I have the support of Origen and Milton, that the Song consists of 'two persons, and a double Chorus'. The double Chorus comprises 'the watchmen' and 'the Daughters of Jerusalem', who may well be her 'mother's children' (1:6). The two persons are He and She. What then becomes of her mother (3:4), her sister (8:8) and his mother (3:11)? I shall stretch the principle of economy to its utmost, by arguing that her mother, her sister and his mother are not new characters, but are all aspects of the Beloved, the Female of the Song. Whatever the justice of this, roles interchange in the Song as frequently as metaphors. Indeed, there is little distinction between role and metaphor. The various subworlds of the text, the language of the Song – dream, desire, praise, grief and so on – are as 'real' as any 'actual' event recorded there. One sympathises with those who see the Song as a dream, except that the only way to define a dream is as a series of 'similes, metaphors, symbols and other figures of speech'.[29] It follows, at least, that we cannot construct an argument from the sequence of the Song as if this encodes the linear time of simple narrative. The 'events' of the Song repeat and mirror each other, are as prone to transference as the metaphors. And the 'main event' is the discourse itself: this is truly a song of songs.

I believe that this is an inevitable conclusion given that so much as the Song is unmarked: it is radically difficult, and I should say – remembering the commentators' disagreements – impossible to tell who is the speaker of some key passages. The speaker is often unmarked and often ambivalent. There is also the deliberate interweaving of male and female lovers: the female cuts in on the male and takes over in mid-sentence in 7:10. It follows that the gender of the speaker is often equally uncertain. In 8:6 and 8:7, the climactic statement in the poem's metaphorical tussle between love and death, there is no marking of speaker: the competing, interchanging voices of the Song combine, in a text that remains, none the less, double-voiced:

> Set me as a seal upon thine heart, as a seal upon thine arm: for love is strong as death; jealousy is cruel as the grave: the coals thereof are coals of fire, which hath a most vehement flame.

The sensuous imagery of the poem gives way suddenly to abstraction; yet we are offered, again, a set of metaphorical equivalences – me, love, seal, jealousy, fire/flame – in opposition to death. And the Hebrew here may offer a hint of something more, which English translations – like the King James Bible here quoted – commonly omit: a word standing for the absent name of God. It occurs as a mere particle of a word, '*salhebetyah*': the coals of the flame of Yah. The particle is generally taken as an intensifier: 'coals of fire, which hath a most vehement flame'. The modern Jewish scholar Francis Landy provides a different translation: 'its sparks are the sparks of fire of the flame of God'. He comments:

> The anaemic insistence that *salhebetyah* is a mere superlative deprives it of all content, and reflects a reductive and circular approach, both to poetry and the Song. In other words, since it is a secular poem, there can be no divine references; since there are no divine references, it must be a secular poem.[30]

On this reading, divinity is a part of the text of the Song. We need look no further for the tenor of Rabbi Aqiba's punning similitude of the Song of Songs and the Holy of Holies: 'All the scriptures are holy, but the Song of Songs is the Holy of Holies'. God is present, in metaphor, not in real presence, as law and covenant ('seal'), and as love (flame): dwelling – in and as absence – among fragments of writing, the broken tablets.

A symbolic and mysterious interplay between male and female, enshrining an oblique allusion to the nature of God: this, to my mind, points towards religious myth. The prevailing cultic mythologies in the world surrounding the Jewish nation were mythologies in which divinity has both male and female plural characteristics. Pope's Anchor Commentary is a masterly documentation of their possible relation to the Song; and we should not be quick to dismiss them. The Song is surely, among other things, like the mythologies, a mutability myth; and it seems to me that it freely crosses the boundary between life and death. (Or is it only a post-Blakean reading that senses a figure of death when the female dreams of the lover knocking at her door by night (5:2), telling her: 'My head is filled with dew, and my locks with the drops of the night'?) Pope's account ranges from the cult of Tammuz and Ishtar (Venus and Adonis), through various versions of the black goddess, to the Shekinah or Matronit of the Qabbalah, who – like the Virgin Mary who 'bore Jesus to God, and several other sons and daughters to her husband Joseph, yet . . . remained The Virgin'[31] – paradoxically retained her virginity while being the lover of gods and men. But there is no need to invoke the esoteric or the anachronistic. All is to hand in the Egyptian and, later, Roman cult of Isis and Osiris. Osiris is betrayed and dies, yet has already sired his son Horus (time, the seasons) on Isis (often adored as the black Isis). Horus will grow up to assume the role of Osiris, and will marry his sister, who assumes the role of Isis. This account of mutability links the seasons with love, death and rebirth; and it could hardly be more incestuous. To express the two generations as one relationship: Osiris is the husband, son, father and brother of Isis; Isis is the wife, daughter, mother and sister of Osiris. The myth is also related to kingship, because Pharoanic succession is based on it. If kingship is the royal metaphor, this is the royal myth.

'Come into the garden, my sister, my spouse.' There is no need to claim that the male of the Song 'is' Osiris and the female of the Song 'is' Isis; but the Song is a text full of love, death, rebirth and mutability written at such a time and in such a way that we cannot ignore its overtones of divinity. One might look again at the male's description of the female in Chapter 7: she has joints of thighs like jewels, a navel like a goblet, a belly like a heap of wheat, two breasts like two young roes that are twins; her neck is a tower of ivory; her eyes are like the fishpools in Heshbon, her 'nose is as the tower of Lebanon which looketh toward Damascus'; her head is like Mount Carmel, 'and the hair of thine head like purple; the king is held in the galleries'; her stature is like a palm tree and her breasts are like clusters of grapes (that is, like an earth-mother's, like the breasts of the Diana of Ephesus, herself a type of Isis, and later to be reinterpreted as the Virgin Mary). It may be too easy to set this down as hyperbole; Pope quietly states that it would not necessarily be hyperbolical if it were the description of a goddess, a goddess who, like the multiple divinities of all the world around the obstinately mono-theistic Jews, freely associated with humans in and out of love.

Then there are the complications of incest and role reversibility in the Song. There is, in the Song, a mythological transference of relationship. 'The King hath brought me into his chambers' (1:4); in 3:4 he speaks of having brought him 'into my mother's house, and into the chamber of her that conceived me' – a common matrix; in 3:11 she urges the daughters of Jerusalem to 'behold king Solomon with the crown wherewith *his mother* crowned him *in the days of his espousals*'. He speaks of her in these terms: 'My dove, my undefiled, is but one; she is the only one of her mother' (6:9); in 8.1 she says of him 'O that thou wert as my brother, that sucked the breasts of my mother'. And she proceeds to mingle the mother/sister/spouse roles in 8.5: '*I* raised thee up under the apple tree: there *thy mother* brought thee forth: there she brought thee forth that bare thee' (my italics).

Lastly, the Song ends with what most commentators have taken to be a misplaced fragment, concerning the little sister and her marriage contract; but I would suggest that the little sister/daughter is the new Isis who will be the wife of the new Horus-Osiris (8:10). By verse 12, 'My vineyard, which is mine' – and is also Solomon's (v.11) – 'is before me', her role has merged with that of her mother, and she has become the female lover of the first chapter, calling on her lover in the last verse of all ('Make haste, my beloved') to begin the process anew.

Traditional exegesis is not embarrassed by the theme of sacred incest; in fact, it draws attention to it. Hebrew commentary on the Song cites Isaiah 66:7–15, where mother Zion gives birth to the son Israel; the bride, then, is also the mother. For Christian testimony, we need look no further than the title of William of Newburgh's treatise, 'The sacred epithalamium for the mother of the groom'. Twelfth-century exegesis makes the Shulamite a figure of the Virgin Mary because both are the daughter, the mother, the sister and the bride of God.

168

Sir Edmund Leach reads the Isis–Osiris pattern as a major structural recurrence throughout the Bible, from Genesis into the New Testament. His essay is persuasive mythology partly because it is good theology. This is the formula: 'If God the Father and God the Son are consubstantial and co-eternal then "the mother of God" is also "the spouse of God" and the mother is spouse to her own son.' Its extension is then that 'the relationship between the male aspect of deity A and the female aspect of deity M may then be viewed either as mother/son, or wife/husband, or daughter/father, or sister/brother. The Osiris, Isis, Horus mythology combines all these possibilities.' One of Leach's illustrations, *en route*, is the Song of Songs, which he glosses from the narrative of 1 Kings 1–3 and 2 Samuel 11. His gloss is short enough to quote:

> Solomon becomes co-ruler with David before the death of the latter, and the very first thing that is reported after 'the kingdom was established in the hand of Solomon' is that Solomon marries Pharoah's daughter. Solomon is the son of Bath-Sheba ('daughter of Sheba'), a lady improperly seduced by David before he marries her. Later Solomon is visited by the Queen of Sheba, whom Josephus describes as 'Queen of Egypt and Ethiopia.' According to Ethiopian legend, Solomon married the Queen of Sheba . . .
>   There is also the story by which Abishag the Shunammite first becomes a virgin spouse to David in his extreme old age. Thereafter the issue as to whether Solomon or one of his brothers shall finally succeed to the Kingship is made to turn upon a dispute as to who shall inherit the virgin Abishag.[32]

David, then, is Osiris; Solomon is Horus; and structurally equivalent in the role of Isis are Bath-Sheba, Sheba and Abishag, the 'Shunammite' (Shulamite). Is this typological metaphor or metaphorical typology? It is certainly a form of transference. The Song of Songs is the Song of Solomon because Solomon's relationship with Abishag the Shulamite – and the myth that undergirds it – perfectly capture the intricate networks of roles and relationships, human and divine, that is the metaphoric life of the Song of Songs.

We approach a structural reason why the Song of Songs should be the Holy of Holies. For the Jewish reader, it captures allusively the most important themes and historical relationships of the Old Testament. For the Christian tradition, it does a little more. Where Judaism emphasises

169

mutability and continuity towards an unrealised goal, Christianity presents an all-encompassing, one-off event: recurrent metaphors in the Old Testament are re-presented on the syntagmatic axis of the New, as events. The rebirth of the Song of Songs therefore becomes the promise of resurrection – appropriately, because the first Shulamite in the Bible is not Abishag but the woman in 2 Kings 4 whose dead son Elisha raises to life. The love of the Shulamite in the Song is Solomon who is, mythologically, David reborn; typologically, therefore, a type of Christ (as Lover–Shepherd–King); and an ancestor of Christ according to the curious genealogy of Matthew 1 (curious, because it leads to Joseph, not Mary, and is undone by the parthenogenesis of the next chapter). For both Jewish and Christian traditions, the Song of Songs would then be an exquisite lyric miniaturisation of the whole of the rest of the Bible: in Landy's word, its nucleus.

It would be fascinating to follow this chain of transference. To look no further than Leach's essay, we need the Song of Songs to understand why Mary Magdalen takes to the tomb of Jesus those well-known aphrodisiacs, frankincense and myrrh. Leach gives further parallels from the Old Testament: Abraham and Sarah, the Joseph story, and particularly Moses (to whom God appeared as the burning bush: the flame that burns without consuming, the '*salhebetyah*' of the Song); his Ethiopian, that is, black wife (Numbers 12); and his sister Miriam, whose punishment for contesting this marriage is to be stricken with leprosy, so that she is 'as one dead', 'white as snow', and is cured by exclusion for seven days – the very period later prescribed (Numbers 19) for those who have been in contact with a corpse, a direction followed immediately (20:1) by Miriam's own death. The implication, using Leach's method, is that Miriam, the sister who was dead/white, is reborn at one with the black spouse; sister and spouse are one – as earlier Miriam is structurally equivalent, Leach argues, with Pharoah's daughter, i.e. Moses' (surrogate) mother. This pattern of transference explains why the Koran identifies Miriam with the Virgin Mary. And so one could go on, through the patriarchs, all the way back to the chapter seen by some excellent modern critics as the natural correlative of the Song, as *Paradise Lost* is to 'Paradise Regained': Genesis 2, to which the Song is overtly linked by the supporting image of the apple tree. We return to creation because creation is an act of union and of word, and because 'history is confounded by a series of identical moments'.[33] In fact, we return beyond human history and beyond union – to Genesis 1, to the division of the waters that are Chaos, because, in the words of the Song, (8:7), 'Many waters cannot quench love, neither can the floods drown it'.

I hope that I have gone some way towards justifying my *ad hoc* use of a psychoanalytic term, transference, to describe the difficulty of the Song of Songs. It is an intense, unstable and original coupling between metaphor and typology. It anticipates all possible narrative and all possible history in and as lyric. How one interprets it will depend on where one stands. In the Christian tradition, the meeting of metaphor and typology is the Incarnation, and so remains, however paradoxically, a syntagm; for a Jew it is pure paradigm – the last word and the first, whose name cannot be spoken. I know of no other text that invites us to glimpse past, present and future as though through God's eyes: as a passionate and patterned simultaneity. I am aware that 'transference' is merely a Latinised version of 'metaphor'. None the less, I see the need for a term other than metaphor. In this text, language as play encodes God as desire, and the divine Other appears in a woman's voice.

To make this sort of statement is to rediscover the canonicity of the Song of Songs. But it is not, or should not be, to obscure the human, for what is most interesting of all, if I am right about the mythic relationships of the Song of Songs, is the easy association between human and divine that it would seem to postulate, far from the formal and the fearful distance between the leaders of the Jewish community in the Old Testament and their patriarchal God. That is why for modern readers the Song of Songs is also the greatest example of the genre reinvented by Barthes, 'A lover's discourse', in which states of feeling expel and annihilate narrative coherence in a polyphonic dance of metaphor.

Apocalypse and closure

To read the Song of Songs is to discover an infinitely open text, one whose metaphoric suggestiveness and multiplicity of meaning appear inexhaustible. Yet it is true that the canonicity of the Song of Songs

171

depends upon the possibility of interpretative and institutional closure of that open text, the possibility, that is, of aligning the metaphors of the text along the axis of a coherent system of belief, however esoteric. There is therefore a tension between the role of reader and the role of believer in approaching the Song of Songs, even when one person occupies both those roles. In some ways, the Book of Revelation appears to be the opposite of the Song of Songs. Where the Song of Songs is a masterpiece of lyric disjointedness, the Book of Revelation has a fearful narrative clarity. No text could be more associated with the notion of closure, in both its textual and historical senses. The Book of Revelation transforms what we mean when we say: 'The End'; and it is the Book of Revelation more than any other part of the Bible that licenses the most frequent modern type of interpretative closure in aligning the Bible as text with a particularly rigid form of purported Christian belief basing itself squarely on the literal truth of that text. It would be hard to find a historical reading of the Song of Songs that is as closed and as threatening as the following modern reading of the Book of Revelation:

> On at least five occasions in the last four years, Ronald Reagan has referred to his belief that Armageddon may well occur during the present generation and could come in the Middle East. He associates Armageddon with 'the end of the world'. As authorities for this premonition he cites Bible prophecies and unnamed theologians.
>
> None of the president's statements about Armageddon have been precise or detailed. What he has said sounds a good deal like the commentaries of fundamentalist theologians who have made specific predictions of an imminent final battle between good and evil involving the Middle East, nuclear weapons, and miracles predicted in scripture, followed by the second coming of Christ, a millennium of peace, the end of the old world and the beginning of a new one.
>
> The White House declined requests for an interview with Reagan to put written questions about Armageddon to the president. But in light of what Reagan has said already, Americans could fairly wonder if their president – almost all-powerful on questions of war, peace and 'pushing the button' – is personally predisposed by fundamentalist theology to expect some kind of Armageddon beginning with a nuclear war in the Middle East.[34]

It seemed for a while during the Reagan presidency that we were in danger of seeing inscribed in the world history of our own times the ultimate dispute over literary interpretation. The Book of Revelation has much to answer for.

Yet in many ways the Book of Revelation is not the opposite of the Song of Songs; it is its New Testament counterpart and complement. Whereas in closed readings of the Song a pattern of narrative is constructed from its imagery, in closed readings of the Book of Revelation the narrative coherence is used as a key with which to unlock the highly enigmatic symbolism of the text. And the recurrent symbols in both the Song of Songs and the Book of Revelation are closely related, and form one of the central and most anguished myths of the Bible. They are variant versions of the myth of the garden. That garden is a garden of love, but is is also a garden of death. It is an enclosed garden, and in another guise it is the city that men have constructed – in defiance of divine command. Both as garden and as city, this significant place is an expression of human disobedience. Not accidentally, it is generally characterised in terms of the feminine. In the Book of Revelation the Great Whore is the city of Babylon. The bride of Christ is the new Jerusalem. The double image of the feminised city, one good and one evil, corresponds to a profound ambivalence throughout the entire Bible. Modern scholars tell us that land occupation is at the root of the genre we know as apocalyptic.[35] Apocalyptic arises out of exile from the land, from the garden kept by God. That land is the beloved, desired by God; but some fear that we have been displaced into the false city which is the Whore. The dream is one of reoccupying the promised land, where YHWH is keeper of the vineyard. That reoccupation will be the consummation of the love described in the Song of Songs. It will be at once the founding of the new city, and the restoration of the garden. But is the image one of destruction, or of construction? How are we to view the coming harvest of the earth? Is the promise of resurrection not also a guarantee of impending environmental meltdown?

The word ambivalence is too mild to express the contrasting faces of the apocalyptic options. On the one hand, there is the vision of hell in what may be the earliest example of apocalyptic in the Bible, Isaiah 24–7.[36] I call this a vision of hell although it is a vision of hell on earth, and I am conscious when I do so that Christ's word for hell, *gehenna*, was the name of Jerusalem's municipal tip:[37]

173

Behold, the Lord maketh the earth empty, and maketh it waste, and turneth it upside down, and scattereth abroad the inhabitants thereof.

And it shall be, as with the people, so with the priest; as with the servant, so with his master; as with the maid, so with her mistress; as with the buyer, so with the seller; as with the lender, so with the borrower; as with the taker of usury, so with the giver of usury to him.

The land shall be utterly emptied, and utterly spoiled: for the Lord hath spoken this word.

The earth mourneth and fadeth away, the world languisheth and fadeth away, the haughty people of the earth do languish.

The city of confusion is broken down: every house is shut up, that no man may come in.

There is a crying for wine in the streets; all joy is darkened, the mirth of the land is gone.

In the city is left desolation, and the gate is smitten with destruction.(Isaiah 24:1–4, 10–12)

How do we align such terror with the vision of Revelation, Chapter 21?

And I saw a new heaven and a new earth: for the first heaven and the first earth were passed away; and there was no more sea.

And I John saw the holy city, new Jerusalem, coming down from God out of heaven, prepared as a bride adorned for her husband.

And I heard a great voice out of heaven saying, Behold the tabernacle of God is with men, and he will dwell with them, and they shall be his people, and God himself shall be with them, and be their God.

And God shall wipe away all tears from their eyes; and there shall be no more death, neither sorrow, nor crying, neither shall there be any more pain: for the former things are passed away.

And he that sat upon the throne said, Behold, I make all things new. And he said unto me, Write: for these words are true and faithful.

And he said unto me, It is done. I am Alpha and Omega, the beginning and the end. I will give unto him that is athirst of the fountain of the water of life freely.

He that overcometh shall inherit all things; and I will be his God, and he shall be my son. (Revelation 21:1–7)

Verse 8 of this chapter is very different in tone, and I shall return to it later. The above passage is perhaps the most influential piece of literature ever written: judged, that is, by its historical impact. No other passage has ever been so powerful a public dream; no other passage has inspired more ideals or caused more death. The terrible ambivalence of

174

the apocalyptic genre has impressed itself across western European history to this day. Christianity did not invent the apocalypse; it inherited it, from Judaism and from many sects operating in Palestine around the time of the life of Jesus. Nevertheless, apocalypse is a late genre in the Old Testament itself, and one that marked the enormous shift in Judaism that made a Jewish heresy like Christianity possible. The Book of Job exemplifies that much of the spiritual value, the ideology, of the Old Testament is remarkably different from modern impressions of what it should be like. Particularly, it is not a prerequisite of the Old Testament God that he should be pre-eminently or in any all-embracing way, just. On the contrary, he is irascible; and he is partisan – toward his chosen people. Even they must expect hardship, a fair share of earthly suffering; and among that earthly suffering, unquestioned, is death. Death is, so to speak, an end in itself; the otherworld is Sheol, not heaven, and Sheol is is a place of fairly miserable and insignificant shades. Belief in resurrection is first expressed clearly in the Book of Ezekiel, in the prophet's dream of dry bones being raised to life; but this clearly is the resurrection of the Jewish people. The concept of personal resurrection, and of a significant personal afterlife, is a very late development – coming not more than 300 years before the birth of Christ. It occurs for the first time, in fact, in the Book of Daniel, which is one of the latest of the Old Testament books, though it pretends to be of great antiquity; and the Book of Daniel was written in the years of the Maccabean uprisings in which many young men died – apparently in vain. It is as if these wartime deaths produced a cultural upheaval in the public need to believe in an afterlife; how else to justify so much death? (In recent times Iranian Ayatollahs sent 9-year-old children to die in the battle against Iraq with the promise that they would be transported immediately to heavenly bliss.)

So the Book of Daniel is of immense significance, and remains the best of the apocalypse books – most of which never made their way into the canon. The Book of Daniel gives for the first time the idea, or ideal, of a personal resurrection; it gives the idea of a God who is biding his time to dispense, to the living and to the massed legions of the dead alike, universal justice before a Divine Tribunal; and, in its seventh chapter it gives the promise of 'the One in Human likeness', called the 'Son of Man', who is quickly interpreted as the coming Messiah. It also gives, for the first time, the image of God that has become standard: as an old man with white hair and a long white beard whose name is not YHWH, the ineffable, but 'the Ancient of Days'.

But the Book of Daniel does more than this: it produces a new genre, the apocalyptic, that sits very oddly among the Scriptures. For the great majority of the Old Testament looks like a written transcription of actual speech. Jeremiah, for example, did no writing: he had a scribe at his elbow to copy his words. True, Moses was an accomplished scribe and was 'lame of speech'; but he was given Aaron as his 'prophet', or spokesman. Prophecy is the staple Old Testament communication model: that of speaker and auditor(s). The message is addressed to all; the voice is that of the speaker. In apocalyptic, by contrast, the model is that of writer and reader. The message is couched in esoteric language and is addressed to the few who are privy to its code (the vision of Daniel 7 ends with the writer's statement 'I kept the matter to myself' – that is, I wrote it down); and the 'voice' of the writer is that of a *persona*. Daniel did not write the Book of Daniel; no more did 'St John' write the book of Revelation. Apocalyptic writings are either pseudonymous or, very often ascribed to a famous author who lived before the time of composition. The Book of Daniel purports to relate to and record historical events of the seventh century and sixth century BCE; it is attributable to Daniel, as a legendary figure of the past; and it was in fact written around or a little before 164 BCE. There is no possible dispute about this, for the historical events recorded in the Book of Daniel are demonstrably wrong. There was never a world-empire of the Medes, and there was no historical Darius in this period. The Book of Daniel claims to be true when it in fact records fictions. Apocalypse is fiction; unlike much of the rest of the Bible, it is literature by the very narrowest definition of the term, to be compared, not with myth, like Genesis 2, or legend, like Genesis 22, or partisan history, like the Book of Kings, but with, say, *Robinson Crusoe*, or *David Copperfield*. What the author of the Book of Daniel claims to have Daniel prophesy had already happened – or should have happened, if only he had got his facts right. This sort of prophecy after the event is a fraud, a lie – 'literature'.

The characteristics of apocalyptic literature, then, are these: pseudonymity, necessitating the use of a (narratorial) *persona*; the survey of history as if from an earlier point in history; the use of visions, esoteric codes and symbolism; prophecy after the event; the privileging of writing over speech; the content presented as a privileged revelation sent from or through an angel; content that is eschatological and climactic, with messianic woes, the final judgement for God's enemies and salvation and resurrection for his friends; and a total break between the two ages, now and the time imminent. The Book of Daniel was written at a time of violent persecution in the reign of Antiochus IV Epiphanes. It is written to hearten other hard-pressed opponents. Hence another characteristic of apocalyptic: it is political resistance literature. And the more outrageously supernatural and cosmic its wish-fulfilment, the more dogmatically does it assert that it is *revealed truth*. It does so with a stridency and an intolerance that is at odds with much of the rest of the Bible, especially the teachings of Jesus in the Gospels. The stridency is simply characteristic of the genre.[38]

Concerning the genre, Albert Schweitzer was one of many biblical scholars to believe that apocalyptic was the matrix of all Christian theology. Christianity is a midrash, a gloss of Daniel 7. This much can surely be said: Christianity is a direct outgrowth of Jewish apocalypticism, and would have been inconceivable without it. The discovery of the Qumran scrolls, and other twentieth-century research, has shown the proliferation of apocalyptic movements in Palestine before, and contemporary with, Jesus. In Mark 14:63 Jesus specifically quotes Daniel 7:13, and applies to himself the title 'Son of Man', that stood in Daniel as a symbol for 'the holy ones of the most High', the faithful Jews who withstood the persecution of Antiochus; and Jesus applies the title as it had come to be understood, as a claim to be the Messiah. Yet while it is clear that John the Baptist and his followers were essentially apocalyptic – John's message is one of harvest, fire and baptism, classic apocalyptic imagery – Jesus is on the whole more cautious, sounding the note of an eschatology already fulfilled in himself. Jesus preached that the coming of the kingdom would occur in the lifetime of some of his disciples, and in Matthew 25:31–46 he foretells the last Judgement. Nevertheless, the *parousia* of Jesus is different from the apocalypticism of John the Baptist; and different too from the sequences of events foretold in the Book of Revelation, with which Christ's teaching is now too commonly conflated. Jesus in Luke

17:21 explains that 'the kingdom of God is within you'; and he speaks of the second coming of the Son of Man as a revelation, the day when the Son of Man is revealed (17:30) as a night when the righteous will simply disappear:

> I tell you, in that night there shall be two men in one bed; the one shall be taken, and the other shall be left.
> Two women shall be grinding together; the one shall be taken, and the other left.
> Two men shall be in the field; the one shall be taken, and the other left.
> And they answered and said unto him, Where, Lord? And he said unto them, Wheresoever the body is, thither will the eagles be gathered together. (Luke, 17:34–7)

Reverend Jerry Falwell has assimilated this prophecy to the quite different sequence in Revelation that leads through Armageddon. Here is Falwell's nuclear nightmare, in which Falwell looks forward to what he calls the Rapture:

> You'll be riding along in an automobile. You'll be the driver perhaps. You're a Christian. There'll be several people in the automobile with you, maybe someone who is not a Christian. When the trumpet sounds you and the other born-again believers in that automobile will be instantly caught away – you will disappear, leaving behind only your clothes and physical things than cannot inherit eternal life. That unsaved person or persons in the automobile will suddenly be startled to find that the car is moving along without a driver, and the car suddenly somewhere crashes . . . Other cars on the highways driven by believers will suddenly be out of control and stark pandemonium will occur on every highway in the world where Christians are caught away from the driver's wheel.[39]

This is chilling, but it is also a quite confused mish-mash of *parousia* and the Book of Revelation, with all its modern American adjuncts of skyscrapers, nuclear weapons and freeways: how fitting that the world should end on a freeway.

The Book of Revelation may perhaps have existed before any of the Gospels, and is quite a different affair from the *parousia* – which it never mentions.[40] It falls into four parts: letters to the churches (Chapters 1–3 and the end of 22); the revelation to 'John' (4–11); the revelation concerning punishment and global destruction (12–19), which almost certainly are examples of prophecy after the event and refer to the siege and destruction of Jerusalem by the Romans in AD 70 (Jerusalem is equivalent to Babylon, which is equivalent to the Great Whore); and three chapters to do with the resurrection of the first-born (20–2). These last three chapters are especially problematic, since they raise ideas which do not occur in the rest of the text: the 'millennium', the 1,000-year-rule of the saints, a truly just society, between the defeat of the beast and the false prophet in Chapter 19 and the loosing of Satan, the final battle and the coming of the new Jerusalem in Chapter 21, which marks the final end of the world; Gog and Magog as the enemies of Chapter 20; and two resurrections, not one.

One can refer to the Anchor Bible Commentary for further discussion; and it is a particularly important reference, because the commentator, J. Massyngberde Ford, writing in 1975, makes a most plausible, controversial and explosive argument about the origins of the Book of Revelation. She notes, and in my opinion overstates her case, that Jesus is not an apocalypticist in the Gospels: his charismatic ministry occurred late in life and was for the service of others. Certainly he showed no interest in cosmic history or in the division of history into epochs which is central to the Book of Revelation and all apocalyptic writing. She notes that the figure of Jesus is entirely absent from the Book of Revelation, in fact that 'the Revelation is the only [book of the New Testament] in which Jesus is not the central figure'. The Lamb of God in the Book of Revelation is more important than the Christos, the anointed one; and the Lamb of God is associated in the Gospel only with John the Baptist (see John 1:29, 36). Not only is Jesus absent; so is his whole doctrine of the *parousia* (the word never occurs), and of the sovereignty of God, the lordship of Jesus. There is an almost complete absence of Christian pneumatology, that is, theology relating to the person of the Holy Spirit; there is no explicit reference to any of the Christian sacraments, and no Christology in the hymns of the Book of Revelation. It is the only New Testament book in which Jews are not the opponents. Moreover, Ford argues, the motif of two resurrections is Jewish, not (otherwise) Christian, as is that of the millennium; the harlot is a Jewish Old Testament theme depicting Jerusalem: Chapter 11 is concerned with the temple and the ark of the covenant, specifically Jewish concerns. All other apocalypses of the period are Jewish, and the general ambience of the Book of Revelation, as Ford argues, has less in common with the rest of the New Testament than with the Qumran scrolls, which represent, as it were, 'pre-Christian Christianity'. The drift of Ford's argument leads her to suggest that all but the letters to the churches – Chapters 1 and 3 and the end of the Chapter 22, and these churches were not all Christian churches – emanates from the circle of John the Baptist, and reflects his own and his disciples' expectation of 'He that cometh'. These disciples of John would have been Jewish, and may or may not have been Christian converts. In short, then, if Ford is right – and surely given its later use, this would be a crowning irony – the Book of Revelation may never have been a Christian book.

Ford's commentary, however, represents the very final stage in a tradition of commentary that pulls the Bible apart. It would seem that the critical pendulum is now swinging in the opposite direction. Whereas Ford sees the Book of Revelation as a series of discrete atomic parts, Bernard McGinn would insist, by contrast, on the essential integrity of the text. Certainly, there is no reason why I should wish to subscribe to Ford's interpretation. It seems to me in fact to have the crucial fault of almost all other interpretations of the Book of Revelation: it is so very precise. The Book of Revelation, like the Song of Songs, appears to me inexplicable, and in that sense it would defeat all interpretation. True, Revelation is cogent and orderly where the Song is the reverse. Yet the narrative structure of Revelation is no more reliable than the lyric structure of the Song of Songs. If the Song seems open, and Revelation seems closed, both historically prove open to a great range of interpretation, and the aim of almost all that interpretation is in almost all cases to close the text. The urge to close interpretation is associated with the structure of an institutionalised belief. As was the case with Bible translation, however, closure is itself paradoxical. In the case of translation, the King James Bible seems open because of the need to maintain institutional mediation, whereas the Geneva Bible seems closed because of the desire of its translators in effect to free the Puritan household from the institutional Church. In terms of interpretation, the inheritors of the kind of openness that marks the King James Bible work in the modern academy; while the inheritors of the closure of the Geneva Bible preach the coming of Armageddon. As McGinn writes: 'The conflict of interpretation between academic readings carried on in schools of divinity and religion and in departments of English on the one hand and the mass of general readers on the other is probably greater now than ever before.'[41] It is characteristic of the genre of apocalyptic, if not to abolish the actual interpreter, to dispense with the need for any further interpretation when the Kingdom makes itself manifest. In that sense, apocalyptic represents the triumph of the believer over the institution; and that sort of triumph wins back a version of openness that is probably not at all what is sought.

How then did the Book of Revelation get into the New Testament? Against a great deal of opposition from the early Church Fathers (especially the Eastern ones who wanted nothing to do with it), and for one reason only: its ascription to St John the Evangelist, confused with St John the Divine. This attribution was certainly mistaken; but it was current enough for the Book of Revelation to become canonical. The Church never liked it: If the world was about to end, the Church was about to be made redundant. And the book was the particular despair of Martin Luther, who at first found it an embarrassment to all Christians and felt that the Bible would look a lot better without it. However, when Luther's mission became more political, and involved extending the powers of German princes, he was to find the Book of Revelation particularly helpful.

How to deal with the apocalyptic timetable? The Church quickly supplied an ingenious answer. Does the Book of Revelation not state that it speaks of 'things which must shortly come to pass'? Simple, then: the millennium began with the full establishment of the Church, which *is* the just society on earth. The claim set impossibly high standards for a political body, but it was taken seriously enough by those waiting for the New Jerusalem to appear in the skies. An eleventh-century Pope opined that the New Jerusalem was unable to descend on the site of the old for the simple reason that the old Jerusalem was full of Saracens; hence the Crusades. Thousands of crusaders nearing Jerusalem saw – and that is what they wrote, *saw* – in the sky the walls and turrets of the New Jerusalem as it circled and hovered, ready to descend.[42]

Apocalyptic expectations in the medieval period and beyond are closely linked to popular religion, and so to social upheaval. I now return to Chapter 21, and to the verse that I previously omitted – verse 8:

> But the fearful, and unbelieving, and the abominable, and murderers, and
> whoremongers, and sorcerers, and idolaters, and all liars, shall have their part in
> the lake which burneth with fire and brimstone: which is the second death.
> (Revelation 21:8)

This may be a shattering change of tone; but it is a marvellous comfort
to the oppressed. Small wonder that there developed in the medieval
period the notion of the apocalypse as the 'revenge of the poor'. I quote
the fourteenth-century Franciscan preacher John Bromyard, who ima-
gines the poor 'speaking with Christ the judge' and detailing their
injuries:

> Our labours and goods . . . they took away, to satiate their greed. They afflicted
> us with hunger and labours, that they might live delicately upon our labours and
> our goods. We have laboured and lived so hard a life that scarce for half the year
> had we a good sufficiency, scarce nothing save bread and bran and water. Nay
> rather, what is worse, we died of hunger. And they were served with three or four
> courses out of our goods, which they took from us . . . We hungered and thirsted
> and were afflicted with cold and nakedness. And those robbers yonder gave not
> our own goods to us when we were in want, neither did they feed us or clothe us
> out of them. But their hounds and horses and apes, the rich, the powerful, the
> abounding, the gluttons, the drunkards and their prostitutes they fed and clothed
> with them, and allowed us to languish in want . . .
> O just God, mighty judge, the game was not fairly divided between them and
> us. Their satiety was our famine; their merriment was our wretchedness; their
> jousts and tournaments were our torments. . . Their feasts, delectations, pomps,
> vanities, excesses and superfluities were our fastings, penalties, wants, calamities
> and spoliation. The love-ditties and laughter of their dances were our mockery,
> our groanings and remonstrations. They used to sing – 'Well enough! Well
> enough!' – and we groaned, saying – 'Woe to us! Woe to us!'.[43]

Norman Cohn's caution is a proper one: 'Needless to say the purpose of
such a sermon was not to incite to social revolt'; on the contrary, if God
will set everything right at the Last Judgement, there is no reason to
revolt now.

But in popular hands the idea did not always work like this:
millennial ideas in general and in the Book of Revelation in particular
are the cradle of European socialism. D. H. Lawrence objected to just
this in his extraordinary commentary on the Book of Revelation:

> We are speaking now not of political parties, but of the two sorts of human

nature: those that feel themselves strong in their soul, and those that feel themselves weak. Jesus and Paul and the greater John felt themselves strong. John of Patmos felt himself weak, in his very soul.

In Jesus's day, the inwardly strong men everywhere had lost their desire to rule on earth. They wished to withdraw their strength from earthly rule and earthly power, and to apply it to another form of life. Then the weak began to rouse up and to feel *inordinately* conceited, they began to express their rampant hate of the 'obvious' strong ones, the men in worldly power.

So that religion, the Christian religion especially, became dual. The religion of the strong taught renunciation and love. And the religion of the weak taught *Down with the strong and the powerful, and let the poor be glorified.* Since there are always more weak people, than strong, in the world, the second sort of Christianity has triumphed and will triumph. If the weak are not ruled, they will rule, and there's the end of it. And the rule of the weak is *Down with the strong!*

The grand biblical authority for this cry is the Apocalypse. The weak and pseudo-humble are going to wipe all worldly power, glory, and riches off the face of the earth, and then they, the truly weak, are going to reign. It will be a millennium of pseudo-humble saints, and gruesome to contemplate. But it is what religion stands for today: down with all strong, free life, let the weak triumph, let the pseudo-humble reign. The religion of the self-glorification of the weak, and the reign of the pseudo-humble. This is the spirit of society today, religious and political.[44]

This is Lawrence at his most fascist, or at least his most Nietzschean. One can go further. The most influential commentator on the Book of Revelation in the Middle Ages was the Spiritual Franciscan, Joachim of Fiore. Joachim's ideas never won orthodox approval, but his was a highly influential commentary on the epochs of history. Joachim divided the history of the world into three ages according to the Trinity: the age of the Father, corresponding to the time of the Old Testament; the age of the Son, corresponding to the New Testament and the early Church; and the third age, the age of the Holy Ghost, which the Spiritual Franciscans believed began with St Francis, the second Christ, and which was to last for the 1,000 years of the Book of Revelation.[45] This is the age of perfect justice. For distant cousins of this idea, one might mention Hitler's Third Reich – which was to last for 1,000 years, or recall that according to Marx in the development of Marxist society the final phase, or third age, will be the dictatorship of the proletariat, an age of total justice and perfection in which government machinery will be unnecessary.

In the red corner, then, we have had the Marxist vision of the third age; and in the blue corner, we have had the Reagan administration, whose views were overtly apocalyptic. As Dugger reported in 1984:

Last October 18, President Reagan telephoned Thomas Dine, the executive director of the American–Israel Public Affairs Committee, to thank him for lobbying to persuade Congress to authorise Reagan to keep the Marines in Lebanon for another 18 months. A transcript was made of the conversation, Reagan told Dine:

'You know, I turn back to your ancient prophets in the Old Testament and the signs foretelling Armageddon, and I find myself wondering if – if we're the generation that's going to see that come about. I don't know if you've noted any of those prophecies lately, but believe me, they certainly describe the times we're going through'.

During an appearance Weinberger [the Secretary of Defence] made at Harvard, a student asked him: 'Do you believe the world is going to end, and if you do, do you think it will be an act of God or an act of man?'

'I have read the Book of Revelation,' Weinberger replied, 'and yes, I believe the world is going to end – by an act of God, I hope – but every day I think that time is running out.'

Even in 1987 it was possible for a zealous if unoriginal exegete of apocalyptic to maintain: 'The mouth of the Dragon is today in the Kremlin.'[46] In the history of our own time we have been at risk of seeing the world end in a dispute over biblical interpretation. Our past has been shaped by the Book of Revelation. We have been living a book, and are in some danger of dying it. Such fears appear to have receded even though the armouries have not; but Antichrist's political message was ever one of false security.

It is worth reflecting on the literary and cultural impact of the Book of Revelation; what it does to the Bible as a whole, and what it does to literature. Immediately it privileges *writing*; it does everything in this respect that Derrida might want, and one cannot resist the feeling that Derrida's criticism[47] is a product of our own age's apocalyptic consciousness: 'Blessed is he that readeth, and they that hear the words of this prophecy, and keep those things which are written therein: for the time is at hand' (Revelation 1:3).

John is told to write what he sees in a book (Revelation 1:11, 1:19;

14:13; 19:9) and he sees the destruction of the world as the opening of a book with seven seals (chapters 5–8). John acquires *his* competence, his understanding of the mystery, his gift of prophecy, by eating a little book given to him by an angel (10:8–10) and he then knows that the book with seven seals is the Book of Life: 'And whosoever was not found written in the book of life was cast into the lake of fire' (20:15). In some medieval cycles of illustration of the Apocalypse, the face of God is itself obscured by the two-edged sword which is identified as the Book, and in one particularly striking early representation of the apocalyptic throne, the place of God is empty save for the Book itself upon the throne.[48] And we have already heard that the opening of the Book is the destruction of the world as we know it. In Revelation, Chapters 7 and 8 the Lamb opens the Book seal by seal and the sequence of the Book and its seven seals is destruction: 'And when he had opened the seventh seal, there was silence in heaven about the space of half an hour' (8:1) – then the sounding of seven trumpets followed by utter and vicious destruction. Again, medieval illustration cycles take the notion of the destructive nature of writing seriously enough to represent towers being felled by as it were pennants bearing the words of the Book of Revelation (Book of Life), which are trailed by angels across the skies. John's book, full of the true sayings of God (22:6), is the book of the Book of Life. It is the same book as the Book of Life: 'and there shall in no wise enter into it any thing that defileth, neither whatsoever worketh abomination, or maketh a lie: but they which are written in the Lamb's book of life' (21:27). This entire sequence occasioned D.H. Lawrence's furious gloss:

> But this is not enough. After the thousand years the whole universe must be wiped out, earth, sun, moon, stars, and sea. These early Christians fairly lusted after the end of the world. They wanted their own grand turn first – Revenge! Timotheus cries. – But after that, they insisted that the whole universe must be wiped out, sun, stars, and all – and a *new* Jerusalem should appear, with the same old saints and martyrs in glory, and everything else should have disappeared except the lake of burning brimstone in which devils, demons, beasts, and bad men should frizzle and suffer for ever and ever and ever, Amen!
>
> So ends this glorious work: surely a rather repulsive work. Revenge was indeed a sacred duty to the Jerusalem Jews: and it is not the revenge one minds so much as the perpetual self-glorification of these saints and martyrs, and their profound impudence. How one loathes them, in their 'new white garments.' How disgusting their priggish rule must be! How vile is their spirit, really, insisting,

simply insisting on wiping out the whole universe, bird and blossom, star and river, and above all, everybody except *themselves* and their precious 'saved' brothers. How beastly their New Jerusalem, where the flowers never fade, but stand in everlasting sameness! How terribly bourgeois to have unfading flowers![49]

Lawrence's vehemence is directed at the textual closure of Revelation – a closure that progressively, and skilfully, privileges the book:

And he said unto me, These sayings are faithful and true: and the Lord God of the holy prophets sent this angel to shew unto his servants the things which must shortly be done.

Behold, I come quickly: blessed is he that keepeth the sayings of the prophecy of this book.

And he saith unto me: Seal not the sayings of the prophecy of this book: for the time is at hand. (22:6–7,10)

John's book then ends with a terrible curse:

For I testify unto every man that heareth the words of the prophecy of this book, If any man shall add unto these things, God shall add unto him the plagues that are written in this book:

And if any man shall take away from the words of the book of this prophecy, God shall take away his part out of the book of life, and out of the holy city, and from the things which are written in this book. (Revelation 22:18–19)

There are two more verses followed by, in the King James Bible, and in effect, the Christian canon:

THE END OF THE NEW TESTAMENT

What is the effect of all this? It is to make the Book of Revelation synonymous with the New Testament and the Bible as a whole; the Christian Bible, containing the Book of Revelation is artfully confused with the Book of Life itself, in which actual salvation and damnation are written. And to doubt the claim of the Book of Revelation that 'these are the true sayings of God' – that is, to doubt in any part the truth of the Bible, to 'take away from the words of the book of this prophecy' – is to be erased from the Book of Life and to be cast into the lake of fire. This has coloured our whole view of the Bible, and indeed of Christianity. Christianity is *par excellence* the religion of the book: so much so that one wonders how Derrida can be right to claim that the Graeco-Christian tradition privileges speech over writing. This is partly to do with the structure of the Gospel narrative, but its unpleasantly oppressive aspects are mostly to do with the Book of Revelation.

There are several outstanding ironies.

The first is that the Book of Revelation, precisely because it is so palpably a *book*, and a book so full of esoteric appeal and symbolic coding, is in historical terms a prime mover of what I suspect its author would have despised: the arts, both written and pictorial. Out of John as observer/narrator/author there grows the *persona* of the dream vision; there grows the most easily accessible model of the imaginative artist who, by means of art, speaks the truth. This model reaches its apotheosis in the revolt of the Romantic poet against organised religion: the book makes war on itself.[50] Moreover, the Apocalypse is celebrated, as the book of faith, in stone, in manuscripts, in stained glass, in tapestry – even in music. Its vision of global destruction is a constant incentive to artistic construction. We celebrate that which we most fear to lose: the ephemeral. Western art, Western civilisation, grows out of, and has never escaped from, the shadow of the Apocalypse.

The second irony is to do with literature and its effects. The Book of Revelation is by far the most pretentious book in the Bible, and the most authoritarian – by which I mean simply that it makes more claims for its own truths than any other book, much more than the Gospels, and enlists the authority of the Book of Life itself as its own authority. It does so because, in a sense inapplicable to any of the rest of the Bible except the Book of Daniel, it is pure and deliberate fiction. The greatest irony of our own age, unhappily and increasingly ignorant of the Bible, is that a particular kind of pseudo-fundamentalism – of the kind that uses the Bible as a pretext for reaction and for sanguinary politics – grounds itself wholly in this fiction. I quote from an example that appeared unsolicited in my letter-box:

A dark picture ahead? Atomic night? No, a glorious dawn, when Jesus Christ the Prince of heaven, the King of kings, your Saviour and mine, will return as He promised to bring

DELIVERANCE FROM THE SKIES. . .
Make no mistake about it. The forces of evil are intent on destroying the human race. The enemy of God has his hand raised, ready to strike the death gong . . . But it is written in the Bible: Deliverance will come! Rescue from the skies!

The authority that this pamphlet claims is perfectly clear: 'It is in your own Bible. The prophecies indicate with unmistakable clarity that this generation – that these eyes – could actually see the fulfilment of these words.'[51]

All the biblical references cited in support come from Revelation and the Book of Daniel. If this is sincere, it is all the worse for that. The Apocalypse is in the Bible; so it must happen. This is a particularly dangerous tribute to the writer of Revelation. Nor, I believe, can it possibly be sincere. The pamphlet from which I have been quoting happens to be an Australian production, though it could well be an American one. It is produced by a foundation that wields no little political influence in Australia, and probably elsewhere: such forms of religion are no longer universal, merely multinational. I can only hope that this book may assist a reasoned response: 'No, actually, it is *not* in my own Bible. It is in your own minds.' I hope too that this book may help foster a real respect for that maligned and traduced Bible through knowledge, by seeing it again as new.

A third irony is to do with language. The apocalypse-mongers of our own day have not learned the most fundamental lesson of all that as students of English we have to learn from the Bible: that is, the power of language itself. Those who would persuade us to arm for Armageddon have undermined our very language. I quote from a notorious British Ministry of Defence brochure: 'Nuclear weapons are designed to the highest safety standards and the greatest care is taken in their handling and storage'. I should not call this a biblical style of utterance. At the risk of sounding evangelical myself, it seems to me that we may still be able to learn from the Bible the words we need to wage war on humbug: the social power of a 'still small voice'.

Are fundamentalist readers of the Bible then entirely wrong? Is the Bible no longer to be valued, a text without the power of prophecy? On the contrary, the Bible is intensely relevant to our reading of our past and our possible futures. As a book radically at odds with itself, the Bible is one of the greatest aids we possess to understanding the extremes, the moral obscenity and the idealism, of our subjectivity and our time. What we find in the figurative language of the Song of Songs and the Book of Revelation is an underlying myth of the Bible, its intensely secret code. It writes of love that is in exile, that sets up cities and destroys them in the name of love; that, whether in the lyric form of the Song of Songs or the stark narrative of the Book of Revelation, represents the possible histories of the world. It is not merely the history of our own cultural tradition that it helps us to understand. I am thinking of a bleak modern example of the purposefully apocalyptic destruction of the enclosed garden that is a city: Tiananmen Square in 1989. We should at least have the courage to read such events in the context of parallels from our own culture, not too far distant ones at that: such as the Peterloo massacre of August 1819, when the Manchester yeomanry on the instruction of the government fired upon a mass meeting in St Peter's Field, Manchester, wounding five hundred people and killing eleven; or the *coup d'état* of December 1851 when Louis Napoleon's troops fired upon the people of Paris. Victor Hugo found an ironic perversion of the New Jerusalem in a woman running along the street screaming: 'They kill! They kill! They kill! They kill! They kill!':

> I reached the boulevarde; the scene was indescribable. I witnessed this crime, this butchery, this tragedy. I saw that rain of blind death, I saw the distracted victims fall around me in crowds. It is for this that I have signed myself in this book AN EYEWITNESS.[52]

The reporter of history, signing such a narrative, becomes one with 'St John', the author of apocalypse.

If the Bible is at war with its own tradition, we as its readers are at war with ourselves, with our past and with the powers that mark us – and in the Bible we read histories of such marking and such conflict, with their ambiguous promise of starting again. Closure is no more than a choice of new beginnings, rereadings: that is why the opening of the seventh seal represents the end of the world but not of John's text. What sort of new beginning are we to read in the enigmatic myth that figures in the Song of Songs and Revelation; and to what end does our reading of it as prophecy or history lead: to restoration or to destruction? To a New Jerusalem, or to Armageddon?

One thing is sure. It will need all manner of people to produce careful readings of all manner of texts if we are to avoid destruction. I should argue that one of those texts should be the Bible, provided only that we are able to read it.

Notes

1. *The Poems of St. John of the Cross: A bilingual edition*, English version and introduction by Willis Barnstone (Bloomington and London: Indiana UP, 1968), pp. 38–41.
2. Marvin H. Pope, *Song of Songs*, The Anchor Bible (Garden City, New York: Doubleday, 1977), p. 19.
3. *ibid.*, p. 116.
4. *ibid.*, pp. 93–112.
5. Pope, pp. 117–18: Rupert of Deutz, *In Cantica Canticorum de Incarnatione Domini Commentarii, Patrologia Latina* 168, 837–932.
6. Origen, 'First homily on Canticles', trans. R. P. Lawson, *The Song of Songs: Commentary and homilies* (Westminster, Md: Ancient Christian Writers, 1957), p. 26, quoted by Pope, p. 185.
7. Teresa of Avila, quoted by Pope, p. 187.
8. Pope, pp. 124–5, quoting the famous tag, '*Si Lyra non lyrasset, Luther non saltasset*', 'If Lyra had not peeped, Luther had not leaped'.
9. Pope, pp. 193–4.
10. *ibid.*, p. 129.
11. Johann David Michaelis quoted in Pope, p. 131.
12. Pope, p. 136, quoting from Samuel Davidson, *The Text of the Old Testament Considered* (London, 1856).
13. Pope, p. 137 (Pope's translation).
14. Phyllis Trible, 'Depatriarchalising in biblical interpretation', *Journal of the American Academy of Religion* 41 (1973), 30–48: p. 46 (quoted by Pope, p. 208); see also her *God and the Rhetoric of Sexuality* (Philadelphia: Fortress Press., 1974) and *Texts of Terror* (Philadelphia: Fortress Press, 1984).
15. Dr James Bennett is quoted by Pope, p. 135.
16. Roland Barthes, *A Lover's Discourse: Fragments*, trans. Richard Howard (New York: Hill and Wang, 1978), p. 13. Julia Kristeva has a reading of

the Song, 'A holy madness: She and he', in *Tales of Love* (New York, Columbia UP, 1987), pp. 83–100, 389–90 (notes).

17. *CHB* III, pp. 8–9.

18. Northrop Frye, *The Great Code: the Bible and Literature* (London: Routledge and Kegan Paul, 1982), p. 87; pp. 154–5. See also Jacques-Raymond Tournay, 'The Song of Songs and its Concluding Section', *Immanuel: A bulletin of religious thought and research in Israel* 10 (1980), 5–14.

19. Pope, pp. 141–53; G. Lloyd Carr, 'Is the Song of Songs a "sacred marriage" drama?', *Journal of the Evangelical Theological Society* 22 (1979), 103–14 and 'The Old Testament Love Songs and their use in the New Testament', *JETS* 24 (1981), 97–105; Michael V. Fox, 'Love, passion and perception in Israelite and Egyptian love poetry', *Journal of Biblical Literature* 102 (1983), 219–28 and *The Song of Songs and the Ancient Egyptian Love Songs* (Madison: University of Wisconsin Press, 1985); and the following essays by Roland E. Murphy: 'Form-critical studies in the Song of Songs', *Interpretation* 27 (1973), 413–22; 'The unity of the Song of Songs', *Vetus Testamentum* 29 (1979), 436–43; 'Interpreting the Song of Songs', *Biblical Theology Bulletin* 9 (1979), 99–105; 'Patristic and medieval exegesis – help or hindrance?', *CBQ* 43 (1981), 505–16.

20. Quoted by Pope, p. 35, from Milton's *The Reason of Church Government*.

21. Pope, p. 41, citing Paul Haupt, 'The Book of Canticles', *American Journal of Semitic Languages and Literature* 18 (1902), 205–6.

22. *Boccaccio on Poetry*, trans. C. G. Osgood, 2nd edn (New York: Bobbs-Merril, 1956), p. 49.

23. Frye, *The Great Code*, (n. 18 above) p. 61.

24. Barthes, *A Lover's Discourse* (n.16, above), pp. 3, 4, 5, 7.

25. See n. 5 above; *William of Newburgh's Explanatio Sacri Epithalamii in Matrem Sponsi*, ed. J. C. Gorman (Freibourg: Freibourg UP, 1960).

26. Francis Landy, *Paradoxes of Paradise: Identity and difference in the Song of Songs* (Sheffield: Almond, 1983), p. 16. For Brightman's Works (published in London in 1644) see Pope, p. 128; for the Targum see Pope, pp. 93–101 and his translation of it with each verse in the notes to his commentary.

27. See Othmar Keel, *The Symbolism of the Biblical World: Ancient Near Eastern Iconography and the Book of Psalms*, trans. Timothy J. Hallett (New York: Seabury, 1978).

28. Pope, p. 220; and, generally, his section on 'Love and death', pp. 210–29. See also Landy's essay on the Song in *Literary Guide* (Chapter 1, note 5, above), pp. 305–19.

29. The words are those of the psychologist Dr Max N. Pusin, who uses the Song in therapy, as reported by Pope, pp. 133–4.
30. The case is argued at length in *Paradoxes of Paradise* (n. 26, above). This quotation is from Landy's note, 'The Name of God and the image of God and man: a response to David Clines', *Theology* 84 (1981), 164–70: p. 170, n. 10.
31. Quoted by Pope, p. 168, from Raphael Patai, *Man and Temple in Ancient Jewish Myth and Ritual*, 2nd edn (New York, Ktav Publishing, 1967), p. 192.
32. Sir Edmund Leach, 'Why did Moses have a sister?' in *Structuralist Interpretations of Biblical Myth*, ed. Leach and D. Alan Aycock (Cambridge: Cambridge UP., 1983), quotation from pp. 40–2; see also pp. 44–5, where Leach emphasises the 'geographic frame of reference' of this paradigm.
33. Landy, *Paradoxes of Paradise* (n. 26, above), p. 208. Landy, however, takes the family relationships of the Song to be unreal and metaphorical: see *Paradoxes* and his 'The Song of Songs and the Garden of Eden', *Journal of Biblical Literature* 98 (1978), 513–28. Luce Irigaray, *Divine Women*, trans. Stephen Muecke (Sydney: Local Consumption Press, 1986), comments on female subjectivity as incorporating the roles of mother and spouse.
34. Ronnie Dugger, 'Reagan's Apocalypse Now', *Washington Post*; published in *The Guardian Weekly* 6 May, 1984, p. 17.
35. Bernard McGinn, 'Revelation', *Literary Guide*, pp. 522–41, including further references on p. 541. On closure generally, see Frank Kermode, *The Sense of an Ending* (New York and Oxford: Oxford UP, 1966); Barbara Herrnstein Smith, *Poetic Closure: A study of how poems end* (Chicago: Chicago UP, 1968); *Concepts of Closure, Yale French Studies* 67 (1984), ed. David F. Hult, especially for Hult's Introduction and Paul Zumthor, 'The impossible closure of the oral text', pp. 25–42. On the ambivalent feminine city, see Norman O. Brown, 'Rome in Psychological study', *Arethusa* 71 (1974), 95–103.
36. For commentary, see Otto Kaiser, *Isaiah 13–39: A commentary* (London: SCM Press, 1974), pp. 173–233.
37. Jerome Deshusses, *The Eighth Night of Creation: Life on the edge of human history* (1978) trans. A. D. Martin Sperry (New York: Dial Press, 1982), p. 8. This is itself a definitive Apocalypse, except that it lacks one key characteristic of the genre: fiction.
38. Shemaryahu Talmon, 'Daniel', in *Literary Guide*, pp. 343–56: A. A. di Lella, *The Book of Daniel*, The Anchor Bible (Garden City, New York:

Doubleday, 1978); Edwin M. Good, 'Apocalyptic as comedy: The Book of Daniel', *Semeia* 32 (1985), 41–70; Lucas Grollenberg, *Rediscovering the Bible* (London: SCM Press, 1978), pp. 255–66 (a fine discussion, and an indispensable introduction).

39. Falwell's vision is quoted in Dugger's article (note 34 above).
40. J. A. T. Robinson, *Redating the New Testament* (London: SCM Press, 1976), has shed much doubt on the dating. The point is made, for example, in J. Massyngberde Ford, *The Book of Revelation*, The Anchor Bible (Garden City, New York: Doubleday, 1975).
41. *Literary Guide* p. 539.
42. Steven Runciman, *A History of the Crusades*, 3 volumes (1951; Harmondsworth: Penguin, 1971); Norman Cohn, *The Pursuit of the Millennium* (London: Paladin, 1970).
43. Quoted by Cohn, pp. 201–2, from the translation in G. R. Owst, *Literature and Pulpit in Medieval England* (Oxford: Basil Blackwell, 1966), pp. 300–1.
44. D. H. Lawrence, *Apocalypse* (1931; New York: Viking, 1966), pp. 17–18.
45. Joachim of Fiore, *Exposition on Revelation*; see Bernard McGinn, *The Calabrian Abbot: Joachim of Fiore in the history of Western thought* (New York: Macmillan, 1985) and Marjorie Reeves, *Joachim of Fiore and the Prophetic Future* (London: SPCK, 1976). See also Elisabeth Schüssler Fiorenza, *The Book of Revelation: Justice and judgement* (Philadelphia: Fortress Press, 1985); R. B. Barnes, *Prophecy and Gnosis: Apocalypticism in the wake of the Lutheran Reformation* (Stanford: Stanford UP, 1988).
46. Respectively: Dugger, 'Reagan's Apocalypse Now' (n. 34, above) and Roger Stokes, *The Jews, Rome and Armageddon* (Adelaide Hills: Christadelphian Ecclesia, 1987), p. 336.
47. See Derrida's own essay, 'Of an apocalyptic tone recently adopted in philosophy', *Semeia* 23 (1981), 63ff.
48. Frédéric van der Meer, *L'Apocalypse dans l'Art* (Anvers: Chêne, 1978). For the Son of Man with two-edged sword, see illustrations on p. 151 (Sainte-Chapelle, Paris), pp. 184–5 (Angers tapestry), pp. 206–7 (Flemish Apocalypse, Paris Bibliothèque Nationale MS. Néerl. 3); and for the Book on the otherwise empty throne, from the Tours Bible of *c*. 840 (British Library Additional MS. 1054, f. 449^r), see illustration on p. 74.
49. Lawrence, *Apocalypse* (n. 44, above), pp. 187–8.
50. See van der Meer, *L'Apocalypse dans l'Art* (n. 48, above), especially pp. 258, 346, for the first 'Romantic' John, from Memling's Bruges altarpiece of the mystic Marriage of St Catherine; Murray Roston, *Poet and Prophet:*

The Bible and the growth of romanticism (London and Boston: Faber and Faber, 1965).

51. 'Rescue from the skies', Questions from 'Here's life' (Sydney: 'Logos Foundation', 1983).
52. Victor Hugo, *The History of a Crime*, trans. T. A. Joyce and Arthur Locker, quoted in *The Faber Book of Reportage*, ed. John Carey (London and Boston: Faber and Faber, 1987), pp. 328–31: p. 331.

Index

Index

Index